Franz Keller

The Amazon and Madeira river

sketches and descriptions from the note-book of an explorer

Franz Keller

The Amazon and Madeira river
sketches and descriptions from the note-book of an explorer

ISBN/EAN: 9783337374242

Printed in Europe, USA, Canada, Australia, Japan

Cover: Foto ©Andreas Hilbeck / pixelio.de

More available books at **www.hansebooks.com**

THE
AMAZON AND MADEIRA
RIVERS

SKETCHES AND DESCRIPTIONS FROM THE NOTE-BOOK OF AN EXPLORER

BY

FRANZ KELLER

ENGINEER

NEW EDITION

WITH SIXTY-EIGHT ILLUSTRATIONS ON WOOD

LONDON

CHAPMAN AND HALL, 193, PICCADILLY

1875

LONDON:
PRINTED BY VIRTUE AND CO.,
CITY ROAD.

PREFACE.

IN June 1867, my father and I, who had been studying the maps and plans of a former expedition in the province of Paraná, were commissioned by the Minister of Public Works at Rio de Janeiro to explore the Madeira River, and to project a railroad along its bank where, by reason of the rapids, navigation was rendered impossible.

Since the end of the last century—when, in consequence of the treaty of Ildefonso in 1777, Portuguese astronomers and surveyors ascended the Madeira—no regular or reliable plans had been executed of the immense forest-covered valley. The bold descent effected some twenty years ago by the American naval officer Gibbon, I may observe, was too hurried, and undertaken with too slender means; and another expedition, commanded by the Brazilian engineer, Major Coutinho, proved to be a complete failure, though certainly not for lack of means.*

Upon the ensuing of peace, after the long war with Paraguay, the old question of a way of communication between the Brazilian coast and the province of Mato Grosso came to the front; and as that clever diplomatist, Conselheiro Felippe Lopez Netto, had also succeeded in concluding a treaty of boundaries and commerce with Bolivia,† by which was secured the prospect of a passage through the valley of the Madeira, it was thought necessary that a thorough

---

* Another voyage of discovery undertaken by Mr. Coutinho on the Purus (an affluent of the Solimões) gave similar negative results. That river afterwards became better known through the daring of Mr. Chandless.

† By this treaty the Brazilio-Bolivian boundary is to touch the left shore of the Madeira under 10° 20′ south latitude, near the mouth of the Beni.

exploration should be made. General attention was, moreover, directed to that remote corner of the vast realm by the sudden appearance of a new Steam Navigation Company on the Lower Madeira, and by the recent opening of the Amazon River to the flags of all nations; the realisation of the full benefit of which latter measure depends on its extension to the lateral rivers as well.

The following pages embrace, in addition to a summary of the most important hydrographic results of the voyage, my remarks on the inhabitants, the vegetation, the products, and other topics of interest in connection with these countries, not in the dry form originally assumed by them of a diary, but in the more inviting shape of chapters, under which easier access may be had to the whole.

The illustrations, which I regard as indispensably supplementary to the description of scenes so foreign to us, are from sketches taken on the spot, and, for preservation of their minute fidelity, drawn on the blocks by myself; and the name of one of our first wood engravers will further warrant their accuracy.

Soon, however, there will be no need of well-equipped expeditions to visit these outposts of *Ultima Thule*. Comfortable steamers from Liverpool will convey the tourist, bent on a trip, to Pará in eighteen days. In seven days more he can be at the mouth of the Madeira; and in another week's time he may get to the first rapid of Santo Antonio, whence, at no very distant period, the locomotive will hurry him to the magnificent forests, which we could reach only after a troublesome voyage of three months' duration, counting from the mouth of the Madeira.

A life of bustle and activity will then be infused there. India-rubber, cacáo, precious timber, dye-woods, and resins will no longer perish for want of means of transport; and agriculture and cattle-breeding will restrict, if they cannot yet supplant, the half-wild existence supported by hunting and fishing. Even before our return home from South America, after an absence of seventeen years, we had the satisfaction of seeing the execution of our railway project as good as secured; a North American contractor, Colonel G. E. Church, thoroughly familiar with this part of the world, having obtained the necessary concessions in that behalf from both the Brazilian and the Bolivian Governments, and having experienced little difficulty in raising the requisite funds in England.

PREFACE.

If the following pages, in which I have endeavoured to observe the true medium between optimist and pessimist views of things, should help to convince some Brazilian in authority who may chance to peruse them, of the continued existence of pernicious abuses and errors, and should show him that, in spite of undeniable recent progress, the career of improvement has not been exhausted; and if they should succeed in inflaming the Old World with interest in the welfare of these secluded corners of the New, some at least of my heartiest aspirations will have been realised. These countries do indeed demand attention, if it be only on the ground that they offer the fair prospect of some day becoming outlets for those fermenting elements which, with increased seriousness, have lately menaced social order in over-peopled Europe.

By the emancipation of slave-born children, from the first day of January 1872, it is true that the abolition of Slavery, which is the chief bar to real progress, has become simply a question of time: but we have to await the political equalisation of the immigrants with the natives, and the concession of the right of civil marriage,* before we can, with clear consciences, advise our farmers of the better class to settle there. Poor labourers and small tradesfolk, however, so numerous with us, will profit by the change to high wages, even under existing conditions.

Only an immigration of German race, that really *settles* in the new home and honestly shares the burdens of the State, can truly help the thinly-peopled country; and Brazil, which sees thousands of Portuguese landing yearly and going back as soon as they have scraped together a few hundred milreis, is specially qualified to judge of this radical difference between Latin and German nations. Energetic representatives, such as we at last seem to have beyond the Atlantic, particularly at Rio, will meanwhile avail sufficiently to protect German residents in Brazil, and in due time effect the removal of all the inconveniences incident to their settlement there.

---

* In June, 1873, the Brazilian Government had come to an open rupture with the Bishop of Pernambuco, or rather with Rome itself, on account of the Encyclical against the Freemasons, who number several of the highest Brazilian officials in their fraternity. In the interests of peace and decency in the Protestant colonies, however, the Government was forced not only to declare the validity of unions effected after the Protestant rite, against the decision of the Bishop, but also to prosecute at law two colonists' wives who had become Catholics in order to marry a second time, together with the Catholic priests who had performed the second ceremony.

PREFACE.

In conclusion, I desire to be allowed here to express my thanks to my father, who was my trusty companion on the weary voyage, and my scientific associate, and to my brother, Professor Ferd. Keller, the historic painter, whose tasteful counsel respecting the illustrations has proved of so much value to me.

FRANZ KELLER-LEUZINGER.

CARLSRUHE,
   January, 1874.

NOTE *to the Second English Edition.*—In the present edition the foreign measurements have been reduced to English, and the translation revised throughout, by Mr. H. W. Bates, Assistant Secretary of the Royal Geographical Society.

CONTENTS.

	PAGE
LIST OF THE ILLUSTRATIONS, WITH SHORT EXPLANATIONS.	xi
INTRODUCTION	1

CHAPTER I.

FROM RIO DE JANEIRO TO THE RAPIDS OF THE MADEIRA.

Rio de Janeiro.—Bahia.—Pernambuco.—Parahyba do Norte.—Ceará.—Maranhão.—Pará.—The Amazon.—The Rio Negro.—Manáos.—The Lower Madeira.—The Seringueiros.—The Praia de Tamanduá 29

CHAPTER II.

THE RAPIDS OF THE MADEIRA AND THE MAMORÉ.

Santo Antonio.—Theotonio.—The Caripunas Indians.—Caldeirão do Inferno.—The "Written Rocks."—Salto do Girão.—An Attack.—Old Caripuna Huts.—Ribeirão.—More "Written Rocks."—The Mouth of the Beni.—Exaltacion . . . 54

CHAPTER III.

CANOE AND CAMP LIFE.

The Start.—The Kitchen.—The Bast Shirts.—The Straw Hats.—Strange Dainties.—Alligator-hunting.—The Camp fires.—The Camisetas.—The Mosquitoes.—The Halting-place 85

CHAPTER IV.

HUNTING AND FISHING IN THE PROVINCES OF AMAZON AND MATO-GROSSO.

The Pirá-rucú.—The Lamantin or Peixe-boi.—The Bótos.—Popular Belief regarding them.—The Minhocao and the Mãe d'Agua.—Different Modes of Fishing: in the Pary, with the Covo and the Timbó.—The Rays, the Piranhas, and the Candirús.—Tapir-hunting.—The Jaguar, the Wild Hog, the Capivara, the Monkeys, and the Birds 93

CONTENTS.

CHAPTER V.

THE VEGETATION OF THE VIRGIN FOREST ON THE AMAZON AND THE MADEIRA.

Transformations and New Formations.—Terras Cahidas.—Orchids and Bromeliæ.—Ferns.—Creepers.—Buttressed Trees.—The India-rubber, and its Preparation.—The Cacáo.—Medicinal Plants.—Oils.—Resins.—Fibres.—The Urary or Curare.—The Peruvian Bark.—The Guaraná.—The Coca 108

CHAPTER VI.

THE WILD INDIAN TRIBES OF THE MADEIRA VALLEY.

The Múras.—The Aráras.—The Mundrucús.—The Parentintins.—The Caripúnas: our First Meeting with them.—Their Huts.—Their Burial-ground.—Former Attacks on the Madeira, Javary, and Purús.—The Unknown Footpads at the Mouth of the Mamoré.—Future of these Indians.—Their Languages.—Their Religious Views.—The Pajés.—An Old Indian Settlement 137

CHAPTER VII.

THE MOJOS INDIANS OF THE FORMER JESUIT MISSIONS IN BOLIVIA.

Founding of a Mission.—The Life there.—Strict Discipline.—Their Decay and Present State.—Bloody Episode at Santa Ana.—Consequences of the Political Storms.—Festivities and Processions.—Visit of the Excellentissimo.—The Chicha.—A Vocabulary.—The Missions on the Paranapanema and Tibagy.—Final Considerations 170

APPENDIX.

Mode of Conducting our Surveys, and their Hydrographical and Hypsometrical Results.—Statistics 204

LIST OF THE ILLUSTRATIONS,

WITH SHORT EXPLANATIONS.

PREFACE.

VIGNETTE: PINEAPPLES, CAJÚ, BANANAS, ETC.

INTRODUCTION.

INITIAL: CROWN OF PALM-TREE WITH FLOWERS AND FRUIT.

CHAPTER I.

INITIAL: GROUP OF CIPÓS (LIANAS) ENCIRCLING A LITTLE PALM.

ENTRY OF THE BAY OF RIO DE JANEIRO, AS SEEN FROM THE CORCOVADO.

From the top of the Corcovado, which can easily be reached in three hours from the centre of the city, a magnificent view spreads before the eyes of the surprised beholder; a wide panorama extending over land and sea, over rocky mountains, the ample harbour, faint-blue islands, villas half-hidden in vivid green, and bustling streets. The sketch gives the entrance of the bay, with the "Sugar-loaf" seen from behind.

THE RUGGED PEAKS OF THE ORGAN MOUNTAINS.

The most interesting portion of the Serra d'Estrella, which rises in the background of the Bay of Rio de Janeiro to a height of 7,000 feet, is the Serra dos Orgãos, with its peaks and needles. Like all the mountains round about Rio, it consists of metamorphic gneiss. The view is taken from a steep, ill-paved mule-path, leading to the little town of Therosopolis, from a height of about 2,500 feet.

THE ENTRY OF THE BAY OF RIO DE JANEIRO.

This view is taken from the shore opposite the city of Rio. In the background the "Sugar-loaf" (Pão d'Assucar), whose altitude is about 1,000 feet; in front of it, the old fort of Santa Cruz, which commands the entry; between both, the far horizon of the blue Atlantic; amid the mountains to the right, the pointed top of the Corcovado, rising to 3,000 feet, immediately behind the city.

A JANGADA IN THE BREAKERS.

The jangada, a light raft especially used for fishing, is in use on the coast from Pernambuco to Ceará; the flat beach and the total want of good harbours, whether natural or artificial, not allowing the landing of heavier boats. In spite of the admirable skill and dexterity of the Indians and mestizoes, who usually manage them, they are often submerged, and even overturned by the high surf, and the passengers seldom escape without a slight bath.

THE DIFFERENT STAGES OF LAND FORMATION.

BURIAL-URN OF THE MANÁOS INDIANS (IGAÇABA).

These igaçabas were found not only in various parts of Brazil, but also in Bolivia, on the other side of the Andes on the shores of the Pacific; these latter, by reason of the dry climate apparently, containing extraordinarily well-preserved corpses.

IGARAPÉ DO ESPÍRITO SANTO, OR, DO CORREIO, AT MANÁOS.

The proud fan-palms on the shores belong to the family of the merity, or Mauritius palm, while the dense row of plants close to the water's edge (the aninga) much resembles our calla, and belongs to the colocasiæ.

THE CRAFT ON THE AMAZON, RIO NEGRO, AND MADEIRA.

A coberta, batelão, igarités, and montarias in the port of Manáos. The large palm-leaves forming the roof of the improvised kitchen are of the uauassú, an attalea. The shore shows a bank of the pedra-canga, the ferruginous, easily-crumbling sandstone of the Amazon Basin.

HOUSE OF A RICH SERINGUEIRO.

In the middle the palm-leaf-covered house; in the foreground, to the right, a group of the banana da terra (pacova), or indigenous plantain, a large bundle of whose yellow fruit an Indian is taking to the kitchen.

TURTLE-HUNTING ON THE MADEIRA.

THE SARARACA; THE POISON USED FOR IT.

VIGNETTE: HARPOON, WITH FISHING-NET AND REEDS.

CHAPTER II.

INITIAL: TRUNK WITH ORCHIDS, BROMELIÆ, AND FERNS.

THE THEOTONIO FALL OF THE MADEIRA.

Owing to the considerable width of the river (700 metres) the principal fall (of 11 metres) appears less high than it really is. However, the mighty waves, the dazzling foam, the black boulders appearing now and again, and the primitive wildness of the shores, which are partly covered with high forest and partly washed by the floods up to the bare rocks, combine to give it quite an imposing aspect.

ONE OF THE SMALLER RAPIDS OF THE CALDEIRÃO DO INFERNO.

To avoid the great break in the main channel, the partly-unladen boats have to pass, close to the islands near the shore, through one of the side ones, which offers the comparative advantage of the slope being extended over a greater length.

FAN-LEAF OF A PALM.

An exceedingly graceful palm, 12 to 15 metres high, with a smooth stem. We saw it only in the region of the rapids.

THE RAPID OF RIBEIRÃO, SEEN FROM ABOVE.

One of the most interesting points in the whole Valley. A rocky reef, wildly torn and broken by narrow foaming channels, stretches across the whole width of the river, which is 2,000 metres. Its highest points, unwashed by the floods, are crowned by dense groves, topped with slender palms waving to and fro in the gale.

CARVED FIGURES ON THE ROCKS OF THE MADEIRA.

Though perplexing enigmas to us, perhaps for ever, they will be of interest as evidencing the degree of civilisation possessed by the ancient inhabitants of these regions.

GROUND-PLAN OF THE FORMER MISSION OF EXALTACION.

VIGNETTE: INDIAN UTENSILS.

An elegantly shaped pot, a few calabashes, a dosser, a maracá (sort of rattle used on solemn occasions), and feather ornaments, with maize, sugar-cane, and the deeply-indented leaves of the mandioca on a broad hand-rudder with gaudily-painted tiller, the most indispensable utensil of the Indians.

CHAPTER III.

INITIAL: EMBAÚBA (CECROPIA) WITH BROMELIÆ.

HALTING-PLACE IN THE SHADE OF A FOREST-GIANT.

If trees of the dimensions of that represented here are not found in all tropical forests, they are not a rare sight in the rich alluvion of the Amazon Basin. They generally belong to the ficus family, with light white wood. A halt in the cool shade of such a giant, covered with hundreds of parasitic plants, from the broad-leaved imbé with its rope-like roots to strange orchids and graceful ferns, when the mid-day sun fills the atmosphere around with its glowing rays, is quite a treat after a morning's hard work.

OUR PADDLERS AT BREAKFAST.

On a well-chosen spot, in the shade of slender myrtaceæ and high cacao-bushes, with their golden cucumber-like fruit budding directly from the stem, our brown fellow-travellers (in their stiff bast shirts, or their more elegant white camisetas) are seated round the large earthen pot, out of which the Capitão is distributing the thick pap of maize, or mandioca flour, mixed with little pieces of meat. The loiterer in the foreground is busily beating a stiff piece of bast with the wooden "maceta," to render it soft and pliable enough for wearing.

TOUJOURS PERDRIX!

Though it is rather the sea turtle that gives the material to the celebrated turtle soup, the river turtle also is used for culinary purposes; and none of the steamers running between Pará and Liverpool leave the mouth of the Amazon without a few of the cuirassed amphibian. Neither soup nor ragout of the tartaruga is to be despised; but those who have partaken of the same dish daily for months and months will understand and pardon the above exclamation.

PREPARATIONS FOR ALLIGATOR-HUNTING.

As the lazy saurian, which usually is very shy near the shore, is always more inclined to run and dive than to attack, the hunt is not half so dangerous as it looks; and as soon as the laço is over its head it is over.

KILLING AN ALLIGATOR.

In spite of its resistance, the mighty animal is drugged on to a sand-bank and finished with a few strokes of an axe. Its timidity notwithstanding, however, Indian women while washing on shore have been carried off, as I was told by eye-witnesses, though immediate help was at hand.

VIGNETTE: FIGHTING MACAWS.

CHAPTER IV.

INITIAL: IMBÉ (PHILODENDRON).

The long straight air-roots, demitted by the pothos and aroideæ from their lofty seats in the crowns of gigantic trees down to the ground, are one of the most striking features of primeval vegetation.

SUBMERGED FOREST.

In December, January, and February a great part of the wooded lowlands is more or less inundated by the annual floods. On these smooth, lake-like sheets of water, whose dark surface vividly reflects the luxuriant vegetation, the native hunter harpoons the mighty pirá-rucu.

THE PIRÁ-RUCÚ (SUDIS GIGAS).

This giant of the rivers is signalised as much by its size (8 metres length) as by the brightness of its colour, each of the big silvery scales being edged by a scarlet line, whence its name,—pirá, *fish;* and rucú, or urucú, *red;* especially the red dyeing-stuff of the Bixa Orellana.

THE LAMANTIN, OR PEIXE-BOI (MANATUS AMERICANUS).

This representative of the cetaceans sometimes reaches the length of 4 metres, and is found on the whole course of the Amazon, up to Perú: but its principal abode is not in the main river, but in the lake-like old courses beside it, which usually are densely covered with wild rice and a sort of long grass with blister-like knots, that serve to keep it afloat.

FISHING WITH THE CÓVO.

The Mojos Indians of the Missions wait, at the edges of shoals or banks, for the periodic ascent (at spawning-time, and in dense swarms) of the fish up the rivers and rivulets; when, by dexterous throwing of the covo (a sort of basket of heavy palm-wood, open below and at the top) they try to enclose a certain proportion of them, which they can readily take out at the opening above.

MOJOS INDIAN RETURNING FROM A FISHING EXCURSION.

These rivers, with their ichthyologic treasures (which can, besides, be acquired in the shortest time at the right season) would at low water level, and at the right spots, below some fall or rapid, indeed make an angler's paradise. The largest of the victims that fell to our Mojos is the spotted surubim or pintado, a species of siluris; the one behind it is the tambaki; while at the other end of the bamboo a brown and yellow-spotted ray drags its armed tail over the rocks, and a peixe-cachorro shows its needle-like teeth on the fisher's left hand. The orchid with the long leaves climbing up the mimosa, to the left, is the vanilla.

HEAD OF SWIMMING TAPIR, PURSUED BY DOGS.

The poor, hard-pursued pachyderm had reached the opposite shore, thanks to its quickness in swimming and diving, and in another moment would have escaped the furious curs, if a ball from the hunters, waiting in the canoe behind over-hanging boughs, had not reached it. The uplifted short trunk discloses teeth of respectable size; but, on the whole, the clumsy animal is a harmless, good-natured creature, and little danger is incurred in hunting it.

CARIPUNA INDIANS, WITH KILLED TAPIR.

Under a dense screen of parasite creepers, blooming orchids, graceful ferns, and stiff bromeliæ, the tapir, pierced by several arrows, has broken down. The lucky hunter, a dark Caripuna, will cut it up, selecting the best pieces for himself; and his faithful companion will carry home the heavy load in her platter of palm-leaves. Her lord and master only carries the weapons, and of these just what he requires to be ready for shooting—a bow and two arrows. The remaining supply of them the humble wife has also to carry.

VIGNETTE: DEAD PARROT, TOUCAN, AND WATER-FOWL; AN INDIAN HEAD-DRESS; BOWS AND ARROWS.

CHAPTER V.

INITIAL: COFFEE-PLANT COVERED WITH BERRIES.

The coffee-shrub, cultivated in immense plantations on the undulating soil of the Provinces of Rio de Janeiro, São Paulo, Minas Geraes, and Espirito Santo, begins to bear in the fourth year, and sometimes is so heavily laden with the red, cherry-like berries that the slender boughs bend to the earth. The snow-white flower, resembling that of the myrtle, exhales a most delicate perfume; and in bloom as well as at harvest-time the bushy shrub, with its glossy, dark leaves, offers a gratifying sight.

TRANSVERSE SECTION OF A BREAKING SHORE, CALLED TERRAS CAHIDAS.

Owing to the homogeneousness of the alluvial layers, the water-washed shore often breaks down, with such regularity as to form perfect degrees, linked at the surface by a sort of network or bridge formed by the tough roots.

BROKEN SHORE ON THE MADEIRA, WITH A GROUP OF SINKING JAVARY-PALMS.

The landscape represented by this sketch, taken at sunset, is quite characteristic of the whole Madeira, in its wild loneliness and majestic calm.

BUTTRESSED TREE.

In order to gain the necessary stability, the gigantic trunk, which has no deep roots, shoots out these huge wing-like buttresses. It is found in the North as well as in the South.

GROTESQUE SHAPE OF A SPECIES OF FICUS.

Forms like these, drawn exactly after Nature, are not a rare sight in these forests, though they are not often seen of that size. The trunk almost suggests a living being by the way it clasps the naked boulders and shoots out supports and props wherever they are needed.

USUAL STRUCTURE OF PALM ROOTS; STILTS OF THE PAXIÚBA.

The radical fibres, entangled to a thick clod with most palms, are developed into perfect stilts with the paxiúba (*Iriartea exorhiza*).

OUR TENT UNDER PALMS.

Though we were not lucky enough often to find such a Paradisaic little spot, still it occasionally fell to our lot, and we always thoroughly enjoyed it.

DIFFERENT TRANSVERSE CUTS OF PALM-RIBS.

BIFURCATED PALM-LEAF.

BOUGH OF THE SIPHONIA ELASTICA (CAOUTCHOUC-TREE).

Very different from the so-called ficus, or gum-tree, often seen in European hot-houses, which also gives a resin, but not the one demanded by commerce.

MOUTH OF A LATERAL RIVER ON THE MADEIRA, WITH AN INDIAN SHOOTING FISHES.

The mighty tree rising above its neighbours is the castanheira (*Bertholletia excelsa*); in the foreground, the round dish-like leaves of the Victoria regia.

A SERINGUEIRO'S FIRST SETTLEMENT ON THE MADEIRA.

On the high shore, but in the immediate vicinity of the moist seringaes (caoutchouc-tree woods), the first household arrangements are made. The richly-embroidered hammock is extended between two trees, and a dense musquiteiro is spread over another, serving for the night, and shaded with a light roof. Immediately to the right is the kitchen, with a tartaruga (turtle), that most patient of all slaughtered animals, which, simply laid on its back, helplessly and noiselessly awaits the fatal stroke. In the foreground, the temporary wife of the owner, a young mestizo lady with raven-black hair, comfortably smokes her cigar, rocking herself leisurely in the hammock.

PREPARATION OF THE INDIA-RUBBER.

The workman, a Mojos Indian, holding his wooden shovel, covered with a fresh layer of milk, in the white smoke which issues out of the chimney-like pots from a fire of uauassú and urucury palm-nuts (which alone consolidates the milk in the proper way), sits in the midst of his simple utensils; the nuts on the ground, the calabashes, and a goblet of bamboo in which he fetched the milk from the seringal, to pour it into the turtle-shell in the middle.

VIGNETTE: SUSPENDED BIRDS' NESTS.

These nests, of elastic fibres solidly interwoven, are made by the guache (belonging to the cassicus species), a black bird of the size of our starling, with a long yellow tail. Sometimes several dozens of them are seen suspended at the overhanging boughs on the riverside, or at the extreme end of the branches of tall palms. Whoever has seen a palm-crown waved to and fro and shaken by the wind will form an idea of the comforts of such a lofty seat. One, verily, must be a guache to find the door of the swinging house.

CHAPTER VI.

INITIAL: FERN-TREE WITH BROMELLÆ AND ORCHIDS.

The graceful fern-trees are, with the palms and musaceæ, one of the most striking forms of tropical vegetation. In Brazil there are at least six very different species of this family. The orchid in the foreground is the sumaré (*Cyrtopodium glutiniferum*, Raddi), whose sticky sap is used by the mestizoes of the interior for birdlime, and the repairing of their mandolines, and for other purposes.

BARK-CANOE OF ARARA INDIANS.

There can be no lighter, simpler, and better-constructed crafts in the world than these bark-canoes of the Araras and Caripunas. Elastic pieces of bark of a finger's thickness, stiffened out in the middle and lightly laced at the ends, they accommodate four persons very well; and two will easily carry one over the rocks of some rapid down to calmer water.

OUR FIRST MEETING WITH THE CARIPUNA INDIANS.

The vegetation in the original sketch was drawn from Nature. Our first sight of our savage friends upon our landing I have tried to reproduce from memory as faithfully as possible.

PORTRAIT OF A YOUNG CARIPUNA INDIAN.

The physiognomy of the young warrior with the long hair and the bunch of red toucan feathers in the nose, may be taken as the type of the whole horde.

CARIPUNA INDIAN HUNTING.

Half hidden in the dark shade of thorny prejaúba palms, his long black hair hanging like a mane over his back, he waits, ready to shoot his game, be it the graceful deer, the wild hog, or the tapir. The straight ropes on the right are the air-roots of the imbé; aroideæ clinging high above in the lofty crown of a castanheira.

VIGNETTE: HUMMING-BIRD DEFENDING ITS NEST AGAINST SNAKE.

CHAPTER VII.

INITIAL: THE MAMMÃO (CARICA PAPAYA) AND SUGAR-CANE.

The mammão, or papaw-tree, is often found in the coffee or sugar-plantations; its fruit, of the size of a child's head, is eaten, though rather insipid.

THE MYSTERY OF THE TRINITY EXPLAINED BY A JESUIT ARTIST.

This representation, painted *al fresco* on the tympanum of the old church at Trinidad "in usum Indianorum," is, in spite of its rudeness of conception and execution, admirably adapted to the childish minds of the red-skinned neophytes.

MOJOS INDIAN OF THE FORMER MISSION OF TRINIDAD.

The dark-brown, strongly-set sword-dancer in the classical garment and the bright feather-crown, dancing (like King David) in honour of the Lord, is rarely to be seen even now: but when we put together all the other emblems of ceremonial pomp and sacerdotal sway—the gold-embroidered banners, the heavy silver crosses and swinging censers, the rich garlands of flowers, and the palm-branches—with the dark blue sky canopying the whole, it must be owned that the High Festivals of the Missions could vie in splendour with any Saint's-day in Europe.

THE FORMER MISSION OF EXALTACION DE LA SANTA CRUZ.

One might almost fancy the severe spirit of Loyola's disciples still hovering about the quiet Plaza and under the decaying verandas with their carved pillar-capitals, which will never be restored when they finally yield to the corrosion of wind and weather. Women in their long tipoyas glide noiselessly by, with their primitive ewers on their heads, and the men pass you with a curt greeting. The convent-like stillness has not yet quite subdued the children, who prattle and play and ask unanswerable questions, as they are wont to do everywhere.

HIGH MASS AT TRINIDAD.

Here are represented genuine red-skins executing—partly on well-known, partly strangely-shaped instruments of their own manufacturing—the masterpieces of old Italian sacred music. With an industry one would hardly give their race credit for, they have kept up the art from generation to generation, in spite of the prolonged misgovernment of the white masters of the land, which would have crushed the art proclivities of a less tough nation. Who after this will deny to them the capacity of further development?

MOJOS INDIAN FROM TRINIDAD.

The noble features of this Indian, belonging to one of our boats' crews, reminded me always of Seume's

"Ein Canadier, der noch Europäer," etc.;

and, if he did not quite answer to that ideal of a red-skin, he was at least one of the most taciturn of the taciturn Indians.

MARIANO: MOJOS FROM TRINIDAD.

A handy, clever fellow, who, under the instruction of our cook, tried hard to enlarge his culinary knowledge, and to catch now and then an extra good morsel. His broad cheekbones, oblique eyes, scanty beard, and disposition to *embonpoint*, gave him the appearance of a Chinese mandarin, deepened somewhat in colour.

CAPITÃO PAY: CHIEFTAIN OF THE CAYOWÁ INDIANS.

The old chief, who, together with his tribe, more than forty years ago left the forests on the Ivinheima and Iguatemy, to play more or less the part of a mediatised prince in the Aldeamento de San Ignacio on the Paranapanema, is to the present day a prototype of the good-natured sly Guarani. The preponderance of the well-armed settlers, always ready for deeds of violence and drawing nearer and nearer his native woods, and perhaps vague reminiscences and tales of the paternal government of the Jesuits, will have brought him to the conviction that it is better to live under the protection of the Pae-guassú (that is the Emperor) than to be annihilated in a hopeless resistance.

CAPITÃO VEI BANG: CHIEF OF THE COROADOS.

A striking contrast to the last is the chief of the Coroados, living in another Aldeamento, that of S. Jeronimo. Only after hard fighting, and when he saw that there really was no help for it, did he submit to the white man; and even now his fidelity is not always to be relied on. The following is a characteristic illustration of his supercilious pride. I once showed him my revolver, and explained that in a short time I could fire six shots with it. Well knowing the style of the braggart, who had some time before assured me, pointing to a round mark on his forehead, that the ball which had caused it had come out at the back of his head, I fully expected he would not exhibit any sign of surprise: but I was almost taken aback when, bestowing a contemptuous sidelook at the weapon, and repeatedly mimicking my "piff! paff!" he gave me to understand that he could far more rapidly dispatch a greater number of whizzing, never-erring arrows!

VIGNETTE: MEANS OF CIVILISING THE INDIANS USED BY THE COMPANY OF JESUS.

INTRODUCTION.

IN Brazil, a country most richly endowed by Nature, and which has, of late, repeatedly attracted the attention of Europe by its long war with Paraguay, and its endeavours to solve the Slave Question, we find all the conditions and modes of life so vastly different from what we are used to ourselves, that the following remarks, intended to give the reader a general idea of the country, will not, perhaps, be out of place.

This immense Empire (it is nearly as large as Europe) is divided into twenty Provinces, differing greatly from each other in size and importance. In respect to trade, its situation is a highly favoured one; the Atlantic, with many excellent harbours, forming its eastern confines for 34 degrees of latitude, and the two powerful nets of the Amazon and La Plata, not yet estimated at their true value, linking the sea-coast with the rich countries of the interior.

Its extent, not easily determinable, by reason of the many undecided contests about boundaries, and of the inexactitude of the maps, was estimated by Humboldt to be 3,072,170 English square miles. The following list shows its division into Provinces; but I must add that the statement is given with all reserve, being the result of approximate calculations, the boundaries between the provinces themselves not being clear for the most part.

Amazonas	576,160 English sq. miles.
Pará	478,360 ,,
Maranhão	191,340 ,,
Piauhy	91,420 ,,
Ceará	46,770 ,,
Rio Grande do Norte	27,850 ,,
Parahyba	20,200 ,,
Pernambuco	39,970 ,,
Alagoas	15,730 ,,
Sergipe	16,580 ,,
Bahia	308,280 ,,
Espírito Santo	23,380 ,,
Rio de Janeiro	28,700 ,,
São Paulo	83,550 ,,
Paraná	71,750 ,,
Santa Catharina	31,890 ,,
Rio Grande do Sul	98,430 ,,
Minas Geraes	239,180 ,,
Goyaz	297,650 ,,
Mato Grosso	595,300 ,,

The climate of Brazil is almost throughout a warm and moist one. There are none of those contrasts caused by high ice-and-snow-covered Cordilleras, as in Peru and Bolivia; on whose slopes you pass in rapid succession the burning heat of Africa, the pleasant freshness of Northern Italy, and the chilling cold of Siberia. The provinces of Rio Grande do Sul, Santa Catharina, Paraná, and a part of São Paulo, enjoy a fine temperate climate, much like that of Southern Europe; but, on the whole, the thoroughly tropical character of the gigantic riverine plains of the Amazon, Paraná, Paraguay, and São Francisco prevails.

In Rio de Janeiro the average temperature of the year, as shown by a six-years' record at the Observatory, is between 73° and 75° Fahrenheit (18° and 19° R.). During summer, that is, during the three winter months of Europe, December, January, and February, it is between 79° and 81° F. (21° and 22° R.); and in July, the coldest month, about 70° C. (17° R.).* In the last twenty or thirty years, the climate of Rio de Janeiro has sensibly changed, doubtless in consequence of the destruction of the forests round about the city. For instance, in the cold season, the

---

* Two and a half or three and a half degrees more must be counted for the city, as the Observatory is situated on the Morro do Castello, several hundred feet above it, where it is swept by the cool sea-breeze.

temperature does not now sink to its former low level; and, instead of a decided dry and rainy season, the rains now fall more equally throughout the year; while the average number of storms during the year is twenty-six, whereas, formerly, they could daily be counted upon with the greatest certainty during the three hot months, as is the case still at Pará.

It is a remarkable fact that, immediately after that period (1850), epidemics, like yellow fever and cholera, unknown before in Rio, made their grim entry, and have demanded their yearly victims ever since. We are unable to determine whether there is any vital connection between the two facts, or whether the ironical *post hoc ergo propter hoc !* is applicable thereto.

Along the whole coast north of Rio, the climate is much like that of the capital, moist and warm, though in many places the sea-breeze injures the wheat. At Bahia the average temperature, in summer, is said to be 82° F.; that in winter, $71\frac{1}{2}$° F. At Pará the average temperature amounts to 79° F., and that on the plains of the Amazon to 82°—84° F., with a minimum of 75° F. in the cooler months.

In the interior, the different seasons show a greater variety. In the southern parts of Minas Geraes, at heights of from 1,500 to 2,000 feet above the sea-level, the average yearly temperature is 66°—68° F.; that of summer, 75°—77° F.; that of winter, 59° F.; but frequently the thermometer sinks to freezing point; and it is not a rare sight to see tropical plants, such as coffee, plantain, and sugar cane, severely damaged by the night frosts. In São Paulo the average annual temperature varies between $71\frac{1}{2}$° and $73\frac{1}{2}$° F.; in Rio Grande do Sul, that of summer, between 77° and $80\frac{1}{2}$° F., while in winter it is sometimes below freezing-point. In the German colony of São Leopoldo the mercury once even showed 50° F. In Donna Francisca, another German colony of the province of Santa Catharina, the average annual temperature is 68°—70° F.; that of the summer months (December, January and February), 75°—77° F. However, 97°—$98\frac{1}{2}$° F. in summer and 34° in winter are not thought extraordinary.

Generally, there are but two distinct seasons in Brazil, the cool or dry one, and the hot or rainy one, whose beginning and duration depend greatly upon the local configuration of the country. The latter usually begins in October or November; at some distance from the seaboard, a little later; and in some parts of Maranhão, Piauhy, and Ceará it sometimes fails to make its appearance at all, to the great misery of the population. Then the country looks like a desert; the trees lose their leaves; the grass on the Campos seems to be burnt up, and the mortality is greatly increased, until the first shower brings back health and life to everything and every one. In most of the other parts, almost all the trees and shrubs preserve their foliage during the dry season, though they all suffer more or less, and would do so more if they were not refreshed every night by a profuse dew.

In the southern provinces, where the climate assumes more and more the character of the temperate zone, the rains set in in winter; that is, in June, July, and August; and the hot season is identical with the dry one; while, on the border of the two zones—in some parts of the province of Paraná, for example—two rainy seasons may be distinguished; the first in January and February, and the second in September.

In Rio de Janeiro and its environs, the annual rain-fall amounts to 50 inches; but at the mouth of the Amazon, with its endless virgin forests, its immense water-sheets, and the rapid evaporation under a glowing sun, it amounts to no less than 200 inches, being more than six times the average quantity in Europe.

On the whole, the climate may be called a healthy one, with the exception of a few riverine plains, such as the Rio Doce, Mucury, and some of the affluents of the Amazon, which are plagued with intermittent fevers. The yellow fever, which first caused great havoc at Rio de Janeiro, in 1850, reappears there almost every year since then, and has even increased in intensity of late; but Brazilians and acclimatized Europeans will easily escape it by a sober, regular mode of life. New arrivals, it is true, incur great danger; and I should advise every one who has not lived for years under the tropics, to show his back, in yellow-fever time, to the cities on the seaboard, and to live in the interior until the terrible visitor is gone. Even now, at the German colony of Petropolis, distant only some eight leagues from Rio, but 2,500 feet above the sea-level, one is perfectly safe from it, as it always keeps near the coast, within a narrow range. But not so the cholera. Although here, as everywhere, it pursues especially the highways of commerce, and has its favourite haunts in populous towns, yet there is not one place (be it ever so much out of the way) in all South America, since its first visit in 1852, where one can

INTRODUCTION.

feel secure from this terrible Asiatic scourge. Particularly the negroes, who do not easily fall victims to yellow fever, are cut off in great numbers by cholera.

It is a singular fact that measles and scarlatina are almost always of fatal issue to Indians, and devastate whole populations, while they are not more dangerous to white people and negroes than they usually are in Europe. Together with the small-pox, they form a hideous triumvirate, that will have not a little increased the awe and hatred felt by the poor red-skins for the white men who introduced these dreadful visitors to them.

Three so widely differing races as the white, the black, and the red are, cannot but form a very motley population. For these three centuries, the white immigrants have driven the Indians—the first owners of the soil—farther and farther back into the interior; and the last red man of unmixed blood will be cut off by civilisation and its gifts, contagious diseases and fire-water, before three ages more are gone. Every attempt, on a large scale, to use them as slaves ended in terrible slaughter, and the destruction of whole tribes; and so the humane device was hit on of fetching over the woolly-headed son of Africa, whose neck bows more easily to the yoke, and who endures hard labour under the tropical sun so much better than either whites or Indians. That it was not a successful hit, any reasonable Brazilian will own now, when the getting rid of the hateful institution costs them so much trouble.

As a general census has never yet been effected (and, indeed, it would not be an easy task in the thinly populated provinces), it is very difficult to state, even approximatively, the number of souls. The official census of 1867 calculated it to be 11,000,000 (1,400,000 slaves and 500,000 independent Indians included);* but this statement is evidently over-rated, as is clearly shown by the latest valuation, in August, 1872; by which the total number of the inhabitants of Brazil is set down as

---

* The above-mentioned number of free Indians, spread over an area of 1,700,850 square miles of virgin forest and prairies, gives an average number of one Indian to 3½ square miles. In the separate provinces, the virgin forest and prairies, or campos with the Indian population on them, average as follows:—

Pará, Amazonas, and Maranhão	1,275,640	sq. miles.
Mato Grosso, Goyaz, and São Paulo	297,650	,,
Paraná, Santa Catharina, and Rio Grande do Sul	106,300	,,
Piauhy, Ceará, Pernambuco, Minas Geraes, and Espirito Santo	63,780	,,

10,094,978, including 1,683,864 slaves and 250,000 foreigners. It is true that neither this nor the first statement can be implicitly relied upon, the number of slaves and of Indians, perhaps, excepted, which may come nearer the truth.

The white race (in the strict sense of the word), although the ruling one, forms only a minor part of the population. Especially in the interior, only a limited number of families can boast of pure descent from the first immigrants, the Portuguese—who even now come over every year by thousands, and have got hold of almost all the retail trade in the land. At the first glance the Brazilian is distinguished from his ancestor. He usually is darker, small and elegantly shaped, while the Portuguese has a much robuster frame, and is heavier and slower in every way. By-the-bye, there is no love lost between the two; and many a characteristic nickname tells of the mutual hatred and contempt of the former oppressor and the oppressed. The inhabitants of the Southern provinces, Minas, São Paulo, and Rio Grande, are (on the whole) much taller and stronger, approaching more the European type, and show more energy and activity than those of the North, where the Indian element manifests itself more clearly.

In respect to colour, the prejudice here is by no means so strong as in North America. In Brazil nobody would think of turning a man out from a public place, an omnibus, or the like, only because he was a mulatto (Indian mestizoes are regarded with still more indulgence): and there are coloured men holding high offices in the Army and in the Administration. However, every one wishes to pass off for white; and it is the greatest possible offence to doubt the pure lineage of a Brazilian of good family.

The many shades of colour, some of them distinguishable only by an experienced eye, have as many different names. Some of these are only local expressions, and many imply contempt; so, if you wish to be polite, say *pardo* (coloured man) instead of mulatto or *cabra*, the latter meaning the offspring of negroes and mulattoes. The descendant of negroes and Indians is called *cariboca, cafuzo,* or *tapanhuna;* and the offspring of whites and Indians *mameluco,* very likely intended originally as a nickname. The word *crioulo* (creole), used generally in Europe for those born of European parents in Transatlantic colonies, is applied in Brazil only to negroes born there, be they slaves or not, to distinguish them from the *Negros da Costa,* the blacks brought over from the coast of Africa.

There is no doubt but that the slave population of Brazil is gradually decreasing, in spite of the official census that says the contrary; the number of births being greatly below the number of deaths, and the country not having received any fresh supplies from Africa these twenty years. By the convention with England the slave trade ought to have ceased ever since 1826; but the great gains were too tempting an inducement. Any one who succeeded in safely landing his freight of "ebony" on any point of the Brazilian shore became at once a wealthy man; so, notwithstanding the English cruisers that out of a hundred slave-vessels could hardly capture more than three, on account of the great extent of the Brazilian and African coasts, about 28,000 slaves (at a moderate estimate) were annually brought over. Only during the reign of Don Pedro II. was the supply stopped, owing chiefly to the urgency of England, by searching on the plantations in the interior for *negros novos* (new negroes), and by imposing heavy fines on the culprits, both sellers and buyers. The consequence was that the price of the "black-ware" rose six and sevenfold, from 300 to 2,000 milreis.

From this moment, and still more after the slave-emancipation in the United States, every clear-sighted Brazilian must have felt that the time was come for rooting out from his own country that hateful relic of barbarous ages, and measures were taken accordingly. By the new law all children born to slaves (the condition of the mother always determining that of the children), after the first of January, 1872, are to be free on attaining their twentieth year. Until then they are to serve their owners as compensation for the care taken of them in their infancy. This measure, though not destroying the evil at one blow, but keeping it up for a number of years, must yet gain the approval of every one who has spent any time in a slave-trading country, and has seen the difficulties of the position. A sudden emancipation of the slaves, if it could be effected at all without entirely ruining the present owners, would certainly be attended with the saddest consequences, not only to the productions of the country in general, but also to the liberated slaves themselves.

If it be a difficult task to educate the rising generation to the degree of obtaining their labour without absolute compulsion, it is an impossible one as to the grown-up slave. Besides this, the evil consequences of the abominable institution will be felt for long years after its entire abolition, in the lax morality of the families, in the total want of intelligent workmen, and the utter impossibility, with existing means, of improving agriculture, which hitherto has been carried on in the rudest and most unprofitable way.

"Of what use is it," said an intelligent, educated landowner once to me, "of what use is it to know that we have not improved our farming one hair's breadth since the time of our ancestors, the Portuguese? Even if we knew better *what* to do, and *how* to get out of that wretched old routine of ours, it would not help us on; for with the hands we employ—a crowd of stupid niggers, who, as slaves, are stubborn, and must bear a grudge towards even the very best of masters—it is quite impossible to effect the slightest change in our ruinous system."

To the coffee and sugar-growing provinces it is, of course, an all-important matter to have new hands in the land as soon as possible, in order to check the dreaded reduction of value in the trade and finances of the empire.

The attempt to settle Chinese coolies proved as unsuccessful as that to induce the planters of the Southern States, after the war, to transmigrate to Brazil. People had the highest idea of the wonders American energy and industry could work there, and they believed the long-looked-for panacea against their own indolence had been found; but they forgot that, in spite of all the hatred towards their victorious neighbours, the Southerners could not but foresee the advantages held out to them by their old home, in which, peace being restored, agriculture, trade, and industry flourished anew, and where, after all, they could prosper so much easier than in Brazil, where everything was quite new to them, except slavery, and where the general indolence would also have been a check to *their* activity. With the aid of some American agents, who volunteered for the obviously lucrative job despite their high military titles—most of them called themselves generals—several hundreds of emigrants arrived. Besides most respectable families, there seemed to be some perfectly organized gangs of thieves amongst them, whose luggage was found, at the Alfandega of Rio, to consist of false keys, rope-ladders, revolvers, and other tools of refined modern burglary. The voyage and the first instalment of the new-comers having cost Brazil some hundred thousands of dollars, almost all—including these gentlemen, I hope—returned disappointed, after a very short sojourn; most of them, too, at the cost of the

Empire, which gained nothing by the whole affair but the tardy discovery that a thriving country like the United States, that has not yet reached its climax of development, and is itself in want of hands, cannot by any means afford to send a considerable number of emigrants even to Paradise.

If the Brazilians had cherished any hopes of reviving the decaying institution of slavery by the settlement of the former slave-owners from the South of the Union, their mistake certainly was a double one; for such a success, if at all possible, would have been but a new disaster. But if the Government would profit by the bitter lesson for which it paid so dear, and would but try to improve the condition of the German emigrants—the only ones that will settle for good in their new homes, differing much in this respect from the Portuguese, who all go back as soon as they have gained a few hundred milreis— the result would yet prove to the advantage of the Brazilians. Unfortunately they are haunted by the notion of the national existence being endangered by too great a preponderance of foreigners, and the proper measures for inducing settlers to come have been withheld. Instead of giving good tracts of land gratuitously to new-comers, making roads for them, and granting to them perfect religious freedom and political equality with the natives, the country was discredited, in the eyes of Europe, by rich coffee-growers being allowed to conclude those *parceria* contracts with German colonists, by which the latter were placed entirely in the hands of, sometimes, most unscrupulous masters. They have allotted to them a certain number of coffee-plants, to which they have to attend, and the produce of which they are to divide in equal shares with the owners of the ground; only, as they have, with *their* share, to discharge the debts contracted for the voyage (the first instalment of payment), and for victuals during the first year, they are kept in a state of dependence, which it is the interest of their masters to prolong as much as they can.

Another drawback to successful colonization is that, everywhere, the lands best adapted for agriculture and trade are scarcely to be bought for any money; and, consequently, colonists get land either poor in itself or too remote from ordinary means of communication. Especially the rich first growth (Mato-Virgem), used exclusively until now for coffee culture, is getting dearer from day to day, and has already become scarce in several provinces, that of Rio de Janeiro, for example, although coffee-culture there dates back only fifty years; for, as the plant (at least with the there usual treatment or ill-treatment) will yield only for some twenty-five or thirty years, whoever can afford it simply leaves the old plantations to cut down new tracks of virgin forest, instead of trying to prolong the period of productiveness * by properly manuring the soil.

Of course, with any activity on the part of the hundreds of thousands of hands busy at this system of robbery, immense districts must be cleared in a comparatively short time, and rendered unfit for coffee-growing, at least. But, even if this were not the case, if the virgin forests of the interior were really inexhaustible and easier of access than they are, it must be of the greatest interest to the planters themselves, as well as to the Government, and to road and railway companies, to keep once-tilled land under cultivation, and not to put the centre of coffee-culture farther and farther from the sea, thus rendering comparatively useless greater and greater stretches of expensive roads.

All this considered, it must be clear that poor, newly-arrived colonists cannot buy any soil fit for the lucrative culture of coffee near the coast; and, in out-of-the-way places in the interior, where it may be had on reasonable terms, it is of no use to them, as they cannot sell the produce. Only after the entire abolition of slavery will and can all this change. The soil will get cheaper, especially if a land-tax be levied; the Government will be able to buy good and advantageously situated districts for new settlers; and then only, the large fazendas with their hundreds of negroes disappearing, and smaller estates, conducted on sounder principles, taking their place, agriculture will develope itself, as it ought, on such a first-rate soil and under such a fertilising climate.

As to the Indians, considered from an ethno-economical point of view, as working material and equivalent for the slaves, the great task of getting them used to fixed settlements and regular work, and of uniting them to some useful community, has already been achieved. The Jesuits have shown by their Missions that it can be done. Lopez also, the ill-famed President of Paraguay, who had reaped the benefits of their long activity, working upon the same principles of absolute despotism,

---

* If any cheap mineral manure could be discovered which would answer this purpose, or would render to the capoeira (second growth, from *eda poeira*, low or thin forest) those elements which it lacks, compared with first growth, the fazendeiros might yet hold up their heads for many years to come.

had brought his Guarani State to such a degree of national development that he could carry on for five years a bloody war against a country of six times the population of his little republic; but whoever knows the indolent character of the Indians, and the tenacity with which they cling to their old habits, will not wonder that in Brazil little or nothing has been attained by the small energy and scanty means allotted to "catechese dos Indios."

The civilising work of the Jesuits was violently interrupted by their expulsion in 1759; and the Portuguese Government, always behind a century or two, could not devise any better plan than the pursuit of the red-skins by fair means or foul. As late as 1808 a decree of the king ordered war against them, especially the Botocudos, with fire and sword, until they "movidos do justo terror das minhas reaes armas," should sue for peace. Since the reign of the present emperor, Don Pedro II., they are protected by law, and spared at least as much as possible; still this protection is not always efficient, by reason of the enormous extent of the country; and the full-blood Indians will disappear in Brazil as surely as they do in North America.

Wherever they come into immediate contact with that set of conscienceless intruders who usually are the "pioneers of civilisation," they must succumb if there is no protecting element to help them. If a nation is bereft at once of everything which, till then, it cherished—its gods, its chiefs, and all its peculiar ways of life—and if it is brought into contact with European corruption; in the state of moral destitution consequent on the loss of all national and religious support, the worst results are unavoidable. The zeal with which the Indians of former Missions in Bolivia cling to the present day to the rites of the Catholic Church, may partly have its source in their childish taste for outward pomp and gaudy shows; but certainly a good deal of it arises from their striving to gain some equivalent for their lost nationality.

The gradual disappearing of this ill-fated race, numerous tribes of which certainly bore in them germs of civilisation that might have been developed under proper management, is the more to be regretted as the solution of many ethnographic problems will thus become more and more difficult. After all the most valuable notes gathered and published by Humboldt, Spix, Martius, D'Orbigny, Moke, and others, many facts have not yet found satisfactory explanation, and probably never will find it; the more so as there are so few monumental remains of former periods, and scarcely anything written by the hands of the autochthons, a few unintelligible hieroglyphs excepted.

On the South American Continent we find Indian tribes living close together—not separated by any barriers, such as ice-covered heights, impenetrable jungles, or dreary deserts—which differ so materially from each other in language, character, and customs, that they have scarcely anything in common but their brown skin and black lank hair. A new-comer, deceived by this outward similarity, will think them of the same kin and kind; but, on closer observation, he will find that they are totally different nations, living generally in deadly feud with each other; and by-and-bye he will also discover their physiognomies to be of quite another type.* So in the Southern provinces we saw in the closest vicinity two entirely different nations—of course, at war with each other from times immemorial. One of them, the Guarani, of the widely spread Tupi tribe, showing the well-known eagle profile of the North American Indians, first-rate pedlars and fishers, generally keep near the large rivers; while the other, the Coroados, or Ca-en-gangues (forest-men), as they call themselves,† more warlike and high-handed, carrying off and enslaving whomsoever they can, do not use canoes at all, and prefer the wooded ravines of the lateral valleys or the grass-grown ridges of the Campos, where the fat tapir, the wild hog, and the nimble deer fall an easy prey to their never-failing arrows and heavy lances. Their oblique eyes, short nose, and high cheek-bones, strongly remind one of the Mongolian type, though by this remark I would not imply their direct Asiatic origin.

A few years ago they fought a bloody though unsuccessful war against the white intruders, and were pursued and punished for it by the Portuguese Government in the most ruthless way, while many tribes of their hereditary foes, the softer Guarani, bent their necks without much difficulty beneath the heavy yoke of the Jesuits.

These Guarani, although their outward appearance and character recall the old Mexican tribes, seem to have come, in all probability, from the South, the Paraguay of to-day, and the Southern provinces of

---

* The slave population of Brazil, scraped together from all parts of Africa, and showing a great variety of types, also seems to newly arrived Europeans to be wrought after one and the same model—a sort of primitive negro; the general similitude of colour and hair causing the marked differences of physiognomy and cranium to be overlooked.

† Martius calls them Camés.

Brazil, and to have spread thence all over the continent. Close to the descendants of these brave wanderers, divided into a great number of vastly differing tribes (many of which have created for themselves idioms quite unintelligible to the rest), we find the usually more barbarous tribes of the real aborigines; and we must needs ask ourselves,—without finding a satisfactory answer though,—the reason of these different modes of life under the same outward conditions; why, of two nations of the same race, one should spend half its life on the water, while the other, living but a few miles off, can neither build a canoe nor handle a paddle.

Considering the Babylonish chaos of Indian languages (Martius counting for Brazil alone about two hundred and fifty different idioms), the valuable labours of the Jesuits can scarcely be too highly estimated. They first formed and fixed grammatically the Guarani or Tupi language (lingoa geral), and introduced it in their Missions; and now it has become the popular language in all the North of Brazil, especially in the provinces of Pará and Amazonas, where it is used, almost exclusively, by all the Indian settlers and half-castes of the most diverging tribes.

Martius has given a most valuable account of Indian customs, and vocabularies of a great number of their languages.

That anthropophagy is still practised by several of these tribes, unfortunately, is a fact which cannot be doubted. So with the Miranhas on the Amazon, and the Parentintins on the Madeira and Rio Negro; but equally certain it is that very many tribes have been falsely accused of it by the intruding whites, who sought to have an excuse for their cruel treatment of them. Usually, only those slain in their combats, or prisoners of war, are served at these horrid banquets; and this not without a certain choice, as a woman of the Miranha tribe assured us at Manáos. She vowed that they never ate "Christãos," that is, civilised people, whose flesh does not savour well, on account of their eating salt! But such assertions cannot be implicitly trusted, as Indians very often take a pleasure in deceiving or making fun of their curious white questioners. So they have a trick of returning for answer one of the words of the question proposed, which often gives rise to the queerest misunderstandings.*

* We took with us as servant a young Cayowá Indian, from the Aldeamento de Santo Ignacio, in the province of Paraná, who answered to the name of "Chamá,"

Only a few of the independent tribes have fixed abodes. Most of them pull down or burn their light sheds, whenever they think fit, and then wander forth, often for many miles,—the wives carrying all the household implements, the stores, and even the spare arrows of their husbands,—in quest of better hunting-grounds, to gather the ripe, wild fruit, or to visit their own plantations of Indian corn and mandioc, which this unsteady, wandering life does not hinder them from growing.

These two plants, which certainly had been cultivated for ages before the discovery of America, still number with the most important productions of Brazil, both for Indians and Europeans. The corn (milho), grown especially in the South as fodder for horses and mules, yields a coarse flour (fubá), which, cooked to a thick pap—a sort of polenta—is, together with black beans, the chief dish of the working population of the provinces of Minas Geraes and Rio de Janeiro.

Of the Mandioc root, which flourishes throughout the country from North to South, there are two kinds—the Aipim (*Manihot aipi*), much like potatoes when boiled, and the Mandioca brava (*Manihot utilissima*), of which, after extracting the very poisonous juice,* the farina is prepared, —a coarse-grained meal which, without any further preparation, takes the place of our bread on the tables of Brazilians, both high and low. Wheat and rye are only grown in the German colonies of the South, and not in sufficient quantities for the demand of the towns, which are chiefly supplied from North America and Europe. Rice, of several excellent qualities, is largely cultivated, particularly in Maranhão. It is, together with black beans (feijão) and sun-dried meat (carne seca), a daily dish with almost all classes of the population.

All these articles are rather high-priced, as their culture is not so lucrative as that of the exported articles, coffee, sugar, and cotton; and it is, therefore, neglected on the large estates.

Coffee can be grown almost everywhere, though, in the hottest districts of the North, it must be planted in the shade of larger trees, to get a good crop; and in Rio Grande and Paraná it thrives but poorly, and is grown only for domestic use. The provinces that export most are São Paulo, Rio de Janeiro, and the Eastern part of Minas Geraes.

---

that is, when it just suited his convenience. On closer investigation we found out this was believed to be his name, from his regularly answering "Chamá," to the question, "Como se chama?" (What are you called?)

* The fine starchy sediment of this juice is the tapioca.

INTRODUCTION.

Cotton, several varieties of which are indigenous to the soil, and were cultivated by the Indians long before the discovery of America, flourishes in the North (where, however, the quality is second-rate), as well as in the South, where it is acquiring greater importance as an article of export, in spite of the considerable fluctuations in price to which it has been subject.

Spread over almost as wide a range is the sugar-cane, which was introduced by the Portuguese as early as the beginning of the sixteenth century; as sugar, and páo brazil, the well-known dyewood which gave the whole country its name,* were the articles first exported by them. The work in the sugar-cane fields is said to be very laborious and irksome; and Brazilians will be found to assert that sugar-cane culture will come to a sudden stop, upon the abolition of slavery, as free workmen never would undertake it.

Another indigenous plant, of exceedingly wide range, whose culture might be much improved and increased, is the tobacco, which is held in high esteem to the present day by many of the wild Indian tribes. The big cigars, more than two feet long, with which their Pajés (usually the cleverest of the tribe, uniting the treble dignity of priest, magician, and medicine-man) besmoke their patients, certainly are the originals of the "weeds," which no Christian gentleman can do without nowadays.

Some attempts to cultivate Chinese tea in São Paulo and Minas proved a sad failure, as the quality produced was a very inferior one; whether from the effect of the climate or bad management, I cannot tell. Certainly the patient, slender-fingered son of the "Celestial Empire" seems to be better suited to the subtle work of gathering and sorting the leaves than the negro. But they have an excellent equivalent for it in Brazil—the Paraguay tea (*Ilex Paraguayensis*), also called Herva Maté, or Congonha, growing wild everywhere in the Southern provinces, and forming already a considerable article of export. An infusion of the dried and pounded leaves, imbibed through a delicately plaited little tube (bombilha), is the indispensable national beverage of all classes in the La Plata States, Paraguay, and the South of Brazil, while the North has cacáo and guaraná instead. Of these and other productions of the forests of the North, such as the cacáo and the caoutchouc, hereafter.

* The first discoverers called it Terra da Vera Cruz, or Terra da Santa Cruz (Land of the True, or of the Holy Cross), and not till long after was this denomination changed for the name of the much-appreciated wood.

By reason of excellent natural pastures of great extent (campos or prairies), the Southern provinces, Rio Grande, Paraná, Santa Catharina, and São Paulo, are particularly well adapted for cattle-breeding. The interior of Piauhy and Pernambuco, and the isles of Marajó and Goyaz, also breed fine cattle; but, on the whole, this branch of farming has not yet obtained the attention it merits, and Brazil is much in the rear even of its next neighbours, the Spanish Republics, in respect not only of the quality of the cattle, but also of utilising the different parts of the slaughtered animals, the tallow, hides, bones, hoofs, and horns.

However, it was neither the fat pasturage nor the fertility of the soil that proved the strongest allurements to the first immigrants after its discovery. It was the metallic wealth of the country. We owe the first descriptions of the interior to small troops of gold-greedy adventurers, who had set out to seek the Dorado, a fabulous land of gold and diamonds, created by their own vivid imaginations. Especially the settlers of the former Capitania de São Vicente (the present São Paulo), distinguished themselves by their bold explorations; and the province of Minas Geraes bears, to the present day, the name they gave it for its mines.

Although these latter are no longer thought of such high importance, the due development of agriculture being considered (and with reason) to be a much sounder basis of progress for the country, yet several large mines are successfully worked at Morro-Velho and its vicinity by English companies. Mato Grosso also is very rich in ore; and the old mines near the sources of the Guaporé, for example, were abandoned only on account of the difficulty of communication and of the fevers.

Diamonds also were found shortly after the discovery; and here again the province of Minas ranks foremost, with its diamond-washings in the Jequitinhonha, the Diamantina, and the Bagagem, where the renowned "Estrella do Sul" was found. Though in the last century the European merchants, anxious not to overstock the market, and so lessen the value of their Indian supplies, would not recognise Brazilian diamonds as such, they yet have forced their way; and it is not saying too much to assert that the greater part of the diamonds worn throughout the world come from Brazil.

Of course there is no question yet of cutting them there, as manufacturing activity, no matter on what scale, cannot be thought of in a country where hands are so scarce and where wages and provisions are so high. Everything that demands "mão d'obra," from the silk dress and the piano down to the palito (tooth-pick), is still imported from Europe and North America, and, in spite of the long voyage and the enormous custom-house duties, is cheaper than if it were manufactured on the spot.

The greater the distance from the sea, the greater, of course, are the difficulties of conveyance. The want of good, easy ways of communication has been one of the chief drawbacks not only to Brazil, but to all the South American States. Nowhere in the whole Continent, a hundred miles from the coast, is there a regular carriage-road to be found; and the mule, or, at best, the creaking ox-cart, with its enormous wooden wheels fixed on the axletrees, are the indispensable vehicles. It is true that conveyance on mules' backs is the only one possible on paths which, in the rainy season, are knee-deep, and sometimes breast-deep, with mud, which show ascents of twenty or thirty feet in a hundred, and which sometimes are obstructed by huge masses of loose rocks and stones; and very often it requires all the sagacity of the tropeiro (mule-driver), and all the tough perseverance and sure-footedness of his mules, to bring themselves and their loads whole and sound to their several destinations.

In consequence of these difficulties, and of the exceeding slowness of progress (scarcely ten or twelve miles a day), this mode of transport is so dear that even valuable products, like coffee, do not pay the cost of conveyance to a seaport, if the distance exceeds three hundred miles; and as the freight, moreover, necessarily packed in small colli, and loaded and unloaded so often, is exposed to all sorts of risks, it is clear that the central parts of the continent are in a sort of continual blockade, that allows neither agriculture nor trade to prosper.

In Brazil considerable exertions have been made, within the last eighteen years, to remedy this state of things; and these efforts are to be rated the more highly, seeing that the cost of fresh means of communication is very great—about three times more than in Germany—and immediate financial advantages can scarcely be expected from any such enterprises. But as they are indispensable for progress, and as the gain from an ethno-economical point of view cannot be denied, it certainly devolves on the *Government* to build roads and railways, to intersect rivers with canals, and to establish lines of steamers, be the pecuniary sacrifices never so great.

Since the opening, in 1854, of the first Brazilian railway (the Little Mauá Railroad) that leads from Rio de Janeiro to the foot of the Serra, a distance of 17 kilometres, five other railroads of 634 kilometres have been constructed up to 1867. The most considerable of them, the Don Pedro II., is without any doubt the largest enterprise of this kind in South America. Leading from Rio de Janeiro over the Serra do Mar, it has already an extent of more than 200 kilometres, and will certainly on some future day be the chief mode of communication for the provinces of Minas, Goyaz, and Mato Grosso.

Next to it in importance ranks the São Paulo Railway, leading from the port of Santos to the interior of the province, the passage of the Serra being effected by means of stationary engines and a steel rope. In the present day, when any declivity may be freely encountered after Fell's system, it certainly would have been constructed otherwise. Then follow the Bahia and Pernambuco railroads, with an extent of about 124 kilometres each up to the present date, both designed for the purpose of connecting the upper São Francisco Valley with the coast. They prosper even less than the others, leading for the most part through waste, uncultivated tracts. A little better off is the Cantagallo Railroad, of about 50 kilometres, leading from the Villa Nova, in the province of Rio, to Cachoeira at the foot of the Serra. It is to be conducted up to Novo Friburgo, an old Swiss colony. Besides these, preparatory surveys have recently been made for new lines in the provinces of Rio Grande do Sul, Bahia, Rio Grande do Norte, &c., by which new districts, now almost worthless, will be opened to industry and trade.

The above-mentioned Little Mauá Railroad is connected with a carriage-road leading up the steep Serra to Petropolis, a little town in which flaxen-haired children playing in the streets, and their native accent, though mixed up with a sad Portugüese, remind the German strongly of "Home, sweet Home," on the other side of the ocean. Unfortunately this colony, founded in 1845, is very ill-adapted for agriculture, the ground being rough and rocky, with steep slopes on which it is impossible to work with the plough. The inhabitants depend chiefly on the foreigners, who, following the example of the Imperial family, there spend the summer months, to escape the heat and sometimes the yellow fever of the capital.

From Petropolis the normal carriage-road of the Company União e Industria, constructed by my father from 1855—1862, leads to Juiz de Fora, in the province of Minas, a distance of 147 kilometres. It was designed to be extended to Ouro Preto, the capital of the province, and to be connected with a line of steamers on the Rio das Velhas. It crosses the richest coffee-growing districts of Rio de Janeiro and Minas, and has long ago repaid the vast outlay involved in large rock-blasting operations in the Serra do Mar, and in the construction of an iron bridge over the Parahyba of 150 metres length, and the like works, by augmenting the value of the land and increasing the productiveness of the whole district.

With the great extent of the coast of the Empire, the steam navigation is, of course, of the greater importance, as the land communications are by no means easy. Considering that, before the time of steamers, a Government order took on an average about a month to get from the capital to Pará, or to any seaport of Rio Grande do Sul; and again, that at least six weeks elapsed before the decree reached Manáos, and about the same time, or more, before it got from Rio Grande, by the River Plate and the Paraguay, to Cuyabá, the capital of Mato Grosso, one can form a slight idea of the difficulties to be surmounted by the Central Government. Just as in China, the president of some distant province might have been driven away and the Government overthrown without the capital being aware of it for two months or more; and indeed, at the time of the Declaration of Independence, the Northern provinces, with Pará at their head, were on the eve of siding with Portugal, while at Rio and in the whole South the Revolution had long got the upper hand.

Now all this is greatly changed. Besides several Transatlantic lines (from Southampton, Liverpool, Antwerp, Hamburg, Bordeaux, Marseilles) and a New York line, all of which touch at Rio, Bahia, and Pernambuco, there is also a Brazilian line of steamers, which links all the minor ports, and corresponds with the Amazon line and with those on the River Plate and Paraguay. A voyage along the coast, revealing in quick succession the rocky cones of the Serra, proud cities like Bahia and Pernambuco, idyllic fisher-villages half hidden under palm-groves, and dreary stretches of sandy beach, is certainly one of the most captivating that can be fancied.

But while the blue Atlantic with ease bears the mightiest steamers on its broad bosom, and while this part of it generally deserves the appellation given to it by the Portuguese, *um mar de leite* (a sea of milk)—as neither frequent squalls nor dangerous cliffs imperil the vessels —the rivers of the Empire, with the exception of the Amazon and the

Paraguay, together with the La Plata, have their full share of currents, crags, and obstructions.

If the Paraná, with its large affluents that reach to the heart of Minas, the São Francisco, the Rio Doce, the Jequitinhonha and the affluents of the Amazon, the Tocantins, Araguaya, Xingú, Tapajos, Madeira, &c., were perfectly navigable, Brazil would not indeed have to look out for railways and roads just yet. Unfortunately all these rivers have, at different points of their course, either real falls—as the São Francisco, not far above its mouth, has the grand fall of Paulo Affonço—or currents that scarcely allow a canoe or a flat boat to pass; and thus thousands of square miles of the richest soil have continued for ages to remain unexplored, uncultivated, and almost totally uninhabited.

Incredible as it may appear at first sight, it is nevertheless true that the fate of the Southern provinces of Brazil, the western parts of São Paulo, Paraná, and the south of Minas and Mato Grosso, would be a very different one if strong currents and the lofty falls of Sete Quedas, unvisited by any European for two hundred years since the missionary expeditions of the Jesuits, did not render the Paraná unfit for navigation. If on that chief arm of the La Plata Brazilian men-of-war had been stationed, if men and war material could have come by its affluents, the Iguaçu, Paranapanema, and Tieté, the war with Paraguay would have come to an end much sooner, or probably would not have been begun at all.

Notwithstanding the magnificent water-net of the South American Continent, that strikes any one on the map, as yet only the La Plata and the Paraguay, and the Amazon, with the Lower Madeira, are ploughed regularly by steamers; and, in all likelihood, steam navigation in the interior will, for many years to come, be limited to these chief arteries, unless the upper navigable parts of the Araguaya (a tributary of the Tocantins) and the Amazon are connected by some economical railroad with its lower course, as is proposed to be done on the Madeira.

If, from the preceding pages the reader has gathered that in Brazil there is a wide field for human intelligence and energy, the following short historical sketch will show why the country has as yet failed to reach a higher degree of development, with all its great gifts of Nature.

INTRODUCTION.

From the period of the discovery of Brazil by the Portuguese* to the Declaration of Independence in 1822, it was always kept under by the mother country, to the extent indeed of preventing all progress. No less a personage than a Portuguese king himself, Don João IV. (who died in 1656), in a conversation with the French ambassador, with singular sincerity called Brazil his *vaca de leite* (milch-cow). Every measure that might have tended in the least to strengthen the colony, was strictly suppressed, however advantageous it might have proved. Of course nothing was done for schools, Portugal never having distinguished itself in that respect; and, in the most inconsiderate fashion, immense tracts of land, so called capitanias, were given away to courtiers who never intended doing anything in the way of colonising or cultivating them, or to young noblemen who had become objectionable to their families by the extravagance of their lives, and who, of all men, were least fit for the difficult duties of colonisation and administration, though it must be remarked that, among these first Donatarios, there were some excellent men, such as Duarte Coelho, founder of Pernambuco, and Martin Affonço de Souza, renowned for his deeds in India, and founder of the city of São Paulo.

One of the privileges of these Donatarios was to enslave "Indios or Gentios," wherever they or their subordinates could get them, and to sell certain numbers of them "tax-free" at Lisbon. Of course, the settlers made large use of this right; and, also of course, the Indians sought to revenge themselves by sudden attacks and all sorts of cruelties; for which they were, in their turn, pursued only the more pitilessly. By-and-bye the Order of the Jesuits, that soon after its establishment had got a sure footing in Brazil,—especially at Bahia,—became a mighty aid to the settlers, protected their run-away slaves, and generally knew how to arrange things so well that a Carta Regia (Order of the King) gave them the right to plan laws for their regulation. In due time these appeared, and were not to the disadvantage of the Padres, as may be imagined. They ordained, for example, among other things, that any settler asserting a claim to a slave, without being able fully

---

* Alvares de Cabral landed, in 1500, first near Monte Pascal, close to Porto Seguro, and, in the following year, he and the Italian, Américo Vespucci, set out with a small flotilla to sail round the supposed isle. They went along the whole west, and discovered, in January, 1502, the magnificent bay of Rio de Janeiro, which they believed to be the mouth of a large river. This error generated the name of the city and province.

to substantiate it, should lose it entirely, and that the slave should then be the property of the Order; and as, besides, by another Carta Regia, only the Indians captured in "just" war could be considered as slaves, the colonists were entirely in the hands of the Holy Fathers, and naturally embraced with great zeal the proposal of the "philanthropic" Mexican bishop, Las Casas, to import African slaves, the right of whose possession it would be easier to prove. They availed themselves, on a large scale, of the permission given in 1511 of introducing negro slaves, without payment of any duties, into the new colony; the more so as, from continual pursuit and ill-treatment, the Indian tribes living near the sea either were annihilated or had retired to the forests of the interior. Nor were they in security there, for, in spite of Papal Bulls which declared them to be free, greedy hordes of Paulistas (down to the seventeenth century) made great raids as far as the Jesuit Missions on the Paraná and Uruguay for the purpose of fetching Indian slaves; and, even to the present day, many an Indian child is sold in the forests of the Amazon and Pará for a knife, or a hatchet, or a few beads.

The difficulties of the young colony were soon increased by outward foes. The Governador Geral, Men de Sá, appointed in 1549, and residing at the Cidade do Salvador (the present Bahia), had immediately to make preparations against the French; who, under the leadership of the Huguenot Villegaignon, and with the aid of some Indian tribes, their allies, had erected an intrenched camp on the bay of Rio de Janeiro (then Cidade de São Sebastião). In January, 1567, a great battle was fought there, which cost the brave Men de Sá, nephew to the Governador, his life, and which ended in the defeat of the French; and Maranhão, which they had taken in 1614, was re-conquered by the Portuguese.*

The Dutch were more pertinacious in their desire for annexation. In 1624 they took Bahia; in 1630 Pernambuco, which began to prosper well under the brief rule of the Prince Maurice of Nassau; and in 1641 Maranhão; but, as they were not seconded sufficiently by the mother country, just when difficulties arose, the Portuguese succeeded, with

---

* During the war of the Succession to the Spanish throne they revenged themselves, however, for all these failures. In 1710 there came a French fleet under Duclerc; and, in 1711, a stronger one under Duguay-Trouin, who bombarded, ransacked, and plundered Rio de Janeiro.

some difficulty, in mastering them, and finally driving them away in 1654.

Unfortunately the period of peace which followed these victories, and during which the internally effervescing condition of things began to clear and settle, was used by the Portuguese Government only to get up a kind of old Japanese system of isolation, by which it was intended to keep the colony in perpetual tutelage. In consequence of this even now, after the lapse of half a century since it violently separated itself, Brazilians generally entertain a bitter grudge against the mother country. All the trade to and from Brazil was engrossed by Portugal; every functionary, down to the last clerk, was Portuguese.* Any other European of scientific education was looked at with suspicion; and particularly they sought to prevent by all means the exploration of the interior, as they feared not only that the eyes of the natives might be opened to their mode of administration, but also that such travellers might side with the Spaniards in their long dispute regarding the boundaries of the two nations, as the French astronomer, La Condamine, had done.

This question, which arose shortly after the discovery, and was hushed up only during the short Union of both the Crowns (from 1581—1640), broke out with renewed vigour every now and then, maugre the Treaty of Tordesilhas in 1494; according to which, by a bull of Pope Alexander VI., the infamous Borgia, the transmarine possessions of the two nations were to be divided by a meridian drawn arbitrarily over land and main; and in spite of a subsequent confirmation of this strange partition of the terrestrial globe by Pope Julius II., in 1506. Both these extraordinary documents dating from a period when the real extent of our planet, and the situation of its various parts, were utterly unknown, either a stout belief in their own infallibility, or a strong dose of sublime audacity, was certainly required to induce the successors of St. Peter ever to impose such an award.

---

* To the present day the Brazilian calls the Dutch cheese *queijo do reino*, cheese from the kingdom, that is to say, from Portugal; brown Indian pepper, *pimenta do reino;* because these articles and many others, by no means produced on Portuguese soil, reached the colony only through Portugal, of course at three times their original price. Formerly in Brazil, as still in Bolivia, the costliest plate might be found in opulent houses, but not enough knives and glasses, since plate of true Portuguese manufacture could be had more easily, and comparatively cheaper, than steelware or crockery.

By the Treaty of São Ildefonso, in 1777, both parties having long felt how impracticable the old arrangements were—at least, for their American colonies—the boundaries were fixed upon the principle of the *uti possidetis*, at any rate so far as the imperfect knowledge of the interior allowed; but this effort also proved to be vain, as the opportunity of a peaceful understanding between the two nations had been permitted to elapse (intentionally, as is thought) by the Portuguese without a final clearing up of the disputed points. Arms were taken up anew, but until now they failed to bring about any durable results; and the unsolved question descended as an evil heritage to their respective heirs, Brazil, and the South American Republics. A few years ago it gave rise to the terrible war with Paraguay; and it will lead to fresh conflicts between Brazil and the Argentine Republic, which, though closely allied against the common enemy, will sooner or later have to fight it out, especially if the districts in question be opened to trade and civilisation by the world-transforming agency of steam.

A new era began for the country in 1808, with the transmigration of the king Don João VI., who sought and found a refuge from the French grenadiers in the long-neglected colony. As it were at one blow, it rose to an equality of rank with the mother country, which, for a time, indeed had to play a secondary part. During the thirteen years which Don João VI. spent in Brazil, he repealed a great many of the short-sighted and narrow-minded measures which had obstructed all progress; such, for example, as one passed so late as 1784, which prohibited the Brazilians to manufacture any tissues, save the very coarsest cotton for the clothing of the negroes. But, unfortunately, he roused to a blazing flame the old hatred against the Portuguese, by filling all the offices with them, and by creating sinecures for the courtiers who had migrated with him.

A Revolution, which broke out at Pernambuco in 1812, was easily subdued, as the neighbouring provinces, headed by Bahia, positively refused to join it; but the so-called Constitutional Revolution of Portugal, in 1820, found a loud echo in Brazil. At Pará and Bahia, and, finally at Rio de Janeiro, the Portuguese troops sided with the insurgents. The Crown Prince himself took the lead, and, in February, 1821, the King was forced to recognise the constitution, yet to be drawn up by the Cortes at Lisbon. But, as this required before all things the return of the King, and, besides, was exactly calculated to reduce the colony to its former state of dependence, the enthusiasm of the disappointed Brazilians suffered a severe shock; new disorders followed; and, after a stormy session of the Chambers, the King was summoned to accept for Brazil the Spanish Constitution of 1812. He assented to everything; but, within an hour after the retirement of the King, the sitting of the Assembly was arrested by a volley fired through the windows by a company of Portuguese riflemen: and Don João VI. availed himself of the panic of the capital to withdraw all his concessions, and to set sail for Lisbon three days afterwards (on the 26th of April, 1821), leaving the Crown Prince, Don Pedro, as Regent, with extensive powers.

The Portuguese Cortes, however, could not yet make up their mind either to abandon their old system of keeping down and tutoring the colony, or to concede to it any privileges. Continual chicanes and encroachments upon his rights drove the Prince Regent at last openly to head the revolutionary party. At Ipiranga, near São Paulo, having received another friendly missive from Lisbon, he raised, on the 7th of September, 1822, the cry of "*Independencia ou morte!*" which was echoed with enthusiasm throughout the country. On his return to Rio, he was unanimously declared emperor on the 21st of September, and crowned as such on the 1st of December. In about a year's time all the provinces were vacated by the Portuguese troops; and in 1825, chiefly through the mediation of England, Brazil was acknowledged as an independent empire.

But the inner commotions continued, and were not even soothed by a new Constitution, drawn up in 1823, and sworn to by the Emperor in 1824. New revolts in Pernambuco, and some of the other Northern provinces, and a war of three years with the Argentine Republic, which ended in 1828 by Brazil giving up Banda Oriental, annexed only eleven years before, disturbed and weakened the land. The foreign soldiers, enlisted for this war, and retained after its conclusion to keep down the Opposition, and the extravagant private life of the Emperor, who recklessly trampled down the honour of respectable families, provoked dissatisfaction and murmurs, which rose to the highest pitch when he insisted upon carrying on a most unpopular war in Portugal to defend the rights of his daughter, Dona Maria da Gloria (in whose favour he had abdicated the Portuguese Crown), against his brother, Don Miguel. In April, 1831, Don Pedro I., so enthusiastically raised to the

Brazilian throne only nine years before, was forced to abdicate it, deserted and betrayed by every one, in behalf of his younger son, Pedro.

The next period was the most disturbed one that the young Empire had yet witnessed. Slave revolts at Bahia, a civil war in the South, which almost cost it the province of Rio Grande do Sul, and the bloody rebellion known as the Guerra dos Cabanos, in Pará and Amazon, from 1835 to 1837, followed each other quickly. In this last revolt, the Brazilians had stirred up the Indians and mestizoes against the abhorred Portuguese, without considering that they should not be able to quench the fire they had themselves kindled. In a short time, the fury of the whole coloured population turned against all whites, Brazilians and Portuguese alike, without any distinction. More than 10,000 persons are said to have perished in this Guerra dos Cabanos; and, to the present day, those terrible times and the barbarous cruelties committed by the Indians, half-castes, and mulattoes, continue to be talked of with awe in the two provinces.

A revolution in Minas, got up by the personal ambitions of a few political leaders, rather than emanating from the spirit of the people, and the war against Rosas, the Dictator of the Argentine Republic, passed over Brazil without leaving deep traces, at least when compared with the last war against Paraguay; which, besides the stimulus of the old differences about boundaries, was occasioned by the endless vexations and restrictions, with which the Dictator Lopez strove to ruin the Brazilian trade on the Paraguay, and to prejudice the province of Mato Grosso. This despot, cracked up by many European journals as a gallant hero and devoted patriot, at first imitated and, at last, surpassed the good examples of his predecessors, Dr. Francia, the first "Supremo" of Paraguay, who, out of distrust, had detained Humboldt's companion, the Botanist Bonpland, for many years in the country; and of old Lopez, his father, who in 1855 directed the firing-upon of the *Waterwitch*, a steamer fitted out by the United States for a scientific expedition. Even before the war, the younger Lopez indulged himself in the strangest encroachments upon the personal rights, not of Brazilians only, but of Germans, Englishmen, North Americans, and Frenchmen; and even his own countrymen, especially those belonging to the better classes, whose opposition he had to fear, were either made away with in one way and another, or expelled.

It is inconceivable why Brazil so long continued to look on inactively while Lopez was erecting his fortress Humaitá, and why it should never have thought of placing its army and navy on a better footing, or, at least, of opening a road to the menaced Mato Grosso, so easily to be cut off entirely. The importance of such a way of communication was proved but too clearly by the fate of a detachment of 3,000 men, inadvertently sent by land, even in the absence of roads, to the ill-fated province, which had been devastated already by the Paraguayan hordes. Two-thirds of them perished miserably on the way; the rest arrived there, after eight months of terrible sufferings, in such a condition that they had, all of them, to be sent to the hospitals. Besides cholera and small-pox, hunger and privations of every kind made sad havoc among the Brazilians, certainly more than the Paraguayan bullets.

Notwithstanding several decided victories over the latter, the Brazilians never knew how to profit by them; and the restless enemy, in whose ranks the Dictator had maintained the strictest discipline and unyielding courage in the face of all privations, always contrived to rally, to take up new positions of great strength, and to receive fresh auxiliary troops and provisions. The heaviest blame in this respect falls to the Marquez de Caxias, who was entrusted with the conduct of the Brazilian army. His total want of energy and of military talent, and his perpetual hesitations, caused the disastrous war to last five long years. Only when he was superseded in the command by the Comte d'Eu, son-in-law of the Emperor, were the operations carried on more actively; and they succeeded at last in surrounding the fugitive despot and rendering him inoffensive for the future.

Well-nigh incredible to Europeans will appear the cruelties of this petty tyrant; who, under a gold-embroidered uniform, bore the wild heart of the Pampas Indian relishing the tortures of his fellow-men. Especially when he saw that there was no help for it but to surrender or to die, his fury became boundless. No one better than a half-wild Guarani could hope to escape his suspicions; and whoever was suspected was doomed. A German engineer (Mr. F. v. T.), a highly accomplished young man who had been chief of the Paraguayan Telegraph system, assured me at Rio de Janeiro, whither he had been brought by the Brazilians, that hundreds and hundreds of prisoners of all nations, superior Paraguayan officers, priests, and ladies, had been cruelly tortured, whipped to death, or shot, very often without the slightest shade of a reason. His woeful tale of sufferings was strictly confirmed by the interesting book of Major von Versen, who spent the last two years of the war in the Paraguayan camp, and who, like v. T., had been sentenced to death by Lopez, and had had a narrow escape. And this ferocious barbarian, who moreover had shown throughout the contest a cowardice and a petty care for his own Ego, surpassing all bounds; who was grand only in respect of the cold selfishness with which he rejected all proposals of peace, as they of course involved his exile, and which enabled him to look quietly on while the whole nation perished for him; this man was praised by a portion of the European press (the Belgian especially) as a gallant hero, as the brave defender of his country against foreign usurpation!

Brazil, it is true, has to make amends for more than one wrong, as well in its external as in its internal affairs; but (omitting Paraguay) in comparison with the other South American States,—Chile excepted,—it shines like a green oasis amid the desert of these so-called republics, which are for ever wavering between anarchy and despotism.

If the Brazilians, in apology for the backwardness of their country, call it a new one, compared with even the United States, they certainly are right in some respects; as, only since its freedom from Portuguese mismanagement could anything be done for its progress and improvement, or any steps be taken for the systematic development of its natural riches.

On the whole, it seems as if, since the departure of the Emperor Don Pedro II., Europe took a livelier interest in the Transatlantic Monarchy. Let us hope that this interest will be durable, and that both parties will derive advantage from it.

CHAPTER I.

FROM RIO DE JANEIRO TO THE RAPIDS OF THE MADEIRA.

Rio de Janeiro.—Bahia.—Pernambuco. — Parahyba do Norte. — Ceará. — Maranhão. —Pará.—Amazon.—Rio Negro.— Manáos. — Lower Madeira.— Seringueiros.— Praia de Tamanduá.

IF the emerging of a flat, dreary coast is hailed with joy by any one who but for a few days has felt himself the football of the waves, certainly the magnificent Bay of Rio de Janeiro, with the bold outlines of its surrounding peaks and its lovely palm-covered isles and islets, must delight the heart of the sea-weary wanderer. The bare, strangely shaped cones of the Sugarloaf and of the Corcovado, the singularly flat top of the Gavia ("round top"), and the rugged blue Serra dos Orgãos and Serra da Estrella, had long been dear old friends of ours: yet they impressed us anew when, in November, 1867, we took a last look at them and other less inviting friends from the deck of the *Paraná*, that bravely fought her way through the blue waves, leaving to her left Santa Cruz, an old fort defending the entrance of the bay, and to her right the Pão d'Assucar, the first of a majestic row of towering cones.

None of the other ports of Brazil can contest the palm of beauty with the Capital, emphatically called the "Cidade Heroica," although the charms so easily imparted by a rich tropical vegetation are the same, more or less, with all of them.

BAHIA is the first of them touched by the steamer on her way from Rio to Pará. It does not offer anything very interesting except its public gardens, whence one may overlook the bay and port from beneath the cool shade of some groups of beautiful old mangueiras.

Still less interesting is the neighbouring little port of MACEYO, the capital of the province of Alagoas.

But at PERNAMBUCO the trouble of going ashore is well repaid either by a visit to the new parts of the city, that are well planned and give a

ENTRY OF THE BAY OF RIO DE JANEIRO, AS SEEN FROM THE CORCOVADO.

more favourable impression than those of Rio, for instance, or by a visit to picturesque OLINDA on its lovely hill.

On the remarkable coral reef that protects the port are a fine new lighthouse and a quaint old watch-tower, dating from the time of the Dutch dominion.

This coral reef, which has given its name (*Recife*) to one of the three suburbs of the town, is extending all along the coast of Brazil, and allows only at a few places—at Ceará, for instance—of a safe entry for large vessels.

PARAHYBA DO NORTE, situated on the river of the same name at some distance from its mouth, has lonely grass-covered streets and some large, dreary-looking convents of Benedictines, Franciscans, and Jesuits.

A lively contrast to this melancholy and desolate town is offered by the picturesque little fishing-hamlet Cabedello, beneath its grove of palms, near the mouth of the river and in front of the anchoring-ground. The surf-washed brick walls of a small fort built by the Dutch give a sort of historical background to the peaceful landscape. Once, perhaps,

THE RUGGED PEAKS OF THE ORGAN MOUNTAINS.

its few iron guns had to defend the entry against the Portuguese Caravelas, and the quiet harbour witnessed scenes of strife and bloodshed; but now they are almost covered with luxuriant creepers, and lie there rusting in the sand. The female portion of the inhabitants, mostly coloured people, keep up an industry of lace-manufacture after somewhat old fashioned but not the less interesting Portuguese patterns.

North of this point the coast of RIO GRANDE DO NORTE and CEARÁ presents itself as a waste of sandy beach, ever swept by the winds and the waves, though the latter province is said to offer rich and picturesque districts in its interior.

In the port, or rather in the open harbour that serves as anchoring-ground for the increasing commerce of the capital, Fortaleza or Ceará,* are seen sweeping along like arrows those jangadas we had first seen at Pernambuco. They are small rafts made of five planks of light timber, upon which daring fishermen, mostly half-bred Indians and mulattoes, venture far out to sea. He who would go ashore at Ceará must trust himself on one of these frail and unstable vehicles, at the risk of having it turned upside down, or, at the best, of being wetted to the skin by the raging surf.

Of MARANHÃO, which, like Parahyba do Norte, gives an impression of decay, there is little to mention beyond the extraordinary number of sharks in the port, attracted thither by the slaughter-houses on shore, and rendering bathing there impossible.

At length, on November 29th, 1867, we reached PARÁ, at the mouth of the Pará River. The port was full of vessels of all sea-going nations, and among them was the elegantly shaped Brazilian steam-corvette *Nitheroy*. The church-towers and convent-turrets, and the far horizon, with the Ilha das Onças, make it a very pleasant picture, although the absence of any commanding height reminds one forcibly of the flat Dutch landscapes.

The commerce of this city has been rapidly increasing since the year 1850, owing to the improved communication with the immense Amazon basin, which extends from this favourably situated place to the foot of the Cordilleras in the West. Steam has been the powerful lever of the commercial development of Pará; and the supporting point of this lever has, until now, been found only in the immense exuberance of the vegetation, the fruits, the resins, and the timber of those colossal forests which extend over nearly 30 degrees of longitude and 20 of latitude. "A Industria do Amazonas é quasi toda extractiva," that is, based on a sort of robbery, say the Brazilians themselves. Bountiful Nature does almost everything there, while man scarcely helps her.

The upper parts of the Amazon, the Solimões, and their mighty

---

* An article of export peculiar to Ceará is the hard brown wax of the carnauba palm, with which the Brazilians make a sort of dull-burning candles.

affluents, were almost a *terra incognita* before steamers divided the yellow floods of the former. There were only a few slave-dealing regatões,* tempted by their illicit gains, or some clerks of mercantile houses at Pará, who braved the difficulties of a weary voyage in small boats for three or four months, to keep up a highly-lucrative trade in caoutchouc, cacao, Pará nuts, several kinds of resin, and dried fish.

Some eight or ten years ago, all this began to improve. The fertility of the land became better known; and the trade gradually lost the character of slave-traffic and robbery, at least in the more peopled regions of the valley, free competition having been, at last, rendered possible.

In the year 1867, the Government of Brazil finally abandoned the old narrow-minded system of colonial exclusiveness, and declared the Amazon free to the flags of all nations.

But the results of this measure will be of imaginary advantage only, until it is extended as well to the various branch streams; for none of the neighbouring states, Perú, Bolivia, or Venezuela—which alone, even now, have the privilege of navigating them under their national colours—have the power to call into life a well-organised steam-fleet. The "Stars and Stripes" only could effect a thorough change there; but, as yet, they are floating on none of those mighty streams.†

The city of PARÁ does not yield a favourable impression, though there are some monumental edifices in the main streets that formerly might have had some pretensions to architectural beauty; but they have gone to decay, and the commerce of to-day is of too recent a date to make any display in public buildings.

The Cathedral, whose wide bare aisles are of striking grandeur; the Episcopal Palace, and the Palace of the President, originally intended for

---

* Regatão, derived from "resgatar," to *liberate* the prisoners of war of the Indians, whose lives were forfeited. On this pretext the Regatões, at the same time the pedlars of those regions, not only kept up a very flourishing and lucrative slave-trade, but they practised all sorts of cruelties and crimes in the huts of the savage and half-civilised inhabitants of these countries. On several occasions Liberal deputies have warmly spoken, in the Chambers at Rio de Janeiro, against this inexcusable abuse, which still continues, though on a minor scale; but in vain. The distances are too great, and the political influence of the interested parties is too powerful for a successful prosecution of the criminals in these out-of-the-way places. To this day Portuguese merchants keep, on the borders of the Japurá, Purús, Teffé, &c., a great number of aboriginal families in such a degree of dependence that it differs from real slavery only by the circumstance that their masters wisely refrain from selling such useful domestic animals!

† I have just learned that the Imperial Government has, as a special favour, conceded permission to the North American Company carrying out our railway project on the Madeira, to send an American schooner up to Santo Antonio under her national flag.

Don João VI.'s residence when he came to Brazil, are the most conspicuous of them.

The streets are large and regular, but they have an abominable pavement of a soft ferruginous sandstone (pedra canga), which is ground down by the wheels to a fine red dust, apt to be extremely annoying.

ENTRY OF THE BAY OF RIO DE JANEIRO, AS SEEN FROM THE OPPOSITE SHORE.

But Pará has one ornament of which it may well be proud; the shady walks beneath plantations of fine trees (mostly palms), known under the name of "Estradas," and forming an agreeable avenue from the city to the country.

Amid the rich vegetation of the gardens there is one species of palm-tree that especially strikes the foreigner with the matchless grace of its slender stem and light feathery leaves, which are waved about by the slightest breath of air. It is the Assaï, whose fruit (a small nut with a dark blue pulp) makes a very popular and, indeed, very refreshing beverage. Similar beverages are obtained from the fruits of the Bacaba and Bataúa palms, by passing the rich pulps through a sieve, and mixing them with water and sugar.

As soon as we had completed our official visits to the President and others, and had made a few private calls, we took our passage on board the *Belem*, a first-rate steamer of the Amazon Steam Company; whose commander, Senhor Leal, formerly in the Brazilian Navy, received us with great kindness.

The steamers of this Company are from 500 to 600 tons burden, and of 200 horse-power. They are well fitted out; the quarter-deck especially is sheltered against sun and rain by a solid roof, thus forming an agreeable lounge. Here the meals are taken; and in the evening the slender iron columns of the roof support the hammocks, which every one prefers to the hot beds in the cabins below.

Our company was a very motley one. There was the Brazilian civil official, deeming it rather hard to be sent to such a place of exile as Serpa or Manáos; there was the Portuguese Vendeiro, unable to take interest in anything save his porcentages; and there was the American colonist from one of the Southern States, who emigrated in disgust at the defeat of his party, tried life at Santarem at the mouth of the Tapajoz, but found it so dreadfully "dull" that he is going to move heaven and earth at Pará to get repaid for the cost of his passage home again. There were merchants from Venezuela and Bolivia, who, coming in their barques for hundreds of leagues through currents and cataracts, have sold their goods at Pará, and bought others to refreight their boats, which they have left at Serpa or Manáos. Then there was the officer of the Peruvian navy, come quietly as a civilian to inspect, in a friendly way, the state of things in his neighbour's home, and to report to his Government how much, or how little, the Brazilians have done within the last few years to protect these regions against a surprise from his countrymen;* and last, but not least, there was the Italian missionary, a long-bearded Capuchin monk, certainly regretting in his innermost heart that blessed time when cassock and scapulary could place themselves as insurmountable barriers between Governments and Indians, and when his Church alone had the privilege of dealing with the latter. These were our fellow-passengers who peacefully extended themselves in their hammocks, side by side, beneath the sheltering roof of the *Belem*, indulging in that dreamy *dolce far niente*, inevitably produced by a glaring sun and the soft rocking of a vessel, or chatting quietly, as the evening breeze slightly roused their drowsy spirits.

The steamer now passed through the large Bahia de Marajó, whose

---

* Tabatinga, the Brazilian frontier fort, against Perú, is in a most dilapidated state. A Brazilian officer of rank once told me, with that openness which characterises the educated Brazilian, "O nosso celebre Tabatinga, o baluarte contra o Perú, que elles chamão uma fortaleza, é antes uma fraqueza!" (Our celebrated Tabatinga, the bulwark against Perú, that they call a fortress, is rather a weakness.)

flat banks are scarcely discernible, leaving us to guess only the wide mouth of the Tocantins to be where sky and water are melting into one blue horizon, into the Estreito do Breves, one of those narrow, intricate channels, through which the powerful Amazon has to send its waters to the Pará. Magnificent groups of Muriti palms line its sides, their broad waving fans silvered by the brightest of moonshine. At dawn the *Belem* touched at GURUPÁ and PORTO DO MOZ, small villages, inhabited by Indians and half-castes, leaving at the right the singularly shaped flat hills of Almeirim, the only ones seen on the whole tour. After PRAINHA

A JANGADA IN THE BREAKERS.

and MONTE ALEGRE, two other stations of little importance, we reached at last SANTAREM, at the mouth of the Tapajoz, a prosperous and pretty little town. There is a certain charm about that sloping hill, covered with whitewashed houses and cottages, and green gardens, and overlooking a white beach full of boats and barques of every size. Tempted by the lovely aspect, we went on shore to stretch our limbs a little, and to gather some statistical notes, if possible; but we had no idea of the difficulties of the latter undertaking. We began by asking the proprietor of a little shop, who was sitting quietly on his doorstep, and inhaling the exquisite fragrance of some melons near him, while he indulged in that broad stare which probably all new arrivals are subjected to at Santarem: "Quantas almas tem aqui?" (How many souls do you count here?) Uneducated Brazilians never being sure of their L's and R's. "Quantas armas?" (How many arms?) replied he, raising a pair of wondering eyes. "Well, almost each of us has a gun in the house, and sometimes two." "Mas não, senhor, queriamos saber quantos homens morão neste lugar?" (No, sir, we wish to know how many men (people) are living here.) "Oh! how many men? Oh, about as many I think as there are women," he said smiling, the while archly giving a customer the required brandy, and pocketing the dirty large coins. "Mas não é isso, meu senhor, quantos *habitantes* desejavamos saber!" (How many inhabitants? we inquire.) "Oh, oh,—isto é outra cousa, quantos habitantes?" (Oh, that is a different thing! How many inhabitants?) Great pause. "Pois, habitantes tem muitos!" (Well, inhabitants, there are many here!) Just then the bell of the steamer began to ring. In despair we hastily purchased some melons, and hurried on board. How much water will have rolled down the broad Amazon before one can get informed at Santarem of the number of its inhabitants?

The next station is OBIDOS, where the breadth of the river is considerably reduced, while the declivity increases, so as to form a sort of current. A little fort on the right is scarcely of any consequence, especially as men-of-war can easily evade it, at least at high water, by passing through a lake on the right bank, which connects itself to the main stream by deep channels below and above Obidos.

The effects of high and low tide are felt here, though 400 miles from the sea; and it is only the increase of elevation that prevents it being felt higher up.

Before passing the mouth of the Madeira, which is not visible on account of the isles, we reached SERPA, a village of a dozen or so of huts and cottages on a high shore, but which may expect a prosperous future from its favourable position near the Madeira.

Here, as well as at the other stations, we took in some fuel, kept ready on shore in long, well-arranged piles.

Formerly the Amazon Company kept at Serpa a steam saw-mill, which they worked with a colony of Portuguese. The number of fine cedar-trunks* swept down every year by the Madeira from the shores of the Beni, is so great that, at the beginning of the high tides, it sufficed for a few weeks to maintain boats on the river, towing the swimming giants ashore, to set the saw-mill going all the year round.

Unfortunately this establishment, of which the best hopes were reasonably entertained, was badly managed, and abandoned after a short time; not without the peaceful inhabitants of Serpa having been kept in a constant agitation by the dissolute workmen, mostly Portuguese, Englishmen, and Germans. But it is to be hoped that this enterprise, with the advantages of having large quantities of the finest Brazilian cedar, and a navigable river to convey it to the very door, will not long be suspended.

Some miles above Serpa, the *Belem* entered the black water of the Rio Negro, which flows on unmixed with the whitish-yellow floods of the Amazon, for a considerable distance. Though of crystalline transparency, it looks quite dark brown when seen in volume; the colour, common to many other rivers of these regions, being caused by decomposed plants, especially a kind of swimming grass, growing in the *lagos* (lakes) on both sides, in incredible masses.

The steamer now shaped its course more and more to the north-west, and left the Amazon to run into the Rio Negro. At its lower course this is 2,000 metres in breadth, its left margin showing the wavy lines of low hills, while the whole of the opposite side, consisting of either *igapó* or *vargem*,† is exposed to inundations.

Now the first houses of MANÁOS come in sight, and in a few minutes

---

* Very similar to bay-wood.

† There are three marked kinds of alluvium in the valley that differ materially from each other in their vegetation.

1. *The Igapó*, the last deposit, may be some ten years old, but never rises to more than five yards above low water; and the vegetation is in proportion to its date. The Embaúba (*Cecropia*) especially thrives on the lowest and most recent Igapó, while the Seringa or Caoutchouc-tree (*Siphonia elastica*) prefers the older one. The Igapó is inundated already by the ordinary level of the water.

2. *The Vargem*. As soon as the Igapó has risen by the deposits of the high waters above the ordinary level of the river, the character of the vegetation changes. The Cacáo, the thorny Murú-murú palm, the slender Páo mulatto, so appreciated as fuel, appear with some other larger trees, that never are found on the Igapó. There is a sort of Vargem only inundated by extraordinary high floods, whose vegetation resembles more and more that of the next degree.

3. *The Terra Firme*, that is nothing else than the former bottom of the sea, into which the waters have torn their way after a general raising of the ground, or the

CRAFT ON THE AMAZON AND THE MADEIRA RIVERS.

the *Belem*, after sheltering us for seven days, is quietly rocking at anchor in the port of Manãos, the capital of the province of Amazon.

The shallow bay on the left shore of the Rio Negro was full of fishing-boats, from beneath whose roofs of palm-leaves half a score of brown faces popped out to have a look at the strangers, and of large batelões (barques), come from Venezuela, laden brimful with hammocks and piassaba, the hard fibres of a palm (*Leopoldinia Piaçaba*), used for ropes and brooms. There were also the two little steamers of the Government, besides one of the Amazon Company, which was to set out on the morrow, instead of the *Belem*, for the frontiers of Perú,—another seven or eight days' voyage.

As the shallow shore did not admit a direct approach even for small boats, and as a landing-bridge seemed to be an unheard-of luxury, there

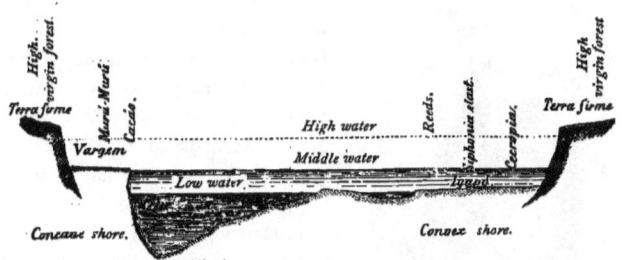

THE DIFFERENT STAGES OF LAND FORMATION.

was no resource but to disembark in two-wheeled carts, standing up to the axle-trees in the water, which took both passengers and luggage safely ashore, though certainly in not what might be called an elegant way.

The ruins of the little Portuguese fort São José da Barra do Rio

bottom of a continental lake, filled by the melted water of icebergs, if we adopt with Agassiz the hypothesis of an ice period for the Amazon Valley.

A sure vestige of the Terra Firme, besides its greater elevation above the level of the river, is the yellowish-red clay, and the rich vegetation of its virgin forests. There the Bertholletia excelsa (*Castanheira*) spreads its gigantic crown; and there also are found most of those precious woods which surpass the best of Europe both in beauty and in durability.

It may be taken as a rule for the lower course of the affluents of the Amazon, that whenever there is *Vargem* on the left concave margin of the river, there will be *Igapó* on the opposite convex one; and *vice versâ* at the next curve.

The *Terra Firme* is generally at some distance from the shore; but sometimes it takes the place of the Vargem for a short space.

Negro,* are seen on the left. But they awake much less interest than an old Indian cemetery, recently discovered on levelling the ground in the neighbourhood of the ramparts. Hundreds of those large urns of red clay (*Igaçabas*), in which the aborigines used to bury their dead, are seen there in long rows, and at no great depth in the earth. In many of them the remains of human bones have been found, whose state of decomposition showed them to be of very ancient date.

In spite of its pompous title, Capital of the province of Amazonas, Manáos is but an insignificant little town of about 3,000 inhabitants. Unpaved and badly-levelled streets, low houses, and cottages of most primitive construction, without any attempt at architectural beauty, and

numerous Portuguese vendas,—where anything may be had, from Lisbon wine and English printed cotton, to Brazilian cheese and dried pirarucú; from Paris soaps and pomatums, to caoutchouc and cacao; from the Belgian fowling-piece to the imported arrow-head—certainly fail to give an imposing *ensemble*; while the population, showing samples of all possible mixtures of white, negro, and Indian blood, also reminds us forcibly that we are in the midst of the South American continent, in the very centre of the Amazon Valley, opened so recently to civilisation and trade. But the magnificent blue sky, a most exuberant vegetation, and the fresh air of careless geniality in the people, tend to make us forget the want of luxuries, and render our first impression of Manáos a very pleasant one, heightened greatly by its igarapés †—bays or channels running far into the land, whose banks are covered with the most luxuriant verdure.

We were lucky enough to find immediately a little house, in which we installed ourselves as quickly as possible, but in which, unfortunately,

---

* The first establishment of the Portuguese on the Rio Negro dates from 1668. It was situated at the mouth of the little affluent Tarumá, and was founded by Pedro da Costa Favella. The fort of São José was built a year later by Francisco da Motta Falcão.

† Igára, canoe; and Pé, road.

we were detained much longer than we had anticipated; for, notwithstanding the efforts of the President, we were unable to get, either there or in the vicinity, the required number of rowers for our expedition, though we offered high wages.

The Indians and Mestizoes of these countries are extremely indolent, and will work just enough to keep themselves from starvation. The Rio Negro being full of excellent fish, which sell well and are caught with very little trouble, and the soil being as fertile as it can possibly be, they spend the greater part of their time lolling comfortably in their hammocks, in a state of pleasant drowsiness, which they would not exchange for regular activity for any money. More or less they are all like the mestizo, who replied to a surveyor, offering him a high rate for his services as guide, paddler, hunter, and fisher: "Return to-morrow, after I have sold my fish in town, and I'll give you double if you will let me alone for the future."

At last we were able to bid good-bye to Manáos, after surmounting innumerable difficulties, caused chiefly by the incapacity and carelessness of the Secretary to the Minister of Public Works at Rio, and the jealousy of the mighty Amazon Steam Company, who saw a dangerous rival in some future Madeira Company.

Through the Bolivian consul, Don Ignacio de Arauz, we had made the acquaintance of an Italian merchant, settled in Bolivia, who was returning thither, and who, for due compensation, agreed to cede to us some of his unwieldy boats* with the required number of Mojos and Canichana Indians. These broad-shouldered sons of the plains of the

---

* Most of the vessels on the Amazon have appellations quite different from those used on the coast. For instance, a schooner with a sort of wooden awning on deck is called *Coberta;* a broad sloop with an arched covering of palm-leaves, *Batelão;* a smaller half-covered boat for rowing and sailing, *Igarité;* while the canoe is called *Montaria,* as it takes the place, so to say, of the horse (montaria, from montar a cavallo). The shape of these vessels, especially of the smaller ones, often recalls the Chinese junks with their peculiarly formed prows. The details of their construction are rather curious. The bottom is made of one piece of the elastic wood of the Jacaréuba (*Calophyllum Brasiliense*), in Bolivia called Palo Maria. To make a boat of two or three yards in breadth, a trunk of about one yard in diameter is carefully hollowed, slowly heated over a coal fire, kept carefully asunder by wooden levers to the required width, and left so till it is perfectly cooled by frequently pouring water on it. The boat will not alter from the shape thus given to it. A few ribs, a stern, a prow, and some benches are put in, a board is nailed all round, and the boat is ready to be launched and to pass through currents and cataracts. It is true these boats are not what could be called elegant, but they answer well for the hard work they have to undergo. The price of an igarité of ten tons is about 300 milreis=£40.

Mamoré and Itonama had struck us already in the streets of Manáos by their singular clothing: straw hats made by themselves, and long shirts without sleeves, of the brown bark of the turury-tree; and by their activity. They were about the only persons we saw working in the streets, carrying turtles and fuel from the shore to the houses, or lending a hand at new buildings. They here gain about ten times as much as they could in their own country, where they live in great misery; and so there is an endless current of emigration from Bolivia to Brazil, in spite of all the reclamations of the former.

After having secured the boats and crew, we had to set about the difficult task of buying provisions for the long voyage before us,—rather a severe trial of our patience, on account of the astonishing indolence of the sparse population, which barely allows it to provide for its own subsistence. Not only are the black beans, that "staff of life" for the greater part of Brazil, brought from Pará, a distance of about three hundred leagues; but even the mandioca flour is imported from the Lower Amazon in thousands of baskets, though that mealy root would thrive just as well in the neighbourhood of Manáos. In respect of meat it is even worse. Instead of the charque, or carne seca (dried meat) of the Southern provinces, which is nutritious enough and easily preserved, they have in the North only an abominable dried fish, the pirarucú, that becomes completely uneatable after a long voyage and in such a moist atmosphere; and, as the limited space of the boats does not allow of making a large provision of live turtles, which (so to speak) take the place of beef in these regions, the traveller must largely rely on his good luck in hunting and fishing.

We took provisions for about four months, the rest of the baggage consisting of tools for canoe-making and repairing, ropes, tents, arms, drugs, and presents for the savage and half-savage tribes in the valleys of the Madeira and Mamoré.

Besides the eighty Indian paddlers, the expedition consisted of my father and myself; a young Brazilian engineer, Joaquim Manoel da Silva, our technical assistant; the Italian merchant from Bolivia; and a young German, P. v. S., whose restless spirit had driven him much about in the world, and who had before accompanied us on a similar exploration, as boat's-mate, carpenter, master of the arms, and assistant of surveys.

Our seven canoes differed greatly in size and freightage. The largest of them was fifteen tons, and had sixteen rowers; while the smallest montaria had three only, the steersman included. Most of them had a sort of half-deck, like the igarités, and a solid roof of palm-leaves or raw hide, to shelter the passengers from the sun and rain.

IGARAPÉ DO ESPÍRITO SANTO.

The two pilots, one at the rudder, the other with a broad pagaia (a sort of short hand-rudder used generally on these rivers, with round, sometimes gaudily painted, tiller) in the hand, stand behind the roof or tolda, at the end of the deck; the cargo having been carefully piled up in the middle, leaving only a small space on each side for the crew, whose dark faces and tall, well-proportioned frames, set off to advantage by their tattered shirts of bark, give altogether a strange appearance to our little flotilla, even to one well-accustomed to the navigation of these rivers.

The voyage from Manáos to the mouth of the Madeira, and on its lower course, when done as we did it—paddling slowly against the current —is, at least, a hard trial of perseverance; and " Paciencia," a favourite word of the Brazilians, which they use to freshen up their courage with, was often in our minds.

The landscape has that character of dull monotony peculiar to the valleys of these gigantic rivers, whose shores consist of alluvium for hundreds of miles. The banks of the lower Madeira, being generally igapó (the newest deposit), the vegetation rarely shows the powerful forms of the virgin-forest; now and then only, the big trunk of a bombacea is seen behind the slender white stem of the cecropia.

On the tops of the highest trees we saw, for the first time, the smooth, light green leaves of a widely-known climbing orchid, the vanilla; and one of our Indians mounted on the boughs, to get us some bunches of the long green fruit, which as yet yielded no trace of its delicate flavour, that ensues on the drying of the fruit.

Very often a broad girdle of swimming grass, Cana-rana (which means sham or false sugar-cane), separating the land from the open water, prevented our landing for miles; and we had to go on until, often late in the evening, a landing-place near one of the few huts on shore rendered it possible for us to descend and pitch our tents.

The inhabitants of these huts—whose straight black hair, dark skin, and quiet, reserved behaviour show them clearly to be of Indian race— live principally on the fish and turtle they catch in the river, while they can easily buy the few clothes they want, their ammunition and fishing-hooks, with the produce of a small cacao-plantation near their homes.

Borba, formerly called Santo Antonio de Araretama, the only village found on the whole length of the Madeira, is about twenty-five leagues above its mouth, and was founded, about the middle of the last century, by the Jesuits as a mission among the Barés and Toras Indians.

The establishment, in its early days, suffered much from the attacks of the savage Arara tribe. In spite of its pompous title of "Villa," it is only an agglomeration of twelve or fifteen low dirty huts round a half-finished little church. The only white man there, a greedy, ambitious priest, is taking advantage of the ignorance of his poor Indian parishioners in the most shameful manner; and unfortunately he is not an isolated example.

These Vigarios, and the superior officers of the Guarda Nacional, must be counted among the greatest drawbacks to the future prosperity of these districts; for the latter have the privilege of selecting men for military service in the line; and they generally abuse this right in the grossest way, leaving unmolested those who will work for them without wages, and sending away those who show a disposition to resist.

The Brazilian Government is more or less acquainted with this state of things; but the Ministers plead the great distance, and take few, if any, measures against these petty tyrants, on account of the number of votes they dispose of at the elections of the Deputies for the National Assembly.

Above Borba, which is said to have formerly produced good tobacco, there are some cacao-plantations, whose fruit at the time of our passing there (in June) were almost ripe and of a bright yellow colour; and about this part of the river also the first high trunks of the caoutchouc-tree are seen—the *Siphonia elastica*, or *Seringa*, as it is called here. On the Amazon and lower Madeira these valuable plants are almost destroyed by continuous withdrawal of their milky sap.

The huts of some caoutchouc-gatherers (Seringueiros) are seen now and then—low roofs of palm-leaves, beneath one end of which there is a raised floor or framework of lath, one or two yards from the ground, to which the inhabitants retire at high water, when necessity obliges them to lead almost an amphibious life.

The next settlement on the right bank of the Madeira is SAPUCAIA-ORÓCA, a few huts of the Mura Indians, a tribe despised and pursued by all others for their thievishness and unsettled, gipsy-like life. Especially the mighty Mundurucú tribe seems to take the task to heart of annihilating them to the last man.

As thence to Exaltacion on the Mamoré, and to Fort Principe da Beira on the Guaporé, there is not one settlement to be found of more than two or three cabins (even at *Crato* there is but one better house, and a few low straw huts); and as larger settlements also never existed before on the Madeira, one cannot but wonder that, on both old and modern maps, there is a great number of towns and hamlets inscribed in these wildernesses.

For instance, the name of Balsamo, marked on them as that of a town, is quite unknown in these regions, even as the name of a river or anything else; while Pederneira, likewise proclaimed as a town, is the name of a current of the Madeira amidst a most desolate wilderness, only trodden by the wild Caripuna Indians. Far and wide there is no vestige of any human habitation, no remains of walls, or other signs of bygone splendour; nothing but the silent forest and the roaring river bounding over dark rocks: and yet the maps show the well-known round mark of a town on this spot, which cannot be mistaken on account of a striking change of direction of the stream, and of the corresponding longitude and latitude.

Even on the lower Madeira, so much more accessible than the regions of the currents, which are visited only by wild Indians, the five thousand inhabitants of the valley are so scattered on a surface of more than two thousand square leagues that we ascended the river often for many days without seeing any kind of human habitation.

The shores of the Amazon itself are so thinly peopled that the whole immense province of Amazonas numbers only some forty thousand inhabitants; while the other great affluents of the right border—the Xingú, Tapajoz, Purús, Teffé, and Javary—which probably have analogous soil and productions, are as yet in the undisputed possession of savages.

Still it is to be wondered at that the population has not increased on the Lower Madeira, seeing its almost perfect navigability up to Santo Antonio, and the exuberance of precious timber, fruits, and resins in its forests.

The Portuguese in the past century had better hopes. They used the river as a way of communication to the province of Mato Grosso, and built the fort of Principe da Beira on the Guaporé, to protect their navigation.

As I mentioned above, the river is almost perfectly navigable below the broad zone of cataracts and currents, which, beginning at Santo Antonio, extends as far as Guajará. The few obstructions to free navigation can be easily removed. At Uroá a few rocks blasted would serve to straighten and deepen the curved channel of 50 feet breadth, which at low water is less than a yard in depth. At Marmelo and Abelhas, near Crato, even simpler operations would suffice.

At CRATO, a lovely Estancia (farm), the natural pastures (campos) extend to the water's edge. Their interior as yet is quite unexplored, but they are probably connected with the plains or prairies of Bolivia.

The cattle of the Estancia, whose first stock had come from Bolivia (descending the Madeira in barques), are thriving wonderfully, and will one day become of importance to the population of the Upper Amazon and Lower Madeira, who, until now, have subsisted chiefly on fish and turtle.

A few years ago, when the first Bolivian caoutchouc-gatherers settled near the Madeira, some raw ox-hides they had brought with them were quite a marvellous sight for their Brazilian neighbours, who used to touch them and to wonder what great powerful animals oxen must be.

Above Crato there are some ten or twelve Bolivian Seringueiros, each of them working with twenty or thirty Mojos Indians, who will make them rich men in a few years. It is true their lives are not very secure, the wild Indians not being the best of neighbours. Only eight years ago the house of one of them was attacked by the savage Parentintin Indians, and the poor victims were roasted and eaten by the cannibals; but as they were surprised on a sandbank at their horrid meal, and severely punished by their pursuers, they have never again ventured out of the depths of their forests. Yet no Seringueiro will dare to penetrate into one of the lateral valleys, be they never so full of the richest seringaes (caoutchouc forests). Sooner or later they would have to dread an attack at dawn of day, and their few fire-arms would be of little avail against the long arrows and heavy lances of the Indians, who, moreover, would not be the only enemies to be dreaded there; for the fevers, sesões (or *febres tercianas*, as the Brazilians call them), are just as bad, or worse, than the fierce red sons of the forest.

More than one settlement had to be abandoned on account of their prevalence, yet they are not so universally spread over the lower levels of these wide valleys as is generally supposed; on the contrary, they are usually restricted to certain localities. At Manáos, for instance, there never was a case of ague, nor in the plains of Bolivia; while it is very frequent on the Upper Rio Negro and Rio Branco, and in the region of the rapids of the Madeira. On the Lower Madeira there are only three places really dangerous, Santo Antonio, Jammary, and Aripuana, though in November, on arrival of the first high floods from the Beni, a fever-blast sweeps through the whole valley.

In 1820, and the following years, when the first symptoms of the revolution showed themselves that finally separated the colony of Brazil from the mother-country, Portugal, there was a sort of Portuguese Cayenne, or Lambessa, called Crato, on the Madeira, which had acquired a sad celebrity for its fevers. But it was not the Crato of to-day, which, on the contrary, enjoys an unusually wholesome climate, in consequence of the extensive grassy plains in its vicinity. That place of exile was situated about thirty-six leagues higher up, at the mouth of the Jammary; and it maintains its unhealthy repute to the present day.

The plague gets more and more malignant and frequent as one approaches the region of the rapids, where a greater elevation and a rocky soil would lead one to suppose it less dangerous and less regular in its appearance. It has happened that Bolivian merchants descending the river have been in danger of losing everything by the sudden illness of all their crew, and the death of some of them. The rest reached Santo Antonio, the last rapid, with the greatest difficulty; but thence the descent can be effected, even with a sick crew, in case of need.

On the extensive plains of Bolivia—between the Beni, Mamoré, Itonama, and Baurés—which are completely submerged every year, and where the subsiding floods leave a great number of stagnant pools, whose water, brown with decomposed organic matter, is used even for drinking, intermittent fevers, strange to say, are scarcely known. Within the last year only the first cases appeared at Exaltacion, on the Mamoré; and the inexperienced inhabitants thought them some contagious disease brought from the Amazon or the Madeira.

It is certain that, on the latter at least, the bad drinking-water, and the muddy floods issuing from the Beni at the beginning of the rainy season, are the chief causes of the ague; but as some places, like Santo Antonio, are particularly afflicted by it without any apparent reason, there must be another agent able to modify existing conditions, at least to a certain degree; and that is no doubt found in the quicker or slower renewal of the atmosphere. This is confirmed by the fact that on many spots the fevers have become less after the forest has been cleared, or cut in a certain direction; and this may explain why the miasmata cause little or no mischief in the swampy plains of the Madeira and Mamoré, where the fresh breezes play. On the whole, it seems that the fevers are decreasing on the Madeira.

Among the poorer caoutchouc-collectors Peruvian bark is rarely found, though it has already come in large hide-covered bags from the

Cordillera through the Mamoré and Madeira to the Amazon and Pará, while formerly it had to be transported over the icy heights of the Andes to the Pacific. Besides a great many most extravagant household drugs, they use commonly the caferana, a herb of bitter taste found in the woods, which is said to be as efficacious as Peruvian bark.

On account of the singularity of the fact, I cannot omit to mention that there is a German among the Seringueiros of the Madeira. He had come over from Holstein twenty years ago, had enrolled himself as a soldier, and fought against Rosas in the La Plata States; and he is now leading a sort of Robinson Crusoe life near the Madeira. He is reported to be a very fast gatherer, and to prepare, with his Indian wife, during the three or four dry months, more than a hundred arrobas (one arroba is equivalent to 32 lb.) of Seringa, while the average produce of a family is only about fifty arrobas.

It was pleasant to see the joyous surprise and the brightened face of the man, when he unexpectedly heard our loud salutation, in German, of " Good morning, countryman ! " from out a canoe full of Indians. We had easily recognised him by his fair hair and beard, the more so, as we had heard of him before, and had been looking out for him for two days. He stood near the water's edge, watching our canoes coming slowly up. Near him was his female companion, a stout, strongly built Tapuya,* and behind them some of their offspring, whose yellow hair contrasted strangely with their dark skins.

A thousand such families, living along the river, soon would completely change the aspect of the country. Especially if an energetic company, fully alive to the position, and sure of adequate support from home, would lead the settlers and protect them against the inevitable jealousies of land and trade monopolists, such a colony might anticipate full success, particularly as facilities of intercommunication will soon give a heavy blow to the old system of robbery.

Some of the hundreds of European workmen, necessary for the construction of the Madeira railway, certainly *will* remain there, in spite of fevers and difficulties; and it will depend only upon the ability of the

---

* In the Tupi language Tapuyo means foreigner and enemy; but nowadays the appellation is given not only to all Indian settlers of the Amazon Valley, of whatever tribe they may be, but, also, promiscuously to all mestizoes; so that very likely, a hundred years hence any one who has a brown skin and catches fish there will be designated by the word.

company and the conduct of the Brazilian Government, whether this number is increased or diminished.

By-and-bye, the monotony of the vegetation, magnificent as it is, and of the landscape, whose uniformity is unbroken by mountain or hill, wearies the eye of the traveller; who, as he paddles slowly up these immense distances in his unwieldy canoe, sees nothing save the blue sky, the smooth water, and a dense girdle of evergreen forest. The appearance of the low-thatched roof of a Seringueiro's wretched home, or the sight of some small Pacóva * plantation, whose vivid soft green contrasts sharply with the gloom of the forest behind, is then regarded as quite a happy event; and we often wished heartily to change the easy navigation on this smooth surface for the variety of troubles and dangers that we knew to await us at the Rapids, and of which we were soon to have our full share.

A remarkable point below Santo Antonio (the first rapid) is the PRAIA DE TAMANDUÁ (shoal of the ant-eater—*Myrmecophaga Jubata*), a long, sandy shoal on the right hand. There, and on similar banks, turtles come in the month of September to lay their eggs, in such incredible numbers that he who sees these cuirassed armies for the first time cannot but feel a sensation of horror and disgust. With wonderful rapidity they dig large holes, one foot and a half deep, into the soft sand, and are often in such a hurry that the eggs of some nest, which had been already covered with sand, are disturbed and scattered about. These shy animals, that generally dive at the slightest noise, are deaf and blind to any danger at this season, and are easily laid on their backs by the fishermen and Seringueiros; hundreds of whom assemble on these occasions, like birds of prey round dead game, to prepare the Manteiga de Tartaruga (turtle-butter). The eggs are dug out and put into the canoes. The thin shells are broken and crushed by treading on them, and the fat yolks, with which they are almost filled, become a thick yellow substance. Under the glowing rays of the tropical sun, the oily parts soon settle on the surface, and

---

* Pacóva, the Tupi name for a species of large plantain, also called *Banana da Terra* (that is to say, the *aboriginal Banana*, to distinguish it from the other species imported, probably from India). This fruit is quite indispensable to the population of the whole Amazon basin. It grows there to the enormous height of forty centimetres, and is eaten both ripe and unripe, raw and cooked. When ripe and dried in the sun it surpasses the fig in delicacy of taste, while it is much like our potato when dried unripe and boiled.

are easily skimmed into large earthen jars. The fat thus gained is not remarkable for delicacy of taste, and is by no means a substitute for butter and olive oil, as one might suppose from the fresh eggs being very agreeable to the palate. The decomposition of manifold impurities, and the circumstance that often some of the eggs have been already half-hatched by the sun, give it an abominable flavour, recalling to mind Russia-leather and tanneries, which renders it thoroughly

TURTLE-HUNTING ON THE MADEIRA.

disgusting to a civilised Christian's palate, at least. Even in the basin of the Amazon the turtle-butter is used only for lamp-oil, and seldom for cooking purposes.

As the exuberant Flora of these countries offers more than one rich oily fruit, yielding excellent material for combustion (the *ricinus* or

Castor-oil nut, for instance), such a war of extermination against the turtles, on whose meat the population largely depends for food, is doubly unreasonable.

It is clear that, with the present procedure, they must rapidly decrease, and that, at no distant date, they will be counted amongst the things of the past, as will be seen by the following figures. On the

Madeira, about 2,000 jars (*potes*) are annually filled with turtle-butter. For each jar about 2,000 eggs are required. Thus 4,000,000 eggs, on a moderate calculation, are destroyed every year. Besides which, three or four thousand female turtles are caught in the laying-season at the Praia de Tamanduá alone, as every Seringueiro takes a few hundred away to keep them as live stock; and, finally, as if such a destruction were not enough, none of the canoes passing there at the right season will omit the opportunity of searching the shoal for newly-hatched turtles of five or six centimetres length, which are reckoned great delicacies; so that comparatively few will come to full growth.

Now, considering that on the Solimões and its tributaries, the Purús, Teffé, &c., a similar process is going on, it can be easily understood why these animals, in spite of their enormous productiveness (a turtle lays from one to two hundred eggs), have sensibly decreased in number within the last five or six years, and that, henceforth, they must necessarily decrease in the ratio of geometrical progression.* A few years ago a good-sized tartaruga of about one metre's length, one metre broad, and thirty-six to forty centimetres thick, equal to the provision of a good dinner for fifteen persons, could easily be purchased at Manáos for two milreis, † whereas nowadays it is very often not to be had at five.

The tartaruga is hunted, like the other species, even out of the laying-season, with bow and arrow, called sararaça, especially adapted for the purpose. The arrow's iron point is loosely stuck into the shaft, and fastened to it by a long, thin string of pineapple fibre (carauá), which unrolls when the wounded animal suddenly dives, bearing away the inserted weapon. The shaft swimming on the surface indicates the exact spot, and is taken up by the fisherman, who thus hauls his prey easily up by means of the carauá-string. As soon as it appears above water, it is finished by a blow with a heavy harpoon, and put into the boat, which not seldom is upset in the efforts of the inmate of the tiny craft to secure his prize.

---

* The different species living on the Amazon and its influents are:—1. The Tartaruga, the largest of all; the male is called Capitary. 2. The Cabeçuda (the big-headed). 3. The Pitiá (Emys Pitia). 4. The Tracajá (Emys Tracajá: *Spix*), considerably smaller than the former. 5. The Matá-matá (Chelys fimbriata: *Spix*), with two deep furrows on the back. By far the most important of them for the population is the Tartaruga.

† One milrei = about three shillings.

Above the Praia de Tamanduá are seen the first precursors of the cliffs, which cause the rapids—small islets of rock, and boulders of granite near their margins, such as we had not seen for all the long months since we left the sea-coast. Soon chains of hills came in sight on both sides; and, after having doubled the next wooded projection of the bank, the Rapid of Santo Antonio, the first of a long series, lay before us.

CHAPTER II.

THE RAPIDS OF THE MADEIRA AND THE MAMORÉ.

Santo Antonio.—Theotonio.—The Caripunas.—The Caldeirão do Inferno.—Inscriptions on the Rocks.—The Salto do Girão.—Our old Mulatto's description of an Attack.—Forsaken cabins of the Caripunas.—Ribeirão.—Other Inscriptions. — The Beni.—The Mamoré.—Exaltacion.—The Return.

THE yellow floods of the Madeira rush, roaring and splashing, at a furious rate over the dark rocks in the middle of the stream, quite a new and refreshing sight after the monotonous scenery of its lower course. Mighty blocks of a gneissose metamorphic rock, their smooth jagged points resembling a wildly waving sea, line continuously both the shore and the isles.

Opposite a rocky island which divides the river into two unequal arms, some straw huts are almost entirely concealed by the dense shrubbery. They are the remains of a Brazilian outpost, abandoned on account of the fevers; but no trace is left of the Mission, Santo Antonio, founded in 1737 by the Jesuits, and transposed after a short duration to Trocano and Araretama (Borba); the buildings, probably, having been only light cottages.

The difference of declivity between the smooths above and below, on an average level, is 4·13 English feet; the division in the left channel is at 164 feet, that on the right about six times that distance. Here the canoes must be unladen, and their contents carried to a point on the left bank above the rapid, while the empty vessels are towed there through a labyrinth of intricate channels, amidst large granite blocks, close to the edge of the right bank.

Over a large shoal and some flat islands, we could see already from Macacos, the next not very considerable rapid, the rising water-spray of the mighty fall of THEOTONIÓ. Between low hills running down to the water's edge on both sides, the river has hollowed a course of 2,300 feet in breadth, through which it dashes at furious speed, terminating in a majestic fall 36 feet high.

Not only the cargo, but the canoes themselves, had to be transported hence on land for more than 760 yards to the quiet water above the fall, a heavy task which took us three complete days of hard labour, our Mojos working with right good will, although the passage of the boats was facilitated by cylinders being placed under them. No wonder, by the way, that one or the other of the canoes, after encountering so rough a transport, was so damaged as to require immediate repair, caulking, and even the addition of new ribs.

On the ridge of a rocky hill on the right bank, we saw the remains of some walls, covered almost completely by shrubs, low palms, and thorny torch-thistles. They date from 1753, when Theotonio Gusmão, by the direction of the Portuguese Government, here founded, in a very good position for defence, a military post, which was, however, soon abandoned. At that time the commerce with the province of Mato Grosso having acquired a fresh impulse from the erection of the Forto do Principe da Beira on the Guaporé, an impulse strengthened by the explorations in 1767 and 1780, such Destacamentos (or military posts) were of the first necessity on that water road, as well for securing the supply of provisions, and for the protection thus gained against the wild Indians, as for the assistance rendered by the soldiers in the hard work near the rapids.

The material of the hills we found to be the same, more or less, over the whole region of the rapids; gneiss, with mostly a very pronounced stratification, and always the same run. We examined it more closely, expecting to find, according to the theory of Agassiz, numerous erratic boulders of different composition lying on the regularly formed rock.

But neither there, nor higher up in Bolivia, could we discover any trace of these "foundlings," even as Agassiz himself was unable to discover, in the environs of Rio de Janeiro, the *"roches striées"* and *"roches moutonnées"* of Switzerland, which testify to an ice-period with its immense glaciers.

Agassiz attributes their absence to the rapid crumbling of the rocks under the combined influence of the tropical sun and rain; but he seems to overlook the fact that they diminish much faster in moderate climates, by the severe disintegrating operation of freezing water penetrating into the smallest crevices.*

While employed as engineer on a road† in the province of Minas Geraes, I had occasion to examine numerous specimens of the spheroidic boulders of diorite, with their concentric coatings of red clay, pronounced to be "foundlings" by Agassiz. To me these shell-shaped crusts appeared to be rather the effect of the cooling process, the more so as the ferruginous clay always was of a more intense hue, like that of burnt ochre, nearest the diorite ball.

Seen from the foot of the projecting hill crowned with the remains of the Destacamento, the many breaks of the THEOTONIO CATARACT, indeed, offer a grand spectacle. It extends across the whole river (760 yards), and has, in general, an angle of 45°. In the middle of it emerges a rocky cone, whose dark colour contrasts sharply with the dazzling white foam and spray. Close to the right bank, where the bulk of the water is discharged, the waves rise to a height of 33 feet, and we there saw the gigantic trunk of a drifting forest-tree tossed and whirled about as if it were a light reed.

From Santo Antonio to above Theotonio there is no great interval between the banks, there being an almost uninterrupted succession of hills from 26 to 40 feet high, densely wooded, as the country generally is, though the vegetation is not so rich and luxuriant as we had found it below Santo Antonio.

The next rapid is MORRINHOS (little hill), where we had to empty the

* In Rio de Janeiro and other Brazilian towns there are a great many cupolas of churches, terraces, vases, and architectural ornaments of every kind, covered only with common mortar, which have successfully resisted the sun and rain of a century or more; whereas, in our own "moderate" climate, they would not last three years.

† This was constructed by the Company União é Industria (President, Marianno Procopio Ferreira Lage; Engineers, Joseph Keller and Bulthos); the first and most extensive road in Brazil (it is 90 miles long). The difficulties of surmounting the watersheds were considerable. The iron girder bridge, 502 feet long, over the Parahyba, near Tres-Barras, after the plans of Joseph Keller, is a remarkable piece of work.

boats again and tow them along against the strong current. Above it the river is between 1,300 and 1,550 yards broad, and is completely navigable for 33½ miles, that is, to the next considerable rapid, which bears the ominous name of CALDEIRÃO DO INFERNO (kettle of hell).

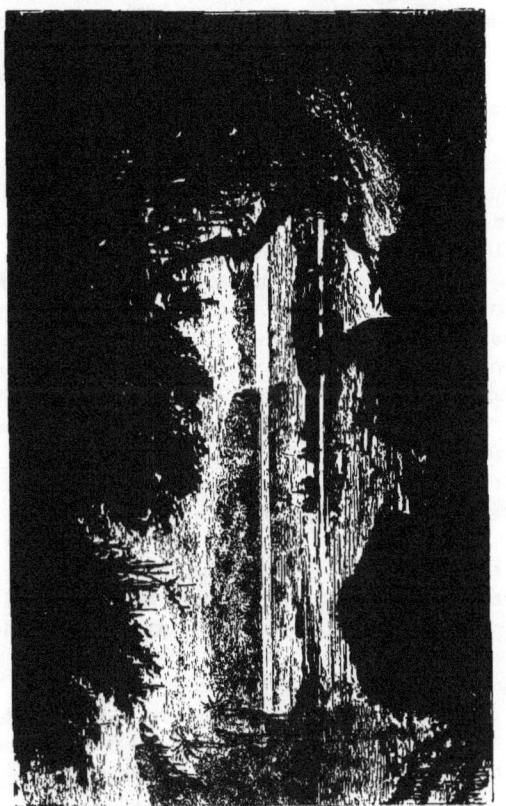

ONE OF THE SMALLER RAPIDS OF THE CALDEIRÃO DO INFERNO.

A horde of Caripuna Indians have settled in the neighbourhood. We paid them a visit in their carefully roofed palm-leaf sheds, though we knew they did not enjoy the fairest reputation for peaceableness, having been engaged in several bloody conflicts with the white-faces.

Whether it was that our numbers imposed on them, or whether in consequence of the little presents we offered them, certain it is that they received us very well, and allowed us at our leisure to examine their arms and implements. We obtained from them some bows made of the heavy wood of the pachiuba palm, long arrows of reed, and several pretty feather ornaments, in exchange for knives, scissors, and white glass beads.

Our Mojos displayed a curious mixture of fear and contemptuous disgust at sight of these naked savage relations of theirs. They reminded me involuntarily of the shepherd's dog and the wolf.

If it were possible, in the next score of years, to make these Caripuna Indians tolerably peaceable neighbours of the white man, the first beginning of colonisation on the Upper Madeira would be made. If they could not be drilled into workmen wielding shovel and axe on roads or railways, they still might be very useful in planting mandioc, Indian corn, and sugar-cane, or as hunters and fishermen. Unfortunately, no steps have been taken as yet to this end. Such things usually remain vain wishes in Brazil, notwithstanding the good-will of some clear-sighted statesmen; and even in this event, the poor autochthons will have to succumb in the conflict with the white race. The particulars of our encounter with the Caripunas will be found in an ensuing chapter.

The CALDEIRÃO DO INFERNO, the next cachoeira or rapid above the Caripuna sheds, is one of the worst of the whole range, not so much on account of its height as of the trouble and dangers of its passage. By seven considerable islands the river is here divided into as many arms, at the entrance to which is the principal fall, or the Caldeirão, the total slope of which is of $19\frac{1}{2}$ feet in an interval of more than 3,280 feet. Here again the weary task of unloading had to be done, trying even to our patient, broad-shouldered Mojos Indians. Bags and chests are heaved and dragged over the sharp edges of stones and rocks, and the vessels are towed up through narrow, tortuous channels, sometimes at the imminent risk of those concerned. Happy indeed is he who leaves that "kettle" safely behind him.

On one of these islands, with the aid of a lantern, I discovered, when preparing to take astronomical observations, some flatly incised designs, some of them spiral lines and others semicircular, on the dark-brown polished surface of several nearly vertically posed slabs of rock, the largest of which was more than $6\frac{1}{2}$ feet in height, with a breadth and thickness of 5 feet. The figures, three quarters to one and a quarter inches high, were incised only one-sixth of an inch deep. Our curiosity being awakened by this discovery, we found afterwards the even more remarkable inscription near the great fall of RIBEIRÃO, which I copied exactly, as well as one of the Caldeirão and one of Lages farther up. And here a reflection I had before made at the dangerous passage of the Caldeirão Falls again proved true, viz., that there is no following implicitly either the counsels of other travellers, or even one's self-acquired experience in former expeditions, as to the best water-way for the boats, which is so easily changed by the slightest variation of level. At all events, it is necessary that the canoes should stop upon approaching a rapid, and a clear view of the channels and of the cliffs to be avoided should be obtained from the shore as near as possible to the obstruction itself. This often is difficult enough; and in the last deciding moment, especially in the descent, the fate of both boat and crew depends chiefly on the quick eye and the strong arm of her pilot.

The Caldeirão do Inferno has, as I mentioned before, the worst reputation among the falls of the Madeira; indeed, more than one richly laden canoe has been dashed to pieces against its black rocks, and many lives have been lost there. The chance solution of a geographical problem found its tragic conclusion, at this ill-famed fall, in the death of the discoverer. Eight or ten years ago, a Peruvian of the name of Maldonado embarked on the Madre de Dios to escape the persecutions of his political adversaries, and by this river had reached the Beni and the Madeira, thus dispelling all doubt as to the course of the Madre de Dios, which for a long time had been taken to be one of the tributaries of the Purús.

Maldonado took his hazardous flight on one of those singular little crafts called Balsas, composed of bundles of a sort of reed, as they are used on Lake Titicaca. As it was in the most wretched condition when he entered the Madeira, he obtained by barter from the Caripuna Indians whom he found there one of their light canoes, in which he continued his descent. Having passed without accident totally unknown regions, inhabited only by savages and wild beasts, he had reached the comparatively safer regions of the Madeira, when his fragile vessel was hurled against the rocks of the Caldeirão do Inferno, and the hardy navigator was submerged in the roaring cataract.

His two companions contrived to save their lives, and to escape starvation on one of the islands, until a descending Bolivian boat took them up and brought them to Manáos. But as they were uneducated mestizoes, who could give but an imperfect account of this remarkable voyage, and as Maldonado's diary was lost with him, the only scientific result was the certainty that the Madre de Dios is an affluent, not of the Purús, but of the Beni, and consequently of the Madeira.

Above the Caldeirão, on the right bank, is a row of hills of about 180 to 200 feet in height, extending to the South-east in an unbroken line as far as the eye can reach. It is doubtless a branch of the Serra da Paca Nova, whose principal chain we were to see farther up, and whose eastern division forms, under sundry local names, the chief watershed between the tributaries of the Amazon and of the Paraguay.

Below the next fall, the SALTO DO GIRÃO, the canoes were again unladen on a favourably situated spot, and, together with the cargo, were conveyed for nearly 1,000 yards on land, through a dense virgin-forest whose undergrowth consists partly of cacao-bushes. The total slope of 26 feet is concentrated on four points, while the width of the river, though very unequal on account of the jagged rocky banks, may be generally estimated at 760 yards. Gigantic drifted trunks lying on the tops of the rocky cones, or suspended amid the branches of the trees on shore, showed the height of the floods in the rainy season; while the dark-brown rocks partly covered by white lichens, the foaming water rushing through narrow channels, and a profusion of light graceful palms, with curiously leaved creepers depending from them and enveloping them in a dense green veil, which only now and again permits a glimpse into the dark interior of the forest, combined to impart to the scenery a charm which was only heightened by the reflection that no human hand had ever disturbed its primeval luxuriance.

At the upper end of the fall, an old mulatto, who accompanied the expedition as hunter, showed us the spot where eight years ago he and his comrades had been attacked by the Caripunas. He related that they had a cargo of salt[*] for Mato Grosso and were

---

[*] While in the sea-ports a bag of salt of about 60 lb. fetches two or three milreis, it is worth fifteen to eighteen in the cattle-breeding districts of the interior, some 150 to 200 leagues from the Atlantic; and, especially before the regular steam navigation on the River Plato and the Paraguay, it was well worth while transporting it there, even in small canoes and over the rapids of the Madeira.

busily engaged in dragging their boat over the rocks, when the treacherous Indians, who had lent them a helping hand, turned upon them.

"Here," said he, "our salt-bags were piled up; and here, from out this shrubbery, the chieftain came with at least fifty of his tribe, armed every one of them with bows and arrows. He professed to

FAN-LEAF OF A PALM.

be dissatisfied with the stipulated remuneration—knives and glass beads that had been handed over to him—and asked for more.

"One of our party, who, understanding a little of their language, acted as interpreter for us, tried to pacify him, and offered him a piece of the succulent tapir roasting hard by at the spit, but he refused it disdainfully; and at this moment, while our companion was yet speaking to the chieftain, he was pierced by an arrow shot at a few paces from behind, which left him just strength enough to shout to us to open fire.

"Discharging our eight guns (we mustered no more), we wounded several of the Indians, the rest of whom retired to the protection of the nearest big trunks, and thence sent a perfect volley of arrows; which, however, wounded but two of our crew, as we had taken shelter behind our salt-bags. But for this bulwark we should have been destroyed, every one of us. When the Caripunas saw that more than one of them would be killed if they tried to take our strong position by assault,—and Indians rarely attack unless sure of success, with only small loss,—they gave in, and slowly retreated into the forest, carefully screening themselves behind the trees; and we saw no more of them. But our poor comrade was dead, despite all our efforts to recall him to life; and we had to bury him here in the wilderness."

Thus spoke the old mulatto. His tale bore the impress of truth so strongly that, though reluctantly, I was forced to modify the good opinion I had conceived of the Caripunas on the occasion of our visit to their shed.

Again our whole crew had to work hard for two days to get the heavy barques to the smooth water above the Girão.

Even with the cylinders placed underneath, the rolling is not easily effected over such an uneven rocky soil; but, as the wood is freshly cut and the sappy bark crushed by the weight of the boats, the rollers soon get smooth and slippery, and the canoes glide over them with tolerable rapidity.

The temperature then was extraordinarily low, having sunk on the 31st of July (in the dawn, between four and five o'clock A.M.), to 65° Fahrenheit—a temperature of rather disagreeable freshness to our skins, accustomed so long to a tropical heat of 80° and 90°.

At the next rapid of Tres-Irmãos (the three brothers), whose name is derived from a hill with a three-headed summit, the Madeira, broken by a large island into two main arms, with a sharp bend suddenly alters its principal direction from South-west to North-east, and runs due East along the parallel of 9° 33".

A porous ferruginous sandstone, called Pedra Canga, which we had remarked at Manáos, and which is found in the whole Amazon Valley, now reappears on the surface. The banks are raised somewhat above the highest flood-level; while the hills, seen at a little distance to the left, attain a height of 330 feet above the base.

The right bank is comparatively flatter; yet here and there are visible the tops of distant hills.

The next rapid, Do PAREDÃO, is caused by a cliff of coarse-grained granite projecting into the river for more than 330 feet. On its uttermost extremity are some blocks of the same material, bordering a deeply-worn channel, whose smooth vertical walls have given it the name of Paredão—that is, supporting wall. The slope is of nearly 6½ feet.

Of about the same height is the next rapid of Pederneira (flintstone), where veins of quartz appear on the surface, and the whole course of the stream is strewn with isolated blocks of various size. At both these rapids the cargo only need be transported on land, the canoes being tracked in the river.

Above Pederneira the Madeira is perfectly free of obstructions. Following its former course from South-west to North-east, up to the mouth of the Abuna, it forms at Pederneira a sharp bend almost rectangular in its deviation.

From time to time, wavy, and in some parts perfectly horizontal, strata of a ferruginous slaty sediment resembling sandstone appear on the banks, which rise to a height of between 50 and 60 feet above low-water level. The chain of hills on the left side, which at Pederneira came close to the water's edge, now disappears from view; and, as far as the eye can reach, extend densely wooded plains, never visited by the white man. The breadth of the river here is nearly 1,100 yards, while the depth averages from 16 to 20 feet, and the declivity is less than 1·30,000; so that, for nearly 37 miles, the river is navigable by the largest vessels and steamers.

The point farthest west of the Madeira River we found to be 3,280 yards above the mouth of the Abuna influent, which has hitherto enjoyed that designation. Here the river again changes its direction, describing from ARÁRAS, the next rapid, a great curve to the Abuna, and thus forming a sort of peninsula between this point and Paredão.

A second horde of Caripunas have chosen this spot for their settlement, evidently for the same reason that induced their relations to build their sheds on the smooth below the Caldeirão do Inferno—the stream, which is free of obstruction, affording them easy communication, and thus facilitating their hunting and fishing excursions. Some old bark-canoes revealed to us the beginning of a narrow path, which leads through the dense forest to their cabins. Hoping to see again some of our old friends, for whom we selected some presents, six of us landed

THE RAPID OF RIBEIRÃO, SEEN FROM ABOVE.

and followed the track, which was kept scrupulously clean and led directly inland. At some hundred paces from the shore, we found an abandoned shed similar in construction to those we had seen at the Caldeirão. The luxuriance of vegetable growth in its interior showed that it had been deserted by its inmates for some time; and we went on, hoping still to find some of the inhabited huts, to which the path evidently led. The vegetation around us was magnificent. Certainly I have never seen a greater variety of palms than there was on the borders of this lonely Indian path. The umbrella formed by the colossal leaves of the Uauassú-palm, by the neat bifurcated fans of a smaller kind of palm, and by the large plantain-like leaves of the Urania or Pacova Sororóca, was so umbrageous, that we experienced not the slightest inconvenience from the scorching rays of the sun.

We walked some four or five miles without finding the least indication of a Malocca* being in the vicinity; so we were obliged, at last, to give up the attempt, and went back to our canoes rather out of sorts with our bad luck.

* Malocca: Indian settlement.

The next rapid of ARÁRAS has an inconsiderable declivity (3 feet 4 in.), and can be passed by full canoes towed up the river. This, though far less troublesome than carrying the load over stocks and stones, is more dangerous, and requires rather more attention than will be thought necessary at first sight. As the unwieldy boats, when held only by one long rope, are apt to drift transversely against some rock, smaller cords are attached fore and aft, to regulate the position of the vessel from the shore, in case of need. The greater part of the crew are up-stream, holding the great cable; and each one has to look out for himself, as the boat comes up, how best he can get from rock to rock, either jumping or swimming; while others stand on either side with the smaller ropes, at one or other of which they pull on word of command. Others stand breast-high in the roaring, hissing foam of the rapid, trying to keep the bow of the fragile craft off the glistening black rocks of gneiss, which would violently open up all its ill-caulked seams. It is perfectly astonishing to witness the ease with which these Indians secure their footing on the slippery, wave-washed stones, carry heavy ropes through the currents, or, if necessary, ascertain by diving whether the boat has grounded, and how best to get her afloat again. The little rapid of PERIQUITOS is passed in the same way as that of Aráras; not so, however, the great CACHOEIRA DO RIBEIRÃO. The river-bed there is, for almost four miles, so obstructed by rocky islands and reefs, and the declivity is so great, that it forms an almost uninterrupted succession of roaring falls and rapids. The breadth of the river, too, has increased, especially at the upper end of the rapid, where is the principal break (to 2,190 yards); and it embraces several larger islands.

Flat rocky hills extend to nearly the water's edge on both sides; and dense virgin forest covers not only the shores but also the larger isles.

While the Indians were working hard at drawing the boats over the last of the rapids, I had taken the meridional altitude of the sun, and found, in climbing over the rocks of the right shore, another "written rock," covered with spiral lines and concentric rings, evenly carved in the black gneiss-like material, and similar to those of the Caldeirão. Looking about for more, I discovered a perfect inscription, whose straight orderly lines can hardly be thought the result of lazy

Indians' "Hours of Idleness." These characters were incised on a very hard smooth block of 3 feet 4 inches in length, and of 3¼ feet in height and breadth. It lay at an angle of 45°, only 8 feet above low water, and close to the water's edge of the second smaller rapid, the CACHOEIRA DO RIBEIRÃO. The transverse section of the characters is not very deep, and their surface is as worn as that of the inscription found farther down. In some places they are almost effaced by time,

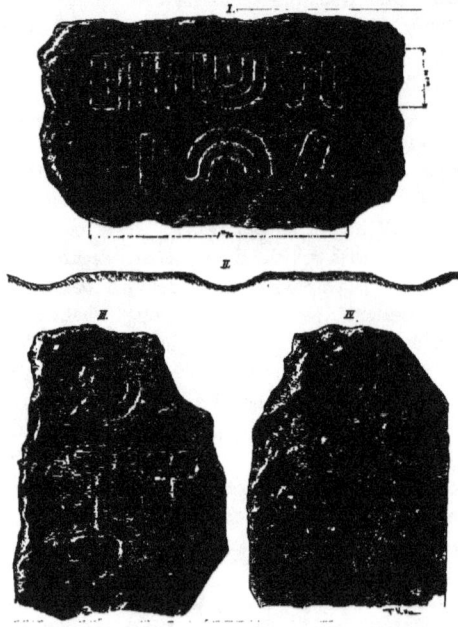

CARVED FIGURES ON THE ROCKS OF THE MADEIRA.

and are to be seen distinctly only with a favourable light. A dark brown coat of glaze, found everywhere on the surface of the stones laved at times by the water, covers the block so uniformly, as well on the concave glyphs as on the parts untouched by instrument, that many ages must have lapsed since some patient Indian spent long hours in cutting them out with his quartz chisel. As the lines of the inscription run almost perfectly horizontally, and as the figures near the Caldeirão and the Cachoeira das Lages are so little above low-water mark, the present position of the block seems to have been the original one. Unfortunately our knowledge of the history of the South-American-Indian races, before the Conquest, is so limited (except, perhaps, some half-mythical traditions respecting the empire of the Incas) that even the most important periods of this history, the wanderings of the Tupis, for instance, bear the character rather of clever hypotheses than of historical facts. We know of great conquering expeditions of the Incas. Can it be that the inscriptions in the Madeira Valley are connected with them; or are they older even than that? Researches and comparative studies of Peruvian antiquities can, alone, best explain whether the origin of these hieroglyphs is to be sought in their empire, that land of a long departed civilisation and grandeur. They could hardly be the work of the forefathers of the Caripunas, if they were, as we may well assume, on the same low level of civilisation as their descendants. A rude nation of hunters is not likely to spend months on the troublesome task of engraving figures on hard rocks with imperfect flint implements. If they, however, took such a fancy, their weak and narrow minds would have chosen rather to delineate what struck them most of all the objects around them; the sun, or the moon, or the animals they hunted; or the alligators, turtles and fishes, which Humboldt found inscribed on the rocks of the Valley of the Orinoco. On the rocky shores of the Araguaya, that huge tributary of the Tocantins, there are similar rude outlines of animals near a rapid called Martirios, from the first Portuguese explorers fancying they recognised the instruments of the Passion in the clumsy representation.*

In passing the long rapid of RIBEIRÃO, we had again to unload everything, even before we reached the real fall at the upper end.

Of the misery and annoyance of such repeated unloading and carrying of heavy chests over glowing, bare rocks, under the burning rays of the sun, against which the stunted growth on the stony soil offers no shelter worth mentioning to the poor Indians, only he can form an idea who has

---

* Unfortunately M. Vallée, who, commissioned by the Brazilian Government, descended the Araguaya a few years ago, does not give even a description of these figures in his official report, which is equally deficient in all other respects. Of the hydrographic results of this voyage my colleagues will form an idea if I tell them that M. Vallée, having made neither levellings nor astronomical observations, simply copied an old inexact little map of the Araguaya on a considerably larger scale, and offered it to the Minister on his return.

seen this kind of "navigation" with his own eyes. Notwithstanding all this, packages of from 500 to 600 lb. are sometimes transported to Bolivia in the same covers in which they came from Pará; and I was told that even pianos have been thus conveyed, and—wonderful to relate —have arrived entire at Santa Cruz de la Sierra.

Great as are these difficulties, they are as nothing compared with those of a transport over the Cordillera, with its Soroche,* its bone-penetrating cold, and its paths leading along precipices which only sure-footed mules can safely pass; not to speak of the vexatious mounting, descending and remounting again, of passes that are nearly 15,000 feet above the level of the sea.

This easily explains the number of Bolivian barques, some sixty or seventy, which annually descend the Madeira with hides and tallow, and take back the products of European and North American industry. The merchants evidently are willing to incur rather the risks and dangers of the rapids than the difficulties and expenses of the Serra.

The narrow forest-path at Ribeirão, along which we had to carry our cargo for more than 1,000 yards, and to the preservation and clearing of which every passing caravan contributes, showed a magnificent vegetation. Lofty torch-thistles, dense cacao-bushes, sappy uranias, strelitzias with large banana-like leaves, and a graceful, slender palm with bifurcated fans, tower in fanciful clusters above the thorny creepers, which form part of the tangled underwood, and through which you can penetrate only with knife and hatchet in hand.

A little influent on the right margin, of 15 or 20 feet breadth, at whose mouth our boats were dragged ashore, to begin their trip on the dry, has given its name of Ribeirão (rivulet) to the whole rapid.

Just above its mouth a rocky ridge, clad with pulpy cactaceæ, extends close to the water's edge; and its prolongation through the whole river-bed (2,000 yards) can easily be followed by the line of the fall and a row of rocky little islets. The fall has a height of 13 feet, and its whole aspect is quite a peculiar and picturesque one. We there found again the round holes in the rocks, called Caldeirões, or kettles, by the Brazilians, which we had already noticed on the Parahyba, in the pro-

---

* Soroche they call, in Bolivia and Perú, the extremely annoying sensation of giddiness, combined with nausea and painful breathing, caused by the extreme rarity of the atmosphere on the Cordillera.

vince of São Paulo, and on the Ivahy and Tibagy,* in the province of Paraná. They are the effects of the loose stones set rolling by the floods in the natural hollows of the cliffs. These pebbles, which are of different sizes, bore into the gneiss-like stone (of metamorphic origin) rows of deep cylindric holes, with smoothly-polished vertical sides, and of all dimensions, from a few inches width, to 17 or 20 feet in diameter and depth.

Whole banks of the hard material have been broken off in this way, as may be distinctly seen by the semicircular incisions of the remaining parts. In other places the process is still visibly going on. A narrow division is left, at first, between the holes, whose sides are gradually perforated at the bottom; and this operation continues until the torrent-propelled stones work the channel deeper and deeper, and finally break off its outer wall. The whole fall must recede in this way, though much less rapidly by this simple erosion than by undermining and breaking off the upper layers, as does the Niagara, which, it has been calculated, recedes at the rate of one foot per annum.

Supposing now that these holes deepen only one fiftieth of an inch every year—which must be thought rather a high estimate, considering the great hardness of the structure and the circumstance that most of the kettles are "worked" only during the three months of the floods, —it will be seen that 12,000 years are required to make a hole 20 feet deep; and this will be the scale of retrogression of the fall.

As at the Ribeirão, the length of the rock-islands, whose upper end is now near the edge of the fall, probably represents the original breadth of the cliff over which the river rushed; and, as this length is of 3,280 feet, two millions of years must have elapsed since the present state of slow transformation has begun. Though such a calculation cannot make any pretension to be regarded as exact, the data being insufficient, still it gives us an idea of the powerful changes wrought in nature during immense lapses of time, by the smallest means, even a pebble set in motion by the water.†

---

* At the Tibagy, a tributary of the Paranapanema and Paraná, these "kettles" are anxiously searched by the diamond-washers; as the precious stone, which indeed is a better "borer" than any other, is often found among the pebbles at the bottom. The material there is a metamorphic sandstone, while close to it doleritic cones raise their rocky crowns.

† In a very interesting work which appeared lately, "New Tracks in North America," by W. Bell, the author gives a detailed description of the gigantic ravines or

Two and a half miles above Ribeirão is the strait known under the name of CORRENTEZA DA MISERICORDIA; the total width of the river being narrowed here to 382 yards. As the steep, rocky shores do not allow of an extension of the floods on either side, and as the whole enormous mass of water must pass through the narrow, and not very deep, opening, the water is necessarily volumed here, and its rapidity is considerably increased.

Thus, while the height of the falls is generally less at high water, it increases in the same proportion in the straits, where the overflow is checked by the limiting ridges.

As there is, besides, a sharp bend in the river, rendering the tracking from the shore extremely difficult; the Correnteza da Misericordia must, indeed, at certain times, be an anxious spot for the Bolivian barques. When *we* passed there, on the 15th of August, the river was low, and we experienced no difficulty in coming up against the current. Above Misericordia the Madeira again reaches its normal breadth of 760 to 880 yards, and is as smooth as a lake up to the Cachoeira da Madeira. Just below this it widens to almost 2,200 yards, and is divided by two isles into three main channels.

The Cachoeira, or rapid, itself, is a chaos of small flat islets and reefs, between which the water rushes with a total declivity of 9 feet 10 inches. We were again compelled to unload here, and to carry the cargo on land till above the rapid.

On the metamorphic rocks of the shore we found concentric circles, like those at the Caldeirão: but the most striking feature of the Cachoeira da Madeira is the enormous quantity of drift-wood deposited on the rocks of the left shore, directly below the mouth of the Beni.

Huge trunks of the cedar, and other giants of the forest, swept down by the floods of the Beni, and driven by currents and eddies amongst the rocks, have stranded there with the fall of the river; and there they will remain until, perhaps, next year's flood may carry them away down-stream. These entangled masses of many hundreds of colossal trunks have doubtless induced the Portuguese to give the name of Madeira (timber, wood) to this rapid; and the enormous

---

cañons of the Colorado and its affluents, where the effects of erosion are striking indeed. The Colorado has hollowed for itself, out of very hard stone, a bed, the vertical walls of which reach the enormous height of 5,000 feet in several places; once even 7,000 feet. The ravine extends for more than 500 English miles.

quantities of floating timber at the mouth of the river must also have served to change its old Indian name of Caiary into Madeira.*

The BENI, whose mouth is above the fall on the left hand, has a width of 1,100 yards, and an average depth of 8 fathoms. As it discharges a volume of 153,386 cubic feet per second, at its ordinary level (being something more than the united volume of the Mamoré and Guaporé), the Beni ought to be considered as the main stream of the Madeira, and the two others as its tributaries; and, consequently, the name of Madeira ought to be given to the river only from below the mouth of the Beni, while above it the name of Mamoré, as that of the larger of the two, ought to be bestowed; not of Guaporé or Itenez, as is generally done in Bolivia.†

The mouth of the Beni, which we found to be on the 10° 20′ of Southern latitude, and on the 22° 12′ 20″ of longitude West from Rio de Janeiro, was designated in the last regulation of boundaries between Bolivia and Brazil as the point where the frontier, running due West between the Madeira and Javary, touches the shore of the former. Consequently the left shore of the Madeira, or Mamoré, is Bolivian territory upwards from the mouth of the Beni, while the right belongs to the Brazilian province of Mato Grosso, far up to the Guaporé. At the time of our sojourn in Bolivia, the patriotic party of the so-called Republic, adverse to Brazil, was highly indignant at this treaty, at the evident victory of Brazilian diplomacy, or, as many said, of Brazilian gold over their always money-wanting and greedy Dictator, Melgarejo. But since this, as well as many other things besides, continued the same after his expulsion and subsequent death, we must suppose that the hot spirits have cooled down again, or that the construction of the Madeira Railroad, the increasing trade of both countries, and the prosperity of the Bolivian provinces East of the Andes, clearly resulting therefrom, are thought a sufficient equivalent.

* The isle of Madeira, now totally denuded of its forests, also owes its name to its abundance in timber; which must have seemed extraordinary to the Portuguese, whose country was already stripped of woods at the time of their discovering the isle.

† These differences in the nomenclature are, on the whole, of little importance, as in these desert, out-of-the-way countries, they mostly depend on the caprices of the travellers and geographers; but it does seem incomprehensible that, a few years ago, maps should have been edited, like the Carte Générale de l'Amérique du Sud, par Brué, on which the Mamoré is marked as a tributary of the Beni; as if such crude errors had not been corrected long before, by the explorations of the Portuguese in the eighteenth century.

Very precise instructions, and the advanced season, did not allow us either on the ascent or on the descent to mount the Beni for any considerable distance. A minute exploration of this powerful and, as yet, totally unknown stream would be of the greater interest, in that the soil on its shores must be of excellent quality, judging from the size of the drifting trunks of cedar, which grows to such perfection only on very rich earth. Besides which, it would be the very best way, under existing circumstances at least, to bring the Peruvian bark, which is gathered near its sources, to the Madeira and Amazon. The reduced quantity of water above the mouth of the Beni (about half) is denoted less by the bed's narrowed width than by the river's decreasing depth.

The next rapid, the CACHOEIRA DAS LAGES (that is, of the slabs of rock), though dangerous at high water, did not oppose to us any serious obstacle, the river having been low when we passed it, in the middle of August.

The prospect was charming; the broad stream being broken up into pays by several small islands, densely clad with rich virgin forest, over which slender palms were waving their graceful leaflets.

On the gigantic slabs of the left shore we came up with more of the buzzling incised figures; but they are so obliterated by time and water that I had some difficulty in copying them.

Low hills greeting the river on the right proclaimed the vicinity of the SERRA DA PACA NOVA, a wooded chain whose extension forms the chief water-shed between the basin of the Amazon and that of the La Plata, and whose steep, projecting buttress we sighted presently, above the next rapid, the CACHOEIRA DO PÃO GRANDE. To pass this fall, whose declivity is of $6\frac{1}{2}$ feet at the river's mid height, was easy work compared with the fatigues of the CACHOEIRA DAS BANANEIRAS, the last great fall of the Madeira. As we had to avoid the deep channel, on account of its breakers and powerful currents, and as the large bed is broken into an infinity of small, shallow arms, we had immense trouble even in getting the barques near the real fall, where we had to unload. After four hours' hard labour, we advanced no more than 220 yards. At several points the boats had to be partly unloaded, one of the smaller canoes serving for lighter, and carrying, by several trips to and fro, the cargo of the heavier barques, till we had got beyond the obstruction. At last we reached the principal fall of BANANEIRAS, which has a height of 20 feet, and where we had to transport both cargo and boats overland, in the usual troublesome way. However, the satisfaction of thinking that we had only two more of this long series of rapids before us gave us new vigour and life. It is true that the first of them, GUAJARÁ GUASSÚ,* was not quite as easy to pass as we could have wished. We had to unload, and to track the empty boats through one of the narrow channels wrought by the floods (as at Ribeirão) into the hard quartzose metamorphic formation; but at GUAJARÁ MERIM, the last one, we could draw them after us, with full cargo, against the strong current.

Every one of us, I believe, took a long breath of relief after it, and thought the terminus of our long voyage—the Missions on the Mamoré,—though still distant some 250 miles, quite at hand.

The river now presents the smooth unruffled surface of a lake; no sound breaks the majestic stillness of Nature; there is neither the lonely cottage of the Seringueiro, nor even the smooth roof of palm-leaves of the Indian malocca, to be seen anywhere. Though the elevation of the river-banks above low-water mark is no more than 23 or 26 feet, and they are therefore inundated every twenty or twenty-five years by extraordinary floods, yet the soil is considerably raised above that level at some distance from the shore; and nothing could be more erroneous than to believe the Valley of the Madeira to be subject to annual inundations, as is the case, for instance, with the shores of the Itonama and the Upper Mamoré in Bolivia.

Not the floods, but the dangerous vicinity of wild, murderous Indians who haunt the forests near the confluence of the Mamoré and Guaporé, together with intermittent fevers and the difficulties of communication with the Amazon, are the chief drawbacks to successful colonisation in these vast countries. The Indians, it is well known, have nowhere resisted the influence of civilisation for any length of time; and here also they will have to recede before it. The fevers, it is true, are hard to bear; but in this respect also the land must improve in the course of time, as the forests continue to be cleared; while the last of the evils I have enumerated will soon be remedied, let us hope, by a line of steamers on the Lower Madeira, the construction of a railroad along the rapids, and a second line of steamers above them.†

* In the Guarani, or Tupi language, guajará means *a wild fruit;* guassú, *large;* merim, *small.*

† Even before we left Rio de Janeiro, a company was formed there for a steam line on the Lower Madeira, and had actually begun regular service.

There, in spite of its numerous and sharp bends, the river is navigable by steamers of 3¼ feet draught, as it has an average depth of 5 feet, a width of from 270 to 330 yards, and a rapidity of from 1 foot to 1¼ feet per second. As most of our canoes were anything but water-tight after their three months' hard work, and especially after their repeated draggings on land over stocks and stones, we resolved to caulk them before we proceeded further. The Castanheira (*Bertholletia excelsa*), whose fruit is known in Europe under the name of Brazil nuts, supplied us with the required material; and, as there was plenty of these gigantic trees rising tall and straight as columns, our Mojos had little trouble to collect a sufficient quantity of their bark. They first made with an axe two horizontal incisions at an interval of 7 feet from each other, and then with wooden wedges loosened a strip of bark of about 2½ feet breadth. With continued beating the outer bark is separated from the bast, and the latter is reduced to a bundle of soft fibres, which, after being washed and dried in the sun, are fit for use. While so employed, one of our paddlers was stung in the hand by a poisonous ant (Tucandeira) of nearly an inch and a half long, and in a short time his hand and arm were swollen up to the shoulder. As I treated him successfully with salmiak, one of the Bolivians told me that in his country the use of balms similar to those of the South African poison-doctors, in such cases, was quite common. He had himself witnessed their efficacy in the case of an Indian wounded by the poisonous sting of a ray. What may be considered the healing principle in these antidotes I cannot tell—*dicant Paduani!*—I limit myself to recording the fact.

In such urgent cases it is only natural that people should invent all sorts of extraordinary drugs in countries where there are neither physicians nor apothecaries' shops. Once, in the province of Minas, while opening a picada through a piece of dense virgin-forest with a few negroes, a fine hunting-dog belonging to a neighbouring planter, which had followed me and had afterwards been hunting upon his own account, came suddenly up with hanging ears and tail, and whining piteously. On inspection, we found a tumour with two small red points on his neck, swelling almost visibly, which the negroes one and all declared to be the bite of a poisonous snake. As nothing else was at hand, a piece of very strong *fumo de Minas* (Minas tobacco) was steeped in water; the wound was washed with some of it, and the rest poured down the dog's throat. As I had not so much faith in the efficacy of tobacco as my blacks, I ordered one of them, a sharp lad of sixteen, to take poor Chamyl to our tent, which was about a mile off, to there saddle one of our mules, and to fetch some ammonia from the next town, a distance of about eight miles. In the evening we returned to our improvised abode, speculating on the fate of our pet, whom we gave up as either dead or dying. But as soon as he heard our voices he came out barking a joyous welcome, and wagging his tail just in his old way, and showing no sign of illness. Our black cook, who, together with an old grey-haired African, had kept house the while, told us on inquiry, with a sly smile, that Pai Sé (that is, Papá José), the old black, had given him "um remedio," a drug, which had cured him instantly. Pai Sé, when asked what miraculous drug this was, showed us rather reluctantly a little parcel or bag of dark colour about two inches long and one broad, which he wore suspended by a cord round his neck, and which was so grimed with dirt and grease that we abstained from closer investigation. He had simply washed the amulet, and the dog had drunk the water! As we asked for the ammonia, he informed us with a derisive grin that the messenger was not yet back, and gruffly added that the dog was well enough now, and would not want the drugs of the whites. This was so true that when the lad, out of breath with the hot ride, returned some time afterwards with the ammonia, we put it aside unopened, for Chamyl was quite well and in the best of spirits, and he, perhaps, lives to the present day.

The belief that men who have scratched their backs all over with the tooth of a poisonous serpent will be uninjured by the bite of any, is spread all over Brazil; and I have seen trustworthy people who assured me that they saw such persons safely touch rattlesnakes. Unfortunately I never could ascertain whether they were imposed on, or whether the human system, being gradually impregnated with the poisonous matter, may indeed be protected by it against a sudden access of it, as is the case, more or less, with the vaccine virus.

We now were near the mouth of the Guaporé, and doubly vigilant for the savages said to haunt these regions. Our arms were held in readiness, and nobody was allowed to wander from the halting-place, lest we should see one of our company pierced by the arrows of an invisible enemy. These daring brigands, in their robbing expeditions, rove even into the neighbourhood of the Forte do Principe da Beira, where they have killed several soldiers under the very guns of the decaying fort; and they have ascended the Mamoré, almost up to the old Mission of Exaltacion; some of whose members, who had gone down stream in a boat to gather cacao, were once driven back by a discharge of arrows, which killed and wounded several of them. Such is the audacity of these dangerous banditti that, a few years ago, they seized upon the steersman of a Bolivian boat who had leaped ashore, as it glided along a sand-bank, in quest of gulls' eggs. Under the very eyes of his companions, and notwithstanding his own desperate resistance, he was dragged into the forest, where the savages lay concealed. The surprise was so sudden that the Bolivians did not fire a single shot after them; and, though they pursued them immediately, and heard the piteous cries of the poor kidnapped man piercing far through the wood, they could not save him, either from being roasted, or from a slavery perhaps worse than even death. The rapidity with which the naked son of the forest makes his way through the thorny shrubberies, without so much as scratching his smooth brown skin, is quite astonishing, and is unattainable, not only by the white man but also by the half-civilised Moxos Indians of the Missions. It is matched only by the swiftness of the tapir and the jaguar

From these repeated attacks, the Bolivians stand in such terror of the treacherous savages that they always encamp on the farthest end of some great sand-bank, so as to have as much open space as possible between the canoes and the forest-border; a position which at least gives them time to take up their arms, unless the red-skins follow their usual tactics of sending, unseen, their murderous shafts from behind the dense screen of shrubs.*

Of course, the danger is much less in the descent, when the canoes glide along in the middle of the stream with the swiftness of arrows, than it is in the ascent; when they advance but slowly, and must, besides, be kept near to the shore to escape the full force of the current.

After all I heard from our companions, I cannot but ascribe it to our good luck—and also, perhaps, to the sharp crack of our rifles, which we used of evenings to fire at the ugly flat skull of some

---

* A Dr. Eiras, of Rio de Janeiro, sent out to Santa Cruz de la Sierra in Bolivia as Brazilian consul, was mortally wounded on the way by several arrows discharged from behind the trees as he stole along close to the shore to shoot some water-fowl.

basking alligator—that we were unmolested during our stay of a fortnight in the domain of these robbers. On the 1st of September we reached at last the confluence of the Mamoré and the Guaporé; the former of which has a width of 330 yards at low, and of 550 yards at high water.

Though the GUAPORÉ is considerably broader than the Mamoré (550 yards at low and 760 yards at high water), its volume is less by a third, as we found upon careful measurings of its profile and its rapidity.*

The shores of both these rivers are low, but not exposed to the ordinary floods. The clear greenish tinge of the Guaporé is striking, while the Mamoré is decidedly yellow. The latter, in its lower course, has an extraordinary number of short, sharp curves, on whose convex sides there are uniformly sand-banks, sometimes of considerable length —the favourite brooding-places of the gulls; thousands and thousands of whose gray brown-spotted eggs we there found in their flat dish-like nests. The vegetation on the shores, which had lost much of its magnificence since we left the regions of the rapids and approached the Campos of Bolivia, became more and more prairie-like and poor. Low shrubs and stunted bushes took the place of the splendid trees of the lower valley. A small cluster of palms, bending over the smooth mirror of the water, enlivened only at intervals the dull monotony of the scenery. Some spots on the left, where the Pedra Canga (a porous sandstone) appeared in horizontal strata, already showed the native growth of the Campos;—nothing but strong, tall grass and thorny dwarf bushes.

In the direction of the Campos between the Guaporé and the Machupo, on which the ostriches and the great stags, that already are getting scarce in the neighbourhood of the Missions, are yet found in innumerable herds, we several times saw dense columns of smoke by day, and the reflection of fires by night, lighted probably by wild Indians. On the left bank of the Mamoré, the Campos undoubtedly extend to the Jatá and the Beni, affording excellent pasture to the last remains of those enormous herds of cattle bred by the Jesuits a hundred years ago, and, after their departure, almost wilfully destroyed, in a manner which hardly admits of excuse.

As I shall have to revert to this theme, I may here only mention

---

* See the hydrographic results in the Appendix.

that, twelve years ago, a fat cow could be purchased at the Missions for three pesos (ten shillings); whereas it now fetches about thrice that sum. Near the mouth of the Matucáre, a small influent on the right, such a fresh breeze set in, inviting us to unfurl our sails, that simultaneously, on all the canoes of our little fleet, preparations were made to profit by it. Masts of every kind—both straight and crooked; some vertical, others bending forward or backward—were set up; and sails, of shapes certainly not to be found in nautical handbooks, were utilised for the occasion; not omitting hammocks and musquiteiros; but our heavy boats glided along under them, nevertheless, with unwonted swiftness. We passed in this way the only little rapid of the Mamoré, with a slope of 2 inches and a length of 660 feet, caused by a ridge of Pedra Canga stretching right across the river. As this Pedra Canga is situated (as on the Amazon) on soft, finely laminated clay, which is easily solved by water, the layer of not very hard sandstone loses its base and tumbles down in large fragments. This process of breaking off, and the consequent receding of the rapid, will go on until the whole bank is destroyed; when the river will quietly flow along in its widened and deepened bed, leaving only the rocks on both the shores as final memorials of the former obstruction. These signs being found on eight or ten places on the Mamoré, I do not doubt that, ages ago, it had as many rapids thus levelled by the river itself in the course of time.

The MATUCARÉ affords an easy road, at high water level, to the former Mission of São Joaquim on the Machupo; the country being a dead flat for a considerable extent, and the little lake, whence rises Matucaré, discharging itself on the opposite side, in the direction of the Machupo.

In the dry months, the voyage between Exaltacion and São Joaquim must be made on foot, by barely accessible paths in the woods; and I cannot omit to mention here, in proof of the hard condition of Bolivian Indians, that two of them, carrying seven or eight arrobas (about 240 pounds), were paid one peso (about four francs) for this trip, out of which they have to provide their own food. In this five days' march they have to cross vast swamps with their heavy loads, cruelly tormented by the mosquitos at night, and moreover, exposed to the attacks of wild Indians, who seem to have taken up their station in this wilderness. In fact, they are no better off than slaves; and this state of things can be remedied only by improving the communications, and thereby destroying the monopoly of commerce in the hands of a few enterprising but unscrupulous speculators.

The Campos on the left bank of the Mamoré are inhabited by the Chacovos, a peaceful tribe of Indians, who used to visit Exaltacion from time to time; but of late they seem to have retired more into the unknown interior. They consider the herds of wild cattle in the Campos between the Mamoré and Beni as their property, and resent any hunting or killing of them by the inhabitants of Exaltacion and Santa Ana.

At two days' journey below the ancient Mission of Exaltacion, we found the first rude beginnings of agriculture, plantains and cacao planted by the Indians of the Mission; in close proximity to which was the first civilised house we had seen for months. It belonged to an old Brazilian, Antonio de Barros Cardoza, the same who rendered such material assistance to Lieutenant Gibbon, of the U. S. Navy, eighteen years ago, and whose aid was so important to us, when preparing to return. He is a good-looking man, of about fifty years; his brown, weather-beaten face and strong frame showing the true Portuguese type, and his vivacity and activity contrasting singularly with his long, grey beard. His house, a low, one-storied edifice, with a large open shed that serves at once as sitting-room, store, bed-room for guests, and kitchen, stands on a projecting rock on the right margin, and bears the name of Cerrito. We spent a couple of pleasant hours with him, talking about the war in Paraguay, the politics of Bolivia, and the future Madeira Railway; and we left him, after having accepted his kind offer to lodge us at a little house of his at Exaltacion.

In the "port" of that Mission, where we landed presently, a few small canoes and two larger barques of the same unwieldy shape as ours, were moored at the foot of the steep slope, while on its top some miserable thatched huts, with stunted bananas and the dwarf wind-torn growth of the Campos around them, mark the place that bears the high-sounding name of PUERTO DE EXALTACION DE LA SANTA CRUZ.

Some Indians bathing, and a couple of brown women filling their large earthen jars, were the only objects that imparted an air of life to the melancholy scene.

On our way over the dry Campos to the Pueblo, distant about a mile and a quarter from the port, we met, soon after its roofs had come in sight over the dense foliage of some tamarinds, a few Indian women, who greeted us in their own language in a peculiarly quiet, not unfriendly way, quite their own. The literal translation of this greeting is: "Well! have you arrived?"—and its proper answer, à *l'Indienne*, is a long-drawn *Hm!* There is a Portuguese saying—

> "Cada roca seu fuso;
> Cada terra seu uso."
> (Each distaff its spindle;
> Each country its use.)

and so we will not deride the poor Mojos for their greeting, queer as it sounds.

The first impression of the Pueblo is rather a dreary one; large, grass-grown streets bordered by mouldering house-posts, showing the former importance of the place, and leading to a lonely Plaza in the centre of the regularly-planned site. The low white-washed cottages have all, both in the Plaza and in the side streets, far-projecting roofs, supported by wooden columns, and so forming a continuous verandah. Only a few of them show the luxury of a small window, shut with a wooden grate; the rest have no opening but the door.

One side of the Plaza, which is about 330 feet in length, is entirely occupied by the Church, with an isolated campanile, and the former Collegium of the reverend Padres, which boasts a large verandah as well on the ground-floor as on the second story. The projecting roof of the gable-side of the church rests on four nicely-carved wooden columns, and serves the double purpose of forming an airy, spacious hall, and of protecting against rain the gaudy paintings of the façade, which is of *adobe* (sun-dried brick) like the whole range of buildings.

Although these do not answer all the requirements of architectural beauty, yet it must be owned that the fathers of the Society of Jesus made the most of such poor material, and erected therewith edifices which have resisted the storms of a century and a half, and have been well adapted to their needs and to the climate. To this day, a hundred years after that other powerful storm, which for ever deprived the Jesuits of their Missions in Paraguay, Brazil, and Bolivia, together with all their rich incomes, these buildings could have been as well preserved as if they had been of stone, if Spanish indolence had not neglected to make even the most necessary repairs. Still, such is the impression of vitality made by these edifices, that we expected every moment to see one of the padres appear from out the dark background of the grey, weather-beaten colonnade.

The absence of trees, and the number of tall crucifixes (the largest of which is erected in the middle of the Plaza), give it the appearance of the dreary interior of a quiet monastery,—an impression which is only heightened by the grave Indians gliding noiselessly along the extensive corridors in their long white camisetas.

The sacristan, an Indian, readily opened to us a side-door of the church, and we passed out of the dazzling light of the declining sun into the mystic twilight of the aisle, after having been amused with the grotesque ornamentation and the gaudy colours of the pilastres and statuettes of the outer hall.

A detailed description of the church, and of the life and doings of the Indians in the Missions, will follow hereafter.

Our task now was—and it was neither an easy nor an agreeable one—to get a sufficient number of paddlers for our return, as those who had come with us from the Amazon had been absent from their families for eight months, and were unwilling to undergo the troubles and dangers of the same voyage again after only a few days' repose. The welfare of the traveller in this regard depends entirely on the good or the ill-will of the Director of the Pueblo, who has the title of Corregidor, and of the chieftain of the Indians, who exercises the greatest influence on them to the present day. But as we had been commissioned by the Brazilian Government, and as the President of the Republic had been notified of our arrival by the Brazilian Ambassador, our relation to both the Corregidor and the Prefect of the Department differed materially from that of an ordinary Bolivian merchant of Trinidad or Santa Cruz, who might be hunting for paddles in the Missions, and we therefore had a right to count on their support. On the morning following our arrival at Exaltacion, we went in person to the house of the Corregidor, a still youthful-looking man of the true Spanish type, who lived on the ground floor of the Collegium, which is kept in rather better repair than the first story. He received us in a wide hall paved with bricks, between which sections of large bones, probably of bullocks, formed simple patterns of a rough mosaic. After we had all been seated on heavy, rudely carved arm-chairs, or on similar benches, and the inevitable cigarros had been handed round by an Indian girl, he informed us that he was charged by the " Prefeito do Departamento " to assist us in every possible way in the exploration of a river which was of as great importance to Bolivia as to Brazil, but that he greatly regretted he could not obtain in the thinly-peopled Pueblo of Exaltacion the whole number of paddles we required, viz., forty-two men, and that we were to wait until the Prefect residing at Trinidad, whither he was about to send an express, should decide out of which of the next Missions the rest of our crew was to be taken.

As we began to apprehend that we were going to have as long a delay here as at Manáos, which, at the then advanced season, would

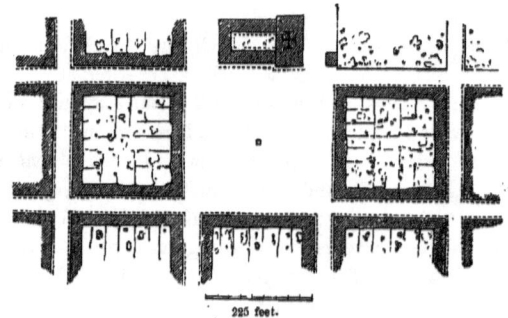

GROUND-PLAN OF THE FORMER MISSION OF EXALTACION.

prove (as it did) of evil consequences to us, I resolved to face the hardships of another fortnight's voyage in a small canoe, and to go myself to Trinidad.

I chose the lightest canoe at hand, and, availing myself of the clear moonlight nights, succeeded in reaching Trinidad (a distance of 150 miles) in six days. There is no rapid in this part of the river, but in some places there is a strong current. Arrived at Trinidad, which is laid out exactly on the plan of Exaltacion, I was kindly received by the Prefect, a Frenchman, and the Chefe da Policia, a true Bolivian of Indian descent (of the Guichoa tribe). Luckily for us all, I was enabled to set out on my return on the second day, with the necessary orders for the Corregidores of San Joaquin and

HALT UNDER A GIANT OF THE PRIMEVAL FOREST (Madeira).

Exaltacion, and with the promise that from Trinidad itself a part of the crew should follow me within three days. Descending the river without intermission, I arrived at Exaltacion in two days and two nights, having on the way encountered a heavy squall and rain of tropical violence, and sustained the loss of the coberta or tolda, the hide-covered awning of the canoe, which was caught by the branches of a low-lying tree as we glided swiftly along the banks. Having immediately despatched a messenger to San Joaquin, we with all haste set about the repairs of four of the barques and the collecting of provisions (chiefly Indian corn-flour and sun-dried meat), in which operations we were so valiantly assisted by old Cardozo that we were enabled to leave Exaltacion after a month's sojourn, and to turn the bows of our barques homewards.

It was the 19th of October, and high time it was for our departure! Already fearful squalls sweeping over the country told us that the rainy season was at hand; and, if this were to find us still in the region of the rapids, we surely should expiate our delay with intermittent fevers.

The disheartening story of the Bolivian merchant overtaken by the floods there, who had to bury eight of his crew within a few days (the rest having had a narrow escape), haunted us incessantly; and we did our best to make the detailed maps of the river-course, and to take the soundings of its depth, with all possible dispatch. Luckily we had already made the astronomical observations on our ascent. We arrived at Santo Antonio as early as the 18th of November, yet not without having, all of us, suffered in various degrees from fits of the fever; which, though subdued, was not cured by repeated doses of quinine, so long as we continued to be exposed to the same pernicious influences.

The labour and trouble of passing the rapids are less, of course, on the descent than on the ascent; but the risks to vessels are greater; and, with the true Indian carelessness of the crew, it is almost miraculous that they escape from being wrecked on the rocks, which are half covered with the bubbling white spray. Several times our barques were in imminent danger, and with them all the results of our troublesome tour; especially once at Guajará, and another time in the currents below Bananeiras.

The unloading at the principal breaks, which in the descent also are unapproachable, the transporting of the freight and vessels over stone and rocks, the frequent breaking and cracking of ribs (of the vessels, I mean), and their hurried repair, are just the same as in the ascent. Suffice it then to say that at last we saw with relieved hearts our boats floating again on the smooth surface of the Amazon, and at Manáos the warmth of the greeting extended to us by friends and acquaintance was intensified by the circumstance that only a few days before the newspapers had stated most positively that one and all of us had been killed and eaten by the Caripunas. On the 14th of December, 1868, we arrived safely at Pará by the same *Belem* which had first brought us to Manáos; and on the 4th of January, 1869, at Rio de Janeiro, which we had left fourteen months before, a little less sunburnt, and unweakened by intermittent fevers.

CHAPTER III.

CANOE AND CAMP LIFE.

The Start.—Preparation of the Bast Shirts and Panama Hats.—Breakfast.—Turtle Soup.—Hunting the Alligators.—Night Camp.

THE lower course of the Madeira presents, for more than four hundred and sixty miles, a picture of grand simplicity and, it must be owned, monotony, which, magnificent as it appears at first, wearies the eye and sickens the heart at last,—a dead calm on an unruffled, mirror-like sheet of water glaring in the sun, and, as far as the eye can reach, two walls of dark green forest with the dark-blue firmament above them; in the foreground, slender palms, and gigantic orchid-covered trunks, with blooming creepers hanging from the wave-worn shore, with its red earthslips, down into the turbid floods. No hill breaks the finely indented line of the foliage, which everywhere bounds the horizon, only here and there a few palm-covered sheds peep out of the green; and still more rarely do we sight one of their quiet dark inmates. Stately kingfishers looking thoughtfully into the river, white herons standing for hours on one leg, and alligators lying so motionless at the mouth of some rivulet that their jaggy tails and scarcely protruding skulls might easily be taken for some half-sunken trunks, are the only animals to be seen; and certainly they do not increase the liveliness of the scene. Dreary and monotonous as the landscape, the days too pass in unvaried succession.

With the first dawn of day, before the white mist that hides the smooth surface of the river has disappeared with the rays of the rising sun, the day's work begins. The boatswains call their respective crews; the tents are broken up as quickly as possible; the cooking apparatus, the hammocks and hides that served as beds, are taken on board together with our arms and mathematical instruments; and every one betakes himself to his post. The pagaias (paddles) are dipped into the water, and the prows of our heavy boats turn slowly from the shore to the middle of the stream. Without the loss of a minute, the oars are plied for three or four hours, at a steady but rather quick rate, until a spot on shore is discovered easy of access and offering a dry fire-place and some fuel for the preparation of breakfast. If it be on one of the long sandbanks, a roof is made of one of the sails, that rarely serve for anything else; if in the wood, the undergrowth, in the shade of some large tree, is cleared for the reception of our little table and tent-chairs.

The functions of the culinary *chef* for the white faces, limited to the preparation of a dish of black beans, with some fish or turtle, are simple enough, but, to be appreciated, certainly require the hearty appetite acquired by active life in the open air. The Indians have to cook by turns for their respective boats' crews; their unalterable bill of fare being a pap of flour of Indian corn or mandioca, with fresh or dried fish, or a piece of jacaré (alligator).

Most of those who are not busy cooking, spend their time preparing new bast shirts, the material for which was found almost everywhere in the neighbourhood of our halting-places. Soon the wood is alive with the sound of hatchets and the crack of falling trees; and, even before they are summoned to breakfast, they return with pieces of a silky bast of about $4\frac{1}{2}$ yards long and somewhat less than $1\frac{1}{4}$ yard wide. Their implements for shirt-making are of primitive simplicity,—a heavy wooden hammer with notches, called macota, and a round piece of wood to work upon. Continuously beaten with the macota, the fibres of the

1. Preparation of the Cáscara or Bark-Shirt. 2. Wild Cocoa.
OUR MOJOS INDIANS AT BREAKFAST (Madeira).

bast become loosened, until the originally hard piece of wood gets soft and flexible, and about double its former breadth. After it has been washed, wrung out to remove the sap, and dried in the sun, it has the appearance of a coarse woollen stuff of a bright whitish yellow or

TOUJOURS PERDRIX!

light brown, disclosing two main layers of wavy fibres held together by smaller filaments. A more easily prepared and better working-garment for a tropical climate is hardly to be found than this, called cáscara by the Indians of Bolivia, and turury* by those of the Amazon. Its cut is as simple and classical as its material. A hole is cut in the middle of a piece about 10 feet long, to pass the head through; and the depending skirt is sewn together on both sides, from below up to the height of the girdle, which usually is a piece of cotton string or liana.

Another branch of industry our Indians were busy at, in their hours of leisure, was the fabrication of straw hats, with the young leaves of a kind of little palm, the same which supplies the excellent hats imported from Ecuador and Perú, and known in Europe under the name of Chile or Panamá hats. Dexterity at all sorts of wickerwork seems to be innate to this race; and the prettiest little baskets, and the finest mats of coloured palm leaves, are to be bought on the Missions of the Mamoré at the lowest prices.†

But all these occupations are left at the call of the first-mate; who has the proud title of Capitano. The boats' crews crowd round their pots; each one receives his allotted portion in a calabash or a basin of horn; and their spoons of the same material are soon in full activity. If a jacaré has lately been shot, or caught in a laço (sling), every one, after roasting his own piece of it on the spit, proceeds to cut at the large slices of the white meat (which, though in appearance like fish, is as tough as India-rubber) with the satisfaction usually produced by three or four hours of hard rowing on view of anything eatable. One tribe especially, the Canichanas, from the former Mission of San Pedro at the Mamoré, think roast caiman the finest eating in the world; while others, the Cayuabas from Exaltacion, and the Mojos, from Trinidad, whose palates are somewhat more refined, prefer beef, fish, or turtle to the musk-exhaling saurian. Notably the turtles, which are not found on the Guaporé and Mamoré (they are not met with above the rapids of the Madeira) are prized by them, though *we* grew rather tired of them, and no wonder. On the lower Madeira, at our fires, there was almost daily going on the cooking of turtles, of all sizes, from the full-grown one of a yard in length to the smallest of the size of a hand; and in every variety of preparation too—whole, and chopped up as for soup; stewed; and roasted in their own shell or on the spit.

* *Curatari legalis*, Martius.
† At Rio de Janeiro a Panamá hat costs twenty and more dollars; in Bolivia about five or six.

Bathing in the river, immediately after meals, is a luxury invariably indulged in by all the Indians; and I never remarked that it was attended by any evil consequences to them.

After a rest of two hours' duration, the cooking utensils, the hammocks, and improvised tents, were carried on board again, and the voyage continued. A second halt was made after rowing for two or three hours, when we came in sight of a good place for fishing, such as the mouth of some smaller river, or an extensive mud bank. Such places

ALLIGATOR-HUNTING.

were usually recognisable from afar, by the multitude of snow-white herons, and of long caimans, which, finding it out before us, crowded there in peaceful unity, and with similar intentions. The vicinity of the scaly monsters is scarcely heeded by the Indians, who fish and take their bath, laughing and jesting, though somewhat hugging the shore, just as if there were no such thing as the tail or the tooth of the jacaré in the world; and, indeed, these creatures are themselves in much greater danger than the red-skins. When the last steak of alligator has been consumed, one of the Canichanas is sure to ask leave to have some fun, and to provide at the same time for their next dinner. Of course the permission is always granted, as the sport keeps up their spirits, and spares our provisions. Without loss of time, then, one of them, having carefully fastened a strong loop of raw hide at the end of a long pole, and having dexterously slipped off his bast shirt, creeps slowly through the shallow water, pole and sling in hand, as near as possible to the alligator, which looks on at these preparations with perfect apathy, only now and then betraying a sign of life by a lazy movement of its powerful tail. But it does not take its eyes off the Indian as he crawls nearer and nearer. The fatal sling is at arm's length from its muzzle, and yet it does not see it. As if under the influence of witchcraft, it continues to stare with its large protruding eyes at the bold hunter, who in the next moment has thrown the loop over its head, and suddenly drawn it to with a strong pull. The other Indians, who the while have been cowering motionless on shore, now rush into the water to the help of their companion, and four or five of them land the ugly creature that with all its might struggles to get back into the water, lashing the sand with its tail and showing its long teeth; but a few vigorous blows with an axe on the tail and skull soon render it tame enough. If, instead of dragging back, the alligator were only to rush forward boldly to the attack of the Indians, they would, of a certainty, leave pole and sling and run for their lives; but this bright idea never seems to occur to the uncouth animal, and the strife always ends with its death. Though there were more than a dozen of them killed during the voyage, I never thought of sending a rifle-bullet through the thick skull of one, except on one occasion, when I was afraid that one of our Canichanas was about to make too close an acquaintance with the hard, jagged tail of an extraordinarily strong monster, which measured full $16\frac{1}{2}$ feet.

Even before the huge spoil is cut up, four musk-glands, placed by twos under its jaw, and on its belly, near the beginning of the tail, must be carefully taken out, to prevent the diffusion, over the whole body, of the penetrating odour of the greasy, brown liquid they contain. These glands, which are about an inch and a half long and as thick as a finger, are carefully tied up and suspended in the sun to dry. Mixed with a little rose-water, their contents serve, as we were told, to perfume the raven-black tresses of the elegant Bolivian ladies at Santa Cruz de la Sierra and Cochabamba, in spite of, or rather by reason of, their strong scent, which gives the headache to all save those

CATCHING AN ALLIGATOR WITH LASSO (MADEIRA).

strong-nerved Señoritas, who love a bull-fight above everything, who know how to roll the cigarito, and to dance the fandango with matchless grace, but who scarcely are able to write their own names.

After such a pleasant interlude of fishing or hunting, the paddles are plied with renewed vigour until the evening, when sleeping quarters are selected, either on a sandbank or in the forest. The canoes are moored by strong piassaba-ropes in some recess of the bank, where they are protected against drifting trunks; the tents are erected, and preparations ensue for the principal meal. Meanwhile, after the very short interval of twilight usual in the tropics, Night almost suddenly throws her dark veil over the valley, and the bright constellations of the Southern sky in quiet majesty adorn the firmament.

While we prepare to take astronomical observations, half-a-dozen large fires are lighted round about, in whose fitful blaze the neighbouring forest trees appear like huge phantoms, looking contemptuously down on us, poor tiny mortals. Our Indians warm themselves in the cheerful glow, smoking, and chatting of the day's adventures, or rather of what are regarded as such—unusual good or ill-luck at fishing and hunting; the casual meeting of some canoe; or the sight of a seringueiro's poor cottage. Work over, they take off the rough cáscara, and put on the camiseta, a cotton garment without sleeves, resembling a wide poncho sewn together at the sides, and whose dazzling whiteness is set off by two scarlet stripes along the seams. The ample folds and the simple cut of the garment, which is made by the Indian women of the Missions on very primitive looms, give quite a stately, classical appearance to the numerous groups round the fires. Such must have been the aspect presented by the halting-places of those daring seafarers, the Phœnicians, who were the first to call into life an international commerce, and whose light-rigged barques first ventured to distant shores, to bring home the precious amber and the useful tin. Only the dense swarms of mosquitos, which set in immediately after sunset, remind us rather unpleasantly that we are far off from those happy Northern regions, where such a nuisance can hardly be well imagined. Especially in the dense forest beneath cacao-bushes, or under the close leafage of the large figueiras, where no breath of air incommodes those light-winged tormentors, it is quite impossible, for the European at least, to close an eye without the shelter of a mosquiteiro (mosquito-net); and we could but wonder at our Indians, most of whom did without it. After supper they simply spread a hide on the ground, on which, with no covering other than the starry firmament above them, they slept undisturbed till the dawn, only occasionally brushing away, as if by way of diversion, the most obtrusive of the little fiends. The capitanos only, and one or other of the older rowers, allow themselves the luxury of good cotton hammocks, which are also made by their wives in the Missions.

Such, with few variations, was the course of our daily life, until we reached the regions of the rapids, when, of course, the hundred little incidents connected with the dragging of the canoes through narrow, foaming channels, and with carrying the goods and the vessels themselves overland, disturbed the monotony of this rude forest life.

CHAPTER IV.

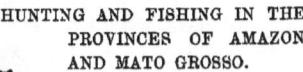

HUNTING AND FISHING IN THE PROVINCES OF AMAZON AND MATO GROSSO.

The Pirá-rucú.—The Peixe-boi.—The Boto.—Fishing with the Covo.—Tapir-hunting.—The Barreiros.

To the inhabitants of the above-mentioned provinces hunting and, still more, fishing are of an importance hardly to be estimated in Europe; and in any, be it the slightest, description of these lands, special attention must be directed to these branches of national economy; which are of small consequence in civilised countries. There the colossal turtles, the pirá-rucú (*Sudis gigas*),* and the lamantin or peixe-boi, are captured, as the tapirs, the wild hogs and deer, are hunted, not for sport, but for subsistence, for the daily food of the inhabitants.

The ox, though no longer an altogether unknown animal in these regions, is still strange enough; and its meat will be rarely met with in the isolated huts of the Indians and mestizoes, for the few heads of cattle, brought up-stream from the lower course of the Amazon by the fortnightly

---

* From pirá, fish; and rucú, red.

steamers, barely suffice to supply the wants of the little towns, such as Manáos, Santarem, etc.* Other of our domestic animals also, such as pigs, goats and sheep, are very rarely found near the huts of the riverines, though the first would thrive excellently. A number of cackling hens, and perhaps a few ducks, are their only live stock; as they

SUBMERGED FOREST.

give no trouble whatever, and find abundant food on the soft earth, and in the roots and fallen leaves near the cottages.

The marvellous bounty of nature, on the one hand, and the innate disposition, confirmed by habit, to do as their fathers have done before them, on the other, will sufficiently explain why Indians and mestizoes so

---

* The population of the Brazilian coast, living on fresh and dried fish all the year round, go to the nearest town regularly on Easter Sunday to buy a piece of beef; for once a year, they say, one must have meat.

HUNTING AND FISHING IN THE PROVINCE OF AMAZON.

markedly prefer the life of hunters and fishers to the less exciting and more settled vocation of breeders of domestic animals. From his earliest years, the young Tapuyo (Indian of the Amazon Valley) accompanies his father either on the open river or on the inundated plains, where, in the cool shade of large trees, or amid the submerged tops of palms which are mirrored in the smooth dark water, they quietly lie in ambush, patiently awaiting the proper moment for throwing their harpoons into the broad back of the pirá-rucú, a fish of 10 to 13 feet long, covered (as if it were armour) with big scales bordered by a sharp scarlet line. When caught, it is dragged on land, opened up the whole length of its back, the vertebræ taken out, and the meat salted and dried in the sun. In its fresh state it is not very palatable; but when prepared in this way, as it is largely consumed by both rich and poor from Pará to the frontiers of Perú, it makes quite an abominable dish, decidedly inferior to cod-fish. And this is not the worst of it. As the meat is very hygroscopic, and the atmosphere, especially in the rainy season, saturated with aqueous vapours, the foul-smelling slices have to be laid out in the sun from time to time; and as the vendeiros (shopkeepers) in small towns like Manáos seem to think no spot more appropriate for that operation than the pavement at their doors, their neighbours and passengers have the pleasure of at least smelling the nasty fish, if they have been lucky enough to escape it at table.

Very different is the lamantin or manati, a fresh-water cetacean, which, despite its Portuguese name of peixe-boi (ox-fish), derived from its broad snout resembling that of an ox, is no more a fish than its gigantic cousin of the sea, the sperm-whale. It abides especially in the quiet lakes on the borders of the large rivers, which are covered with a profusion of long reed-grass and wild rice, the chief food of the peixe-boi. Its flesh is fat and nice, and, when properly prepared, decidedly reminds one of pork.

Although fishing is of far greater importance than hunting to the inhabitants of these countries, for the simple reason that the latter requires powder and lead, and a far costlier weapon than their own bow* or simple iron hook, I will spare the reader the infliction of a dry ichthyologic register of all the species and varieties that people the main stream and its endless ramifications. Their number has been

---

* Bows and arrows are used everywhere on these rivers for shooting fish and turtle; but only wild Indians employ them for hunting on land.

augmented, by several hundreds, by the discoveries of M. Agassiz, in his exploration in 1866, and some future explorer may, perhaps, discover as many more. It is quite a host of fresh-water fish which inhabits the yellow floods of the Amazon and its tributaries. Only some of them spread over the whole length of its course, while the mass (according to the observations of Agassiz) are restricted to certain localities; every section of the stream, indeed, having its characteristic species. A temporary transgression of their proper bounds sometimes takes place; on the whole, however, the enormous water-net may be divided into several regions, which differ more or less sharply in their fauna. Some trifling differences in the vegetation, variety of formation of the banks and of the river-bed, its depth, and especially the greater or minor declivity, doubtless determine these restrictions.

The most constant companions of the traveller on the Amazon are the dolphins, or botos.* From Pará to the rapids of the affluents, and even to the smooths above them, they play around the boat. Being mammifers, like their oceanic brothers, they are compelled ever and anon to come to the surface, to take breath; and they describe therefore, in the water, a peculiar wavy line or cycloid, often leaping high into the air and returning, blowing and puffing, to their native element. One moonlight night, on the upper Madeira—it was at the mouth of the Jammary—our boats were surrounded by a troop of them, that played about, snorting and splashing, and making such a noise, as though hundreds of mermaids were pursued by bearded mermen, that we could not get a wink of sleep all night long.

This noisy play, those sounds that seem so strange for animals of fish shape, and their obvious passion for the society of man (they accompany the boats sometimes for long distances, in troops of thirty and forty), may have given rise to the extravagant tales regarding them, which are stoutly believed by the whole population of the country, from the half-savage Tapuyo and Mameluco to the rich Portuguese vendeiro. The botos are represented to have the property of assuming the human shape from time to time, of walking amongst us like other Christians, and of being especially dangerous to the fair sex. The only tokens which might betray the monsters are their feet, which are turned backward; but such a trifle may be easily overlooked in the dark, which they always choose for their mischievous excursions.

* From a popular Portuguese word, *bote*, jump.

Sly mulatto and Indian women tell their credulous husbands wondrous stories of the adventures they have had with the treacherous botos, which took the shape of their absent spouses so completely that the poor victims only discovered their mistake when the pseudo-husbands took their way to the river and sprang into it with a loud snort. In consequence of this widely-spread superstition, the dolphins are very rarely hunted, though it is so easy to harpoon them, and though they yield an excellent train-oil. They multiply, therefore, within the boundaries assigned by nature.

Another fabulous aquatic monster, in all likelihood a near relation

THE PIRÁ-RUCÚ (SUDIS GIGAS).

of our celebrated sea-serpent, is the so-called minhocão (big worm), a snake of such immense size that the riverines assert with all seriousness that the river rises or falls as the monster either enters or leaves it. It is also called mãi d'agua (mother of waters), which name it shares, though, with a sort of Brazilian Lorelei, haunting the picturesque fall of the Tarumá, a little influent of the Rio Negro. This beautiful maid with golden hair—whether she combs it with a golden comb, like the German Lorelei, has not yet been ascertained—bewitches with her loveliness any man who sets eyes on her. Madness overpowers his senses, and he is deprived of ability ever to find the way back to his cottage. Therefore the narrow glen which the siren has chosen for her

H

abode, and whose umbrageous depth is uninvaded by sunbeam, is regarded with superstitious awe, and no Tapuyo will venture to stay at nightfall at any place within hearing of the roar of the haunted fall.

Another dreaded ghost of the forest, though it be not by far of so lovely a shape, is the Caepóra (Cáa póra, man of the forest), an ugly old man covered with hair, of immense bodily strength, who waylays the hunters and twists their necks. Any unusual sound in the woods is ascribed to the caepóra, and only absolute silence and motionless cowering under bushes and branches will, it is thought, avail to save from his dreadful claws. Incredulous people are forced by urgent entreaties, or, if need be, by menaces, to comply with these arrangements, in order not to rouse the wrath of the totally invulnerable monster. If large

THE LAMANTIN, OR PEIXE-BOI (MANATUS AMERICANUS).

man-like monkeys, such as the gorilla, the chimpanzee, and the orang-outang, were to be found in the Brazilian forests, this widely-spread superstition would admit of easy explanation; but even the liveliest hunter's fancy is not equal to so hideous an exaggeration of such poor representatives of "our cousins" as are howling monkeys, or Barrigudos; and the origin of the fable is certainly to be sought only in the gloomy belief of the Indians, who fancy themselves pursued at every step by demons and witchcraft. Moreover, every tribe has its own hunting-customs, or rather hunting-superstitions, for here also the sons of Nimrod are more inclined to credulity than other mortals. The Coroados of the South will not taste the meat of the deer, lest they should lose their rich black hair; or the protuberance on the neck of the tapir, which is the best morsel, lest they should lose the love of their wives. In the same way they avoid the meat of the duck and of the cutia, a very savoury rodent, lest their children should acquire big, ugly-shaped feet and ears. He who has shot the deadly arrow must not eat of the game if he would have steady aim and good luck for the future; and the women also, to the evident advantage of their selfish, law-giving halves, are prohibited from the eating of many animals.

The fishes apparently are not subject to the same objections, and every means seems lawful for their capture: hooks, bows and arrows, casting nets, and drag-nets, that are spread out in a wide circle and drawn in on shallow sandbanks, sometimes filled with exceedingly rich spoil.* At some points whole tribes will unite, as the above-mentioned Coroados of Paraná, in the operation of forcing them, by raising little stone dykes upon and between the boulders of a current, to take a certain channel so controlled by a plait-work of bamboo that at the upper end the water rushes into it with considerable force, yet leaves it perfectly dry a little farther down, whence it escapes through the interstices. As these "parys" (as the contrivances are called by the Coroados) are usually fitted up at the season of the multitudinous return of the fish after spawning up-stream, few of the larger ones escape their fate; and their profusion would be seriously impaired in streams with parys, if these were not regularly destroyed every year by the floods.

One mode of fishing practised on the Mamoré (though it be not very frequently) is too singular to be passed over in silence. At certain seasons millions of small fish move up-stream in dense swarms. These migrations, which occupy several hours, are awaited by the Moxo Indian, who takes up a standing position in the shallow water, near the shore or near a sandbank, provided only with the cóvo, a sort of conical basket, without bottom, carefully made of laths of a heavy palm-wood joined by plait-work. This basket he throws at the passing fish, which he can afterwards, at his leisure, take out by the smaller opening at the top, provided the water is not higher than the covo itself.

Another method,—the worst of all, since it destroys both the old ones and the spawn, the eatable and the uneatable together, leaving generally the greater part of them as a meal for the urubús (vultures),—can be applied only in smaller sheets of water, in the little lagoons or pools

* The best species for eating are the Surubim, Pintado, Bagre, Tambaki, Tucunaré, Pirá-rára, Piranha, &c.

left by the retiring floods. A poisonous creeper, cipo timbó (*Paullinia pinnata*, L.),* is crushed, and the sap thrown into the water, which in a few minutes will be covered with dead fish of all sizes, the eating of which does not seem to endanger the health. Though I think this mode of fishing worthy only of barbarians, I should not have hesitated once to use the poison, had one of the plants been at hand. It was at the Salto de Theotonio, the most considerable of the cataracts of the Madeira, where a rugged reef of 33 feet in height crosses the river-bed. A great number of pools had been left by the receding floods in its holes and on shore, just about where the fish probably had tried to pass the fall in lateral channels, or by leaping and bounding over the breaks to continue, in the smooth above, their search for an appropriate place to deposit their spawn. In the largest of these pools many hundreds of gigantic fish had been cut off from the main stream, perhaps weeks before our arrival, and were dying slowly in the warm water of the basin, which was impregnated with every variety of putrid matter. We counted already more than five hundred bodies of large dead fish in every stage of decomposition, floating upon the surface of the slimy green water, and emitting pestiferous exhalations. From time to time a huge surubim rose from the depth and

FISHING WITH THE CÓVO.

* Besides this, there are a few other similar plants used in the same way: Goyana-Timbó, Piscidia Erythrina, VELL.; Taraira-Moira, Cocculus inerme, MART.; Conami, Euphorbiæ et Ichthyotheræ, MART.

ONE OF OUR MOJOS INDIANS RETURNING FROM FISHING (Madeira).

moved slowly, almost torpidly, through the thick element. Some dozens of black vultures (urubús) looked sharply and anxiously at us and at the foul pond, their richly-laden table, the while sitting rigid and motionless on the neighbouring rocks with their wide wings opened to the evening breeze, probably to air their feathers. They reminded us, in their immobility, of the bronze eagles on the crown of some old tower. In spite of the sickening aspect, we had the greatest difficulty to prevent our Indians from harpooning the half-dead fish and making themselves seriously ill with this nauseating food, although they had, with but little trouble, succeeded in taking a large quantity of wholesome fish below the fall, in the bays and creeks of the shores, and at the mouth of a small rivulet.

We were taken with the strange shape of the "rays," whose broad wings and projecting eyes are to be met, it is usually supposed, in salt water only. We caught some specimens that measured more than three feet from the extremity of the head to the tail, which is armed with a horny sting, of a finger's length. These rays were of a greyish brown, with black spots encircling a yellow point. They are much feared by the Indians, for their sting, which is indeed well calculated, with its double edge and finely dentated point, to inflict excruciating wounds on the bare foot of some bather, who may incautiously trample upon the creature, as it lies lurking for spoil half-buried in the mud of the shallow banks.

The annexed sketch represents one of our paddlers returning from a fishing excursion, and carrying, besides a ray and a large surubim, another smaller fish, whose sharp curved teeth have given it the name of peixe cachorro (dog-fish). It is not so dangerous to man as the rays or the piranhas,* broad fishes of little more than a span's length, which have literally torn to pieces many a daring swimmer. Their two rows of projecting teeth, which are sharp as needles, are the more to be dreaded, as the terrible creatures are almost always together in hundreds, and they throw themselves upon their victim with the rapidity of lightning, as soon as the water has been dyed with the blood of the first bite, each individual one of the dreadful snapping little jaws tearing off a piece of flesh.

Without any doubt these piranhas are a much greater obstacle to bathing than the jacarés (crocodiles), whose victims are far less numerous than is generally believed.

Another dangerous animal, though in a different way, is the candirú,

* From pirá, fish, and anha, tooth.

an almost transparent, thin little fish, of less than a finger's length, which penetrates with eel-like nimbleness into the orifices of the bathers and causes many fatal accidents, according to the reports of the riverines.

So much for the scaly inhabitants of this immense water-net. I trust I have succeeded in giving an idea of the incredible variety of their forms, which surpass the analogous ones of our rivers both in beauty and in number, even as these gigantic streams surpass our noblest rivers in size.

As for hunting, it is followed much less by the half-civilised mestizo population of the Amazon basin, although its endless forests are full of

HEAD OF SWIMMING TAPIR, PURSUED BY DOGS.

game, than it is in that of the La Plata, in the neighbouring province of Mato Grosso.

The noblest and most generally pursued game is the anta (tapir), that representative of the pachyderms in the New World, which, in the Old, is found at only a few places in India. It flourishes in extraordinary numbers, yet does not herd together in troops, on the densely wooded shores of all the tributaries of the Amazon and La Plata. All the narrow gorges and moist ravines, clad with rich vegetation, and the forests on the shores of murmuring rivulets, and near the roaring cataracts of large rivers, are sure to shelter that diminutive of the elephant. At early dawn it leaves its quiet nook behind thorny bambusaceæ, or leafy bushes, and walks gravely to the river by deeply trodden paths of its ownengineering, for it thoroughly enjoys a cold bath in the morning; and often, when quickly doubling some sharp bend in the river, we surprised it sitting in quiet majesty up to the neck in the water. It swims and dives with astonishing agility; and it may be the sense of greater security in the aqueous element, or it may be a longing for a refreshing bath after a tumultuous flight, which impels it always to take the shortest cut to the river, when pursued by the dogs. But it runs to its own destruction; for there stands the hunter, motionless and ready for his shot, in his light canoe, which is screened from observation by overhanging boughs. Rifle and bow, however, are scarcely wanted. If the river is of any breadth, the snorting and panting animal, vainly diving here and there to escape the furiously biting and barking hounds, is soon overtaken and killed, mostly either with a long hunting-knife, or with a pistol, by the occupant of the nutshell. If possible, it is harpooned before receiving the fatal blow; else it would sink to the bottom, and the hunter would have to await its rising again.

Only the female anta, with her young one, never flies before the dogs. She remains courageously in her retreat, endeavouring to protect with her own body the trembling little creature that creeps between her legs, and vents its anxiety in shrill whistling sounds. Woe to the hardy cur that dares to leave the semicircle of its companions, barking in these cases from a safe distance, and to come within reach of the grim dam. Her elevated short jaw bares some teeth that demand respect, and under her powerful fore-legs the weak ribs of a dog would snap like thin reeds. At last, riddled with bullets, she falls down, a victim to maternal tenderness, on the body of her terrified offspring.

If the hunter succeeds in protecting the latter against the fury of the pack, who are courageous enough now, and if he does not handle it too roughly, it will become as tame as a dog, even on the second or third day of its captivity (as I witnessed myself), and soon will abandon all thought of returning to its native wilds. As its food (grass, pumpkins, fruits, etc.) is easily procurable, it is not only possible but very easy to make it quite a domestic animal.

In Curitiba, the capital of the province of Paraná, a stray tapir ran about the streets, and the negro boys used to ride upon it from morning to night. A temperature of 2° or 3° below freezing point, not uncommon there in June and July, did not appear to incommode it in the least.

Almost all the larger South American animals are easily tamed; the wild hog, the deer, the guaty, the paca, and even the jaguar, not to speak of the monkeys, parrots, and gallinaceous birds. Indeed, there is scarcely a house or cottage in all the Amazon region, that does not swarm with "jerimbabos" (pet animals), such as araras, periquitos, marianitas, jacamins, jacutingas, mutuns, tucanoes, cutias, pacas, monkeys, etc.; which sometimes are of the most troublesome and ridiculous tameness. The half-caste ladies especially are fond of their favourites, and often would not part with them for the world. Even the giboia (a sort of American boa-constrictor) is often set free in the houses, to kill rats, mice, and other vermin, of which there is no lack anywhere. Small lizards, bats and enormous spiders are the most harmless of them; scorpions and lacraias, whose sting is said to be exceedingly painful, being no rare guests, especially in old houses.

Accidents from poisonous snakes are not so frequent as is generally supposed. The bite of the different species of jararacas (*Bothrops jararaca*) and of coral-snakes will produce serious nflammations; but the patient usually escapes if properly attended to; while the rattlesnake of the campos (*Crotalus horridus*) and the surucucu (*Lachesis mutus*) are said to cause certain death. Yet I once saw a negro, at Barbacena in the province of Minas, who escaped with only a stiff leg after having been bitten by a rattlesnake.

All the animals of these forests, birds included (with the single exception of the jaguar), eat clay* with great voracity, and may be found peacefully congregated, sometimes in great numbers, at favourably situated spots, on steep broken banks, for instance, whose reddish yellow walls often show distinct traces of the teeth of a great many species. On moonlight nights particularly, when the whole animal world is awake and more restless than usual, these "barreiros" (clay-pits), easily visible from the river, are excellent places for lying in ambush for all kinds of game; and, if he be lucky, the hunter may kill

---

* Many, especially children, in these countries share the same morbid craving; which often reaches such a degree that not even the certainty of the most painfully miserable death awaiting them can cure them of it. As a desperate expedient, negro slaves sometimes are forced to wear iron masks, which are only taken off during the meals, when the overseer is by.

CARIPUNA INDIANS WITH TAPIR (Madeira).
(Orchids, Bromelias, and Ferns).

even a spotted or black jaguar, in quest, not of the clay, but, like the hunter himself, of deer or wild hogs, which are an easy spoil for its long fangs and powerful paws. Tapirs, that is full-grown ones, do not fall victims so easily. These pachyderms—thanks to their skin of a finger's thickness—dash so swiftly through the shrubs and bushes, with a weight that carries everything resistlessly before them, that, in the first dense thicket of thorns and lianas, they violently disengage themselves of their terrible riders, who tightly clasp them round their necks, before the jaguar's powerful clutches penetrate below their stout skin.

In the endless virgin forests on the shores of the Paraná, before us unvisited by European for two hundred years at least, our hunters shot, at the mouth of the Ivahy, an old tapir, which had evidently had a hard struggle with its sleek enemy. It had one eye only, and its broad back showed deep traces of the jaguar's claws. And thus this poor patriarch of the woods, who had escaped the tooth of the tiger, at last fell a victim to the bullet of one of our half-caste Indians.

The meat of the tapir is excellent, tasting much like beef. The fat hunch on its neck, covered with long black bristles, is a delicacy which would do honour to the table of a Lucullus; and equally esteemed are its short trunk, and the feet, which yield, when boiled, a rich jelly. The Indians and mestizoes usually prepare the head in the following manner; which also serves for whole hogs and other game. A number of pebbles, of the size of one's fist, or larger, are thoroughly heated in the fire, and then carefully placed in a hole prepared for their reception, two or three feet deep. The tapir's head (or the peccari), wrapped in banana or heliconia leaves, is laid thereon; another layer of glowing hot stones, together with more leaves, is put over them, and the hole filled up with earth. At the end of six or eight hours a supply of the best and juiciest roast meat will thus be ready.

Besides the tapir, two species of wild hog, and several kinds of deer, are especially appreciated. Among the latter is an exceedingly pretty one, scarcely three spans high. Stags (and very powerful ones too), whose antlers are much thicker in proportion, and taper much more sharply than those of the European species, are found only in the campos or prairies.

Of the wild hogs, even the larger variety is considerably smaller and weaker than the European class; and, though they are together by hundreds, and the Brazilian hunters generally bring them down at close quarters, we never heard of any damage occasioned by them, beyond badly wounding some dogs. In the middle of the back, these animals have a sort of gland, filled with a greasy, strongly scented substance, reminding one of musk, which, when irritated or hardly pursued by the dogs, they emit through a small opening. As soon as the peccari is killed, it is the hunter's first care to see that this gland is cut out, lest its foul odour should communicate itself to the meat, and so render it uneatable.*

The monkeys, the queerest and nimblest of all the inhabitants of the woods, who with infinite agility swing themselves, in numerous troops, from bough to bough, are often hunted by the Brazilians; but I should not advise a European to partake of the sport. Their piteous cries, if they be not killed on the spot, their desperate, almost human gestures, and their excited examination of the bleeding wound, will more than suffice to spoil the pleasure of the day for any one of sensitive feelings.

Gallinaceous birds, and parrots in endless variety, are found everywhere; yet the latter, especially the long-tailed macaws, are exceedingly shy and very difficult to shoot, while of the former twenty or thirty together may sometimes be seen in the above-mentioned barreiros or clay-pits. Amongst them the jacus (*Penelope cristata*) and jacutingas (*Penelope jacutinga*), of the size of our tame fowls, and the jacamins (*Psophia crepitans*, *P. ochroptera*, *P. leucoptera*), somewhat larger, are considered excellent eating.† When to all these we add the multitude of smaller quadrupeds, such as cutias (*Dasyprocta fuliginosa* and *D. aguti*); coatys (*Nasua socialis* and *N. solitaria*); pacas (*Coelogenys Paca*); and large flocks of ducks, mutuns (*Crax*), herons and water-fowl, the

---

* The capivára (water-hog), a rodent of the shape of the Guinea-pig, but of the size of our tame pig, has a similar gland on the back of its nose, the contents of which smell even worse, if that be possible; and for this reason the capivára is seldom hunted.

† A highly prized because rare bird is the anhuma, or alicorne (*Palamedea cornuta*), whose strange-sounding cry is said to denote a change of weather. It has a horny protuberance on the head of 3 to 4 inches length, which the Tapuyos believe to be a strong talisman. We saw at Manáos a little silver chain, belonging to an old half-caste woman, from which were suspended, besides the horn of the anhuma, the formidable claws of an anteater (*Tamandua bandeira*), a tooth of a jaguar, and bristles of different animals, set in silver; and I really believe the old squaw would not have parted with her treasure for all the wealth of California.

most exacting son of Nimrod will admit that the forests and prairies of Brazil have attractions enough, though the hippopotami, elephants and giraffes of Africa are not found here; and that a ramble on the Amazon or the Paraná, with a good double-barrelled gun, fishing-tackle, and a harpoon, amply compensates for the trouble, even did we omit from the account the aspect of a vegetation of unrivalled magnificence.

CHAPTER V.

THE VEGETATION OF THE VIRGIN-FOREST OF THE AMAZON AND THE MADEIRA.

Changes and New Formations.—Terras Cahidas.—Orchids and Bromeliæ.—Lianas.—Figueiras.—Palms.—The Caoutchouc.—The Cacáo.—Drugs.—Resins.—The Urary.—The Quinquina.—The Guaraná.—The Coca.

EVERYWHERE the decomposing organisms serve as bases for new formations. No particle, however small, is ever lost in the great household of Nature; but nowhere is her restless activity so conspicuous as in the tropics, where the succession of vegetable decay and life is so much more rapid than it is in colder climes; and which will strike the reflecting student more especially in the wide, forest-clad valleys of tropical America, and on the Amazon and its affluents.

On the heights of the Cordillera, the process is already at work. The waste of the mountain-slopes, broken off by rills and torrents, and carried by them into the main river, slowly drifts down stream in the form of gravel-banks, until, scattered and rent asunder in a thousand ways, it finally takes permanent form as light green islands, which are soon covered and protected with a dense coat of vegetation.

As every zone of geologic formation in the extensive valley adds its tribute, these banks are a kind of mineralogical collection, which shows samples of all the rocks on the river-banks; with the exception, perhaps, of light pumice-stone, the produce of the volcanoes of the Andes, which drifts down stream in large pieces, and is highly prized by the Tapuia population (on the lower course) for sharpening and cleaning their weapons and tools. Even when not picked up by hunter or fisher, it is not lost. It will be arrested by some snag or projection of the shore, it will so get embedded in the newly-forming sediment, and thousands of years hence its silicic acid will afford the necessary material for the hard glassy bark of a bambusacea, or the sharp edge of a reed. When the currents are not strong enough to move the larger banks, they at least carry sand and earth with them, and deposit them as shoals or new alluvion at less exposed spots.* But there is no stability in the liquid element, with its periodic rise and fall, and the restless working of the busy waves. Diverted by the obstructing shoal, the river eats away the banks originally formed in the sea basin; and the sharper the bend the quicker the demolition. Then begins to form a serpentine, whose vagrant course gets more and more pronounced by the

TRANSVERSE SECTION OF A BREAKING SHORE, CALLED TERRAS CAHIDAS.

concave bank breaking down and forming new deposits on the convex one; until, at last, an extraordinary flood breaks through the narrow isthmus and opens up a straighter bed for the river, which soon resumes its playful operations afresh.† The convex bank, therefore,

---

* The laws of these movements, the sediments, &c., are of course the same in all climes; but in old Europe all the larger rivers are so controlled, regulated, and canalized, narrowed by dykes and other restraining appliances, that this restless power, the wonderful *perpetuum mobile* of a large river, must be entirely imperceptible, at least to non-professional observers.

† We found places on the Mamoré where three several beds of different periods

always consists of igapó, the newest sediment; while the opposite one may be vargem, or terra-firma.

Trees of soft wood, most of them with white bark and light

OUR TENT UNDER THE PALMS.—PREPARATIONS FOR TAKING THE SUN'S ALTITUDE (MADEIRA).

green foliage, like the embaúba (*Cecropia*), and the siphonia; and herbaceous plants, broad-leaved heliconias and reeds, find the fittest

could easily be distinguished, the oldest of which formed a lakelet connected with the river only by a narrow channel. Natural corrections of the sharpest curves by the breaking through of the narrowest point of the isthmus are not rare.

GROUP OF JAVARY PALMS, ON THE BANKS OF THE MADEIRA.

nurture in the light soil of the igapó, while thorny murú-murús and javáry-palms, cacáo, various myrtaceæ, and fig-trees prefer the vargem; which is flooded for only a short time of the year. The noble castanheira (*Bertholletia excelsa*), the cedar, and all the other splendid timbers of the tropics, thrive on the terra-firma only, above flood-level, in the "drift" of Agassiz.

The undermined concave shores are sometimes a serious danger to the passing barque, as even the slight ripple of a canoe is sufficient to bring down the loosely overhanging earth, often covered with gigantic trunks. These concave sides, with their fallen trees, and their clusters of sinking javary-palms, supported sometimes by only a tangled network of tough lianas, give to the scenery that peculiar character of primeval wildness, which is so charming to foreigners.

When one has climbed up the steep shore, often forming huge terrace-like elevations, and has safely passed through a labyrinth of interwoven roots and creepers into the interior of the forest, which is getting freer from underwood at some distance from the river, he is oppressed with the sensation of awe and wonder felt by man on entering one of the venerable edifices of antiquity.

A mysterious twilight encompasses us, which serves to intensify the radiance of the occasional sunbeam, as it falls on a glossy palm-leaf, or on a large bunch of purple orchid-flowers. Splendid trunks, some of them from 20 to 30 feet in diameter, rise like so many pillars supporting the dense green vault of foliage; and every variety of tall, graceful palms, spare and bushy, and bearing heavy berries of bright yellow or red, struggle to catch a glimpse of the light, from which they are shut out by the neighbouring giants; of which the figueira (or wild fig-tree) is one of the most striking, in the dimensions of its crown and stem, and in the strange shape of its roots, which project like huge outworks. These seem to grow in all directions, forming props, stays, and cross-bars wherever they are wanted, just as if the whole were a soft plastic mass, the sole purpose of which was to supply, with a minimum of material, as much stability as possible to the trunk; whose wood is of extreme softness and whose roots are not deep.* The pachiuba-palm (*Iriartea exorhiza*) and some

* Such are their plasticity and pliancy that a young figueira, taken out and planted with the branches reversed, will take root in this position, its former roots changing into a fresh, oddly-formed but leafy crown. A yet more striking instance

species of cecropiæ, exhibit other extravagances in their roots. They appear as if standing on stilts, the real trunks only beginning at 8 or 10 feet above ground. But, more than all, it is the profusion of orchids and bromeliæ that excites our admiration. These bright children of the tropics envelop with dense foliage as well the fallen and mouldering trunks as those yet upstanding in full vigour and

GROTESQUE SHAPE OF A SPECIES OF FICUS.

bloom, thus forming hanging gardens of astounding magnificence, which reveal leaves and flowers of the most irregular shapes and colours.

of the vitality of a plant I witnessed in the province of Paraná. In a narrow gorge some workmen had built a small log-house of the short trunks of the there abounding tree-ferns. The horizontally placed stems, deprived of their fronds, had grown splendid fresh leaves on both the upper and the lower ends. I must add, it is true, that the site was exceedingly moist and the rainy season, besides, at its height.

A GIANT OF THE FOREST.
BUTTRESSED TREE.

Everywhere, on the branches, and on the ground, and even from out the fissures of the bare rock, light ferns and rich moss spring up and clothe the decaying trunks with fresh green. Of mosses and ferns, especially tree-ferns, we found a greater exuberance and a larger variety, in species as well as in individuals, in the Southern provinces of the empire, São Paulo and Paraná;* but for splendid palms and gigantic dicotyledous, the North is decidedly the richer of the two.† Without the aid of the pencil it is, indeed, scarcely possible to give an adequate idea of the magnificence of this vegetation; especially of the manner in which the different forms are grouped. We may see, it is true, in our own hothouses, well-trimmed palms, beautiful orchids with their abnormal blossoms, and aroideœ with their bright, sappy, sometimes regularly perforated, leaves; but how different is this from the virgin-forest, wherein Nature, undisturbed by man, has created her own prodigies, and where no narrow pots separate her children from the maternal soil, and where no dim roof of glass intervenes between them and the blue ether! Nor, in our carefully tended hothouses, is the eye ever gratified with such agreeable contrasts as are afforded by the silver-grey and rust-brown tints of the decayed leaf of the palm or the fern-tree, or the black bark of the rotting trunk, with the blazing scarlet of some heliconia blossom. How difficult it must be to give to every plant, especially to orchids, the exact quantity of light, warmth and moisture it requires, can be understood only by those who have seen clusters of them hidden in the deep shade of the tree-crowns, while others are exposed to the

---

* In the forests of the province of Paraná, where the Araucaria Brasiliensis and palms and tree-ferns frequently form dense boscages, and where the fernlike zamire with their strangely ornamented bark, whose fossil predecessors we have probably to seek in the so-called stigmariæ, are found everywhere on the shores of little rivulets, we may see a miniature living copy of that antediluvian vegetation whose remains we encounter in our coal-mines. On the shores of these rivers, especially at the mouths of affluents, the formation of charcoal still goes on, though on a minor scale; the immense heaps of leaves and branches being covered by the high floods with sand and mud.

† Excellent timber for building purposes and cabinet-work, surpassing our best oak in solidity, are (besides several canella and laurus species) Jacarandá piranga (*Machærium firmum*), Jacarandá-tan (*Machærium scleroxylon*), Jacarandá-una (*Dalbergia nigra*), Palisander (corrupted from *Palo santo*), Ipé (*Tecoma curialis*), Sucupira (*Bowdichia*), Vinhatico (*Chrysophyllum vinhatico*), Paroba (*Aspidosperma*), Barauna (*Melanoxylon Braúna*), Sapucaia (*Lecythis grandiflora*), Massaranduba (*Lucuma procera*), Cedro (*Cedrela Brasiliensis*), Tapinhoam (*Sylvia navalium*), Muira piranga (*Cæsalpinia echinata*). Angelim rosa (*Paralthea erythrinafolia*).

scorching rays of the sun in the vicinity of a river or in some clearer part of the forest; some species thriving on the bare rock almost, and others clinging fast with their white rootlets to the moist rotting bark of a tree.

As for the temperature in the interior of the forests, it is generally lower by several degrees than on the river, or (of course) on the glowing sandbanks, or the slabs of rock, as in the region of the rapids, for instance, where the thermometer rises to 104° Fahr. even in the shade of a large open tent. The severity of this heat is felt the more acutely that, in the early hours of the morning, the air cools to 68°, and sometimes even to 57°.* Though the difference of level between the mouth of the Amazon and that of the Rio Negro is only 69 feet in a distance of more than 1,000 miles, and 374 feet till above the rapids of the Madeira (the climate remaining, therefore, much the same in spite of the higher latitude of the latter), there is yet a considerable difference observable between the varieties and species of palms, for instance, within the above-mentioned boundaries. Not to speak of the coco da Bahia (the real coco-palm),† that thrives only where the salt atmosphere of the sea reaches it, the noble mauritia, as well as the pretty assaï-palms, are much rarer on the higher course of the Amazon than on the lower; while a small slender palm, with bifurcated fan, whose name I unfortunately could not learn, is found

USUAL STRUCTURE OF PALM-ROOTS; STILTS OF THE PAXIÚBA.

---

* The sensation of cold at this latter temperature was about the same for us as at 1° or 2° under freezing-point in Europe; and, with even my warm cloak on, I was scarcely able to hold the pencil sometimes.

† In the interior of Brazil, in the province of Minas, now and then a coco-palm or two are to be found in front of the house of some fazendeiro (landowner); but they are planted there, and to thrive require to be regularly irrigated with salt water.

Case
A.
Shelf
3

only near the rapids of the Madeira. Other varieties of palm, like the murú-murú, and the creeping jacitára (*Desmoncus*), which grows to the length of 100 feet, while it does not exceed a finger in width, are found everywhere, and are not peculiar to any part of the river.

Though real groves of palms are not found on the Madeira and the Amazon, at least not on the extensive scale of the coco-palm woods on the coast near Pernambuco, or of the palmito groves (*Euterpe oleracea*) in Minas Geraes, São Paulo and Paraná, we often found groups of hundreds of palms, whose noble shafts and light feathery leaves imparted an enhanced charm to the spectacle of white-foaming cataracts, dark reefs, and islets glowing in the light of the setting sun. Of the perfection exhibited by Nature in the most trifling details, the shapes of the cross-sections of the ribs of different palm-leaves give an interesting example. These ribs take a more or less curved shape according to their weight; and, as the fibres themselves more easily resist, as it appears, bruising and pressing than tearing, the upper part of the cross-section is much more developed than the under one; the glassy silicious skin being, besides, much thicker below than above, and more pronounced at the sides, just as is the case with the top and bottom plates of tubular wrought-iron girders. So perfect is the adjustment that the ribs of the uauassú-palm (No. 1), whose

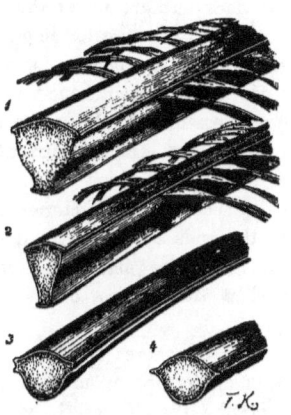

DIFFERENT TRANSVERSE CUTS OF PALM-RIBS.

stiff leaves, standing vertically at the end like those of all the Attalea species, present a large surface to the wind, show a broader cross-section; which imparts greater lateral stiffness. No. 2 does not require this, as the feathery leaves of the murú-murú are horizontally placed, and therefore suffer less from the wind. The ribs of the fan-palm, No. 3, have a roundish shape, as from the peculiar form of their leaves they are more exposed to torsion. As all these ribs, besides, are filled with a soft marrow, and as the hardest fibres are placed on the surface, it is evident that, if the problem had been to construct a rib of the greatest power of resistance with the least expenditure of means, it could not have been solved more successfully.

Another feature of Amazonian vegetation, even more striking than its noble palms, is the urania, called banana sororoca (wild banana) by the aborigines on account of likeness to those chief representatives of the Musaceæ. Its broad fan of mighty emerald-green leaves, mounted on a slender palmlike shaft from 6 to 8 feet in height, forcibly reminds the European of the fans of peacock feathers carried in the grand processions of the successor of St. Peter. In the foreground of the sketch representing our first meeting with the Caripunas, may be seen a urania or strelitzia, whose light-green leaves were set off by the dark background of the forest.

But of far greater importance to the half-civilised riverines than either palms or orchids, for whose beauties they have no eye, are the cacáo and the caoutchouc-tree (*Siphonia elastica*), products of the virgin-forest, essential to the future prosperity of the whole country.

Although India contributes to the supply of caoutchouc,[*] the precious resin which is transformed into a thousand different shapes every year in the factories of Europe and North America, and sent to the ends of the earth, it cannot compete with Brazil, which takes the first place among the rubber-producing countries, in respect as well of the vastness of its export of the material as of its superior quality.

On the shores of the Amazon its production, it is true, has already been diminished by unreasonable treatment of the trees; the idea of replacing the old ones by young saplings never having presented itself, apparently, to the mind of the indolent population; but the seringaes, or woods of rubber-trees, on the banks of the Madeira, the Purús, and other tributaries of the main river, still continue to furnish extraordinary quantities of it. The province of Amazon alone exports more than 50,000 arrobas (1,600,000 lbs.) yearly; while the total of the exports of the whole basin slightly exceeds 400,000 arrobas, or 12,800,000 lbs. per annum.

Even more remarkable than these figures is the fact that, with

---

[*] The word caoutchouc is of Indian origin; while seringa and borracha (of which the former signifies syringe or squirt, and the latter tube) are names given to the same material by the Portuguese, who were first familiarised by the Indians with the rubber, in the shape of tubes which they used as squirts.

THE VEGETATION OF THE VIRGIN-FOREST.

the quantity, the value of the exported ware has steadily risen within the last years, as may be seen by the following statement:—

In 1865 were exported 256,967 arrobas, worth 3,969,036 milreis.
" 1866 " 291,091 " " 5,521,853 "
" 1867 " 301,170 " " 5,937,441 "
" 1868 " 334,975 " " 8,003,550 "
" 1869 " 365,354 " " 9,698,721* "

This increase of price, keeping pace with the increase of exportation, certainly proves that the long list of articles of every kind, for whose fabrication the caoutchouc is wanted, from the old goloshes first made by the Indians themselves to the protecting coats of the telegraph wires, has not yet been exhausted, or, at least, that most of them are in increased requisition.

Unfortunately there has not been until now the slightest attempt made to cultivate this useful tree; and all the caoutchouc exported from Pará is still obtained from the original seringa groves. The trees of course suffer, as they naturally would under the best of treatment, from the repeated tapping and drawing-off of their sap, and the rubber collectors, therefore, must look about for new groves of the tree in the unexplored valleys of the more distant interior.

The planting of the *Siphonia elastica* would be a more profitable investment, as it yields the precious milk in the comparatively short space of twenty or twenty-five years; but, under the combined influence of the indolence of the mestizoes and the shortsightedness of the Government, measures to that end will be adopted and carried into effect only when the rubber exportation shall have diminished with the destruction of the trees, and when European and North American manufacturers shall have found out a more or less appropriate substitute for the too costly resin.

* The total value of the exports of Pará in 1869 was 12,897,598 milreis, somewhat more than £1,000,000 sterling. The distribution over the different countries was as follows:—

The United States . 5,410,015 milreis.   Portugal . . . . . 473,300 milreis.
England . . . . 4,521,520 "   Germany . . . . . 454,643 "
France . . . . . 1,761,178 "   The Brazilian Provinces 276,908 "

The chief articles so exported were:—

Rubber, worth 9,608,721 milreis.   Fish glue, worth 107,503 milreis.
Cacáo, " 1,271,488 "   Copaiva oil, " 101,745 "
Raw hide, " 413,220 "   Stag's hide, " 98,448 "
Brazil nuts, " 348,474 "   Sundries, " 724,038 "
Urucú, " 133,936 "

Near the PRAIA DE TAMANDUÁ we acquainted ourselves with all the particulars respecting the collection and preparation of the caoutchouc, at the cottage of a Bolivian seringueiro, Don Domingo Leigue. As I have already stated, the Siphonia grows, or at least thrives, only on a soil wherein its stem is annually submerged by the floods to the height of 3 feet or more. The best ground for it, therefore, is the igapó, the lowest and most recent deposit of the river; and there, in the immediate vicinity of the seringaes, may be seen the low thatches of the gatherers' huts, wretched hovels mostly, rendered tenantable during the inundations by the device of raising the floors on wooden piles of 7 feet height, in which the canoe, the seringueiro's indispensable horse, also finds a protected harbour. Unenviable truly must be the life of the happy proprietor, who has nothing to do in the seringal during the wet season, and who then has ample leisure to calculate exactly the intervals between his fits of ague, and to let himself be devoured by carapanás, piums, motúcas, and mucuims; under which euphonious names are known some of the most terrible of insect pests.

Narrow paths lead from the cottage, through the dense underwood, to each separate tree; and, as soon as the dry season sets in, the inmate of the palace just described betakes himself with his hatchet into the seringal, to cut little holes in the bark. The milk-white sap immediately begins to exude into pieces of bamboo tied below, over little clay cups set under the gashes to prevent their trickling down the stems. The collector travels thus from trunk to trunk; and, to facilitate operations, on his return visit he pours the contents of the bamboos into a large calabash provided with liana straps, which he empties at home into one of those large turtle-shells so auxiliary to housekeeping in these regions, serving as they do for troughs, basins, &c.

Without any delay he sets about the smoking process, as the resinous parts will separate after a while, and the quality of the rubber so become inferior. An earthen jar, without bottom and with a narrow neck, is set by way of chimney over a fire of dry urucury, or uauassú palm-nuts,[*] whose smoke alone, strange to say, has the effect of instantly coagulating the caoutchouc sap, which, in this state,

---

[*] Two species of *Attalea*, the latter with gigantic leaves.

FIRST SETTLEMENT OF AN INDIA-RUBBER COLLECTOR (MADEIRA).

THE VEGETATION OF THE VIRGIN-FOREST. 119

greatly resembles rich cow's-milk. The workman, sitting beside this "chimney," through which roll dense clouds of a smothering white smoke, from a small calabash pours a little of the milk on a sort of light wooden shovel, always careful, by proper management of the latter, to distribute it evenly over the surface. Thrusting the shovel into the thick smoke over the opening of the jar, he turns it several times to

BIFURCATED PALM-LEAF.

and fro with great rapidity, when the milk is seen to consolidate and to take a greyish-yellow tinge.

Thus he puts layer upon layer, until at last the caoutchouc on both sides of the wood has reached about an inch in thickness, when he thinks the "plancha" ready. Cutting it on one side, he takes it off the shovel and suspends it in the sun to dry, as there is always some water between the several layers, which should, if possible, evaporate. A good workman is thus able to prepare 5 or 6 lbs. of solid seringa in an hour. The plancha, from its initial colour of a clear silver-grey, turns shortly into a yellow, and finally becomes the well-known dark brown of the rubber, such as it is exported.

The more uniform, the denser and freer of bubbles the whole mass is found to be, the better is its quality and the higher the price it fetches. Almost double the value is obtained for the first-rate article over that of the most inferior quality, the so-called sernamby or cabeça de negro (negro's head); which is nothing but the drops collected at the foot of the trees, with the remains of the milk scraped out of the bottoms of the calabashes. The rubber of India is said to be much like this sernamby, and, like it, to be mixed with sand and small pieces of bark. By way of testing the quality, every plancha is cut through again at Pará; by which means discovery is made, not only of the bubbles, but also of any adulteration that might be effected with the milk of the mangaba, that fine plant with dark glossy leaves, now found so often in European saloons under the erroneous name of rubber-plant.

Of the milk of the mangaba also a sort of spurious caoutchouc is made, that has, however, so little of the elasticity and toughness of the genuine article that it has as yet acquired no value in commerce. But, for certain purposes, for making hardened caoutchouc for instance, the mangaba sap would certainly serve quite as well; and, as it can be obtained at a much lower price than the true seringa, it would be well worth the while of European or North American firms to send agents to the Amazon, to establish depôts for the manufacture of the mangaba resin on the spot, more especially as no such enterprise is to be expected from the selfish anxiety of the merchants at Pará. It would amply remunerate commercial houses in this way of business to have local stores and representatives at the chief stations on the Amazon, as Manáos, Santarem, &c., more especially as the navigation of the river is now opened to the ships of all nations, and as schooners and brigs can easily be towed up by steam-tugs. Hitherto most of the goods have been transported by expeditious steamers at very high rates; the conveyance of an arroba of caoutchouc (32 lbs.) from Manáos to Pará, for example, costing 500 reis (about 1 shilling), whereas by tugs and barques it could be easily effected for 300 reis, the passage taking sixteen days instead of seven. Moreover, this direct communication

INDIA-RUBBER MANUFACTURE ON THE BANKS OF THE MADEIRA.

between consumers and producers would tend at the same time to destroy, at least in great measure, the vampire-like dominion exercised by a few landowners and other influential persons over the poorer rubber collectors, who have not established for themselves a correspondence with Pará. These monopolists, for the most part majors and colonels of the National Guard, being able, by virtue of their positions, to bring most considerable influence to bear on the elections of deputies, are caressed by the Government; and, employing with impunity all manner of vexations, they compel the poorer class of collectors to sell to them the fruits of their industry at half-price; to be content with 14 milreis per arroba (about 28 shillings for 32 lbs.), while they themselves dispose

BOUGH OF THE SIPHONIA ELASTICA (CAOUTCHOUC TREE).

of it for 36 milreis at Pará. To make matters worse, even this wretched price being scarcely ever paid in ready money, but rather in goods and provisions charged at thrice their value, it is not to be wondered at that the poor seringa collector, though he works a gold-mine (so to speak), at the end of the year owes more than he can discharge; and from this cleverly designed bondage he is never able to liberate himself. Thus disheartened, these poor creatures, mostly ignorant mestizoes and mulattoes, become even more inconsiderate and frivolous than Nature has made them; and, out of the temptingly arranged stores of their "protectors," they are sure to select the most ridiculous gewgaws, such as high riding-boots, gold watches, and silk jackets, and silk umbrellas for their brown ladies, although they know that the useless articles will cost them a year or more's hard labour.

In this condition of things, it will be readily understood that no thought has been given to improving the preparation of the caoutchouc, either by the use of alum for its solidification, in place of the weary process of smoking it with palm-nuts, which are not always to be had, or by the mixture of ammoniac—a still more important discovery—by which the milk may be kept liquid, and thus would become transportable in casks. And equally evident is it that only with a total change of their commercial conditions, by the establishment of new lines of steamers, by the construction of railways, and by the opening of branches of European firms, can these highly favoured countries be divorced from the errors of their old routine, and led into other and more prosperous ways. These happy changes effected, the cacáo plant also, which grows luxuriantly over an immense range, may be turned to good account, more especially as the preparation of it for export is so simple, the seeds being only dried in the sun. There is also a coarse sort of chocolate made of it, but it spoils easily. It still continues to be planted on a small scale on the Amazon and near the mouths of some of its tributaries, and its quality is said to be first-rate; but, as it was often sold mixed with the inferior seeds of the wild cacáo, its purchasers fell off.

This wild cacáo, with its large lancet-shaped hanging leaves, and its cucumber-like fruit springing directly from the stem, is one of the characteristic features of the virgem, on which it often forms dense thickets, which are all the more impenetrable that the boughs—exhibiting frequently at the same time the small reddish flowers and the ripe golden fruit, in which the seeds lie embedded in a sweet white marrow—bend to the ground and there take root again.

But the india-rubber and the cacáo are not the only treasures worth collecting in these forests. Even now the export of the Pará nuts, the fruit of the *Bertholletia excelsa*, yields an annual revenue of 200,000 dollars; and the copaiba oil and the urucú, the seeds of the *Bixa Orellana*, used for dyeing, about 100,000 dollars. These sums seem small enough, it is true, but there are perhaps a hundred times those values of the rich-flavoured nuts rotting unheeded in the forests, and above a score of other rich oily seeds, at present collected only for the use of the natives, not to mention several resins which yield the finest varnishes, plants giving the most brilliant hues, and others with fibres that would serve not only for the finest weavings, but also for the strongest ropes; besides about forty of the most indispensable drugs, all which might become most valuable articles of export.

For the benefit of readers interested in botany, I subjoin a list of the most important of these plants, with both their Indian and their Latin names, when I could find them out. It is taken partly from V. Martius's works, and partly from my own notes.

OILS SERVING FOR COOKING, LIGHTING, SOAPS, &c.*

Patauá (Oenocarpus patauá. *Mart.*)
Caiauhé (Elaeis melanococca.† *Gaertn.*)
Bacába (Oenocarpus bacába. *Mart.*)
Tucuman (Astrocaryum tucuma. *Mart.*)
Assai (Euterpe edulis. *Mart.*)
Marajá (Bactris marajá. *Mart.*)
Iupaty (Raphia taedigera. *Mart.*)
Ubussú (Manicaria saccifera. *Mart.*)
Inajá (Maximiliana regia. *Mart.*)

Castanheira (Bertholletia excelsa. *Humb.*)
Sapucaia { (Lecythis ollaria. *Velloso.*)
{ (Lecythis grandiflora. *Anbl.*)
Andiroba (Xylocarpus caropa. *Spreng.*)
Pequia (Carica butyrosum. *Mart.*)
Uaucú (Monopteryx uaucú. *Mart.*)
Ucuúba (Myristica sebifera. *Sw.*)

ODOROUS OILS.

Cujumary (Ocotea cujumary. *Mart.*)
Cumarú (Dipteryx odorata. *W.*) (Tonga-bean.)

Puchury (Nectandra puchury. *Nees and Mart.*)
Tamaquaré (Laurinea).
Uixi-pucú (Myristica).

RESINS, GUMS, AND MILK-SAPS.

Carnaúba (Copernicia cerifera. *Mart.*)
Angico (Acacia angico. *Mart.*)
Almecega (Icica icicariba), the so-called sham Elemi.
Jatahy, Jatobá (Hymenaea Martianna), the so-called Animé resin.
Sorva (Colophora utilis. *Mart.*)
Mangaba (Hancornia speciosa) } Substitutes for india-rubber.
Monpiqueira (?)

Cajueiro (Anacardium occidentale. *L.*)
Ucuúba (Myristica Surinamensis. *Mart.*)
Cipó Macaco (?)
Mururé (?)
Maporonima (?)
Pariry (?)
Massaranduba (Lucuma procera), Milk or Cow-tree, with a resin much like gutta-percha.

---

* Though the ricinus, which also gives an excellent lamp-oil, does not grow wild in Brazil, it yields profuse crops with scarcely any trouble, and might become another money-producing article.

† Of the same family as *Elaeis Guineensis* (Jacq.), the Guinea oil-palm, or dendé, whose thick, orange-coloured oil, made of the outer fleshy pulp of the nut, gives that peculiar flavour to the highly peppered national dishes of Bahia, which, from the kitchens of the black slaves, have found their way to the tables of their masters.

‡ As the real coco-nut tree only thrives near the seashore, it cannot well be

Dyeing Stuffs.*

Urucú (Bixa Orellana. *L.*)†
Urucurana (Bixa urucurana. *W.*)
Ucuúba (Myristica Surinamensis. *Mart.*)
Carajurú (Bignonia chica. *Humb.*)

Baracutiára (?)
Tatajúba (Maclura ?)
Muiratinga (?)
Guariuba (Maclura ?)

The most important of the Medicinal Plants.

Ipecacuanha (Cephaëlis ipecacuauha. *Tussac and Richard.*)
Salsaparilha (Smilax Syphilitica. *Mart.*)
Copaiba (Copaifera Jacquini. *Desf.*)
Jurubéba (Solanum paniculatum. *L.*)
Anabi (Potalia resinifera. *Mart.*)
Uixi (Myristica platysperma. *Mart.*)
Canjerana (Trichilia canjerana. *Mart.*)
Jacaréuba (Calophyllum Brasiliense. *Mart.*)
Coajingúba (Ficus anthelmintica. *Rich.*)
Muiratinga (?)
Biquiba (Myristica officinalis. *Mart.*)
Assacú (Hura Brasiliensis. *W.*)
Cupuassú-rana (Pharmacosyce doliaria. *Mart.*)
Sucuúba (Plumeria phagendenica. *Mart.*)
Cajú (Anacardium occidentale. *L.*)

Sassafraz (Ocotea amara. *Mart.*)
Massarandúba (Lucuma procera).
Marupa (Quassia simaruba. *L.*)
Puchury (Nectandra puchury. *Nees and Mart.*)
Jiquitibá, Turury (Curatari legalis).
Caferana (?), substitute for quinquina.
Juréma (Acacia jurema. *Mart.*)
Caaopiá (Vismia micrantha and Vismia laccifera. *Mart.*)
Andiroba (Xylocarpus caropa. *Spreng.*)
Cujumary (Ocotea cujumary. *Mart.*)
Mata-matá (?)
Abutuá (?)
Amapá (?)
Barbatimão (Acacia adstringens. *Reiss.*)
Manacan (Brunfelsia hopeana. *Benth.*)

---

counted among the products of the forests of the interior. Even there the rich oil the nuts contain is seldom extracted. They are usually taken down green for their cool, refreshing water, or sent ripe into the interior for making "doce" (sweetmeats).

* The anil, or indigo, does not grow wild in the woods, and is not indigenous; but it thrives so plentifully there that we may hope to see it planted, and exported on a larger scale in future years. The most valuable of all dyeing-woods—the Pernambuco, or Brazilwood—*Cæsalpinia echinata* (Lamarck), called arabutan by the natives, is frequent in the South—in Pernambuco, Bahia, Minas, and Espirito Santo, and is still sent abroad as largely as ever. The red decoction of the wood gives, with the addition of an acid, a red deposit, while the liquid above it takes a yellow colour. With ammoniac, the deposit will be purple; with alum, crimson; with perchloride of tin, pink; with acid protoxide of lead, dark red; and with iron vitriol, violet. With corrosive sublimate of mercury, or sulphate of zinc, the liquid gets of a bright yellow.

† So called after the daring Orellana, who, in 1544, impelled by the hope of becoming governor of the new countries, was the first to descend the Amazon, from Perú to the Atlantic. The fanciful description he gave of an attack he sustained at the mouth of the Nhamundá, from a horde of armed women, originated the singular name of the river; the whole story certainly being founded on a mistake, and his wish to make the most of his adventures. His Amazons, doubtless, were only the squaws carrying the spare arrows of the fighting warriors, and answering the discharges of the Spanish blunderbusses with fearful yells.

PLANTS MAKING ROPES, CORDS, &c.

Piassaba (Attalea funifera. *Mart.*) ⎫	Uaicima Guaxima (Urena lobata).
Curuá (Attalea spectabilis. *Mart.*) ⎪	Piriquitá (?)
Murity (Mauritia vinifera. *Mart.*) ⎬ PALMS.	Curumicáa (?)
Tucum (Astrocaryum tucuma. *Mart.*) ⎪	Carapato (?)
Carnaúba (Copernicia cerifera. *Mart.*) ⎪	Beribá (Anona ?)
Javary (Astrocaryum Javary. *Mart.*) ⎭	Ituá (?)
Castanheira (Bertholletia excelsa. *Humb.*)	Mamão-rana (?)
Tatajuba (Maclura ?)	Carapicho (Urena sinuata).
Turury (Couratari legalis. *Mart.*)	Cipó (liane) ambé (?)
Tauary (?)	,, ,, pixuna (?)
Curauá (Bromelia), giving a very fine and glossy fibre.	,, ,, timbotitica (Cissus).
	,, ,, pagé (?)
Munguba (Erythrina).	,, ,, assú (?)
Xury (?)	,, ,, preto (?)
Sapucaia (Lecythis ollaria. *Velloso.*)	,, ,, rei (?)
Mata-matá (Lecythis coriacea).	,, ,, titara (?)
Acapurana (Wullschlaegelia. *Mart.*) Rutacea.	,, ,, de cerca (?)

Notwithstanding the fertility of tropical vegetation, I doubt whether any other part of the world, in the same latitude, can offer as great a number of useful plants as does the Amazon Valley; and now, when all-transforming steam is about to open up to us this rich emporium, European industry should take advantage of the hitherto neglected treasures. What might not be done with the fibres—some of which surpass our hemp and flax in all respects? The curauá, for example, a sort of wild pine-apple, gives a delicate transparent flax of a silky lustre, such as is used in the Philippine Islands, on a large scale, it appears. It is sold under the name of palha at Rio de Janeiro. The tucum and the javary would make excellent ropes, cords, nets, &c., well calculated to resist moisture and rot; and the piassaba, the murity, &c., would readily supply solid brushes, brooms, hammocks, hats, baskets, mats; while the snow-white bast of others would give excellent paper.

The lianas, or cipós of these countries are, besides their minor uses, quite indispensable to the half-civilised natives for the construction of their light cottages; taking the place (as they do) of our nails and cramp-irons, beams, posts, and rafters. The whole palm-leaf roof is fastened, and artificially interwoven and intertwined, with tough creepers of nearly an inch thickness.

According to a widespread proverb, the Jesuits, on first settling in Brazil, demanded of the Portuguese Government, as a compensation for the hardships they had undergone in spreading the Gospel, all those countries of the interior "*where the customary nails were to be found.*" This would have comprised pretty nearly all from the Atlantic to the Cordillera, as the lianas are found everywhere in the woods; and

MOUTH OF A LATERAL RIVER ON THE MADEIRA, WITH AN INDIAN SHOOTING FISHES.

though, as is notorious, the Fathers never were timid in their demands, it is scarcely credible that they should have formulated them in so wide a way. But *vox populi, vox Dei;* and *se non è vero, è ben trovato.*

In the above list of medicinal plants, I have not mentioned

one of the most important, the cinchona or Peruvian-bark tree, that gives us the quinquina; because its home, at least that of the most precious species, is not the moist forest of the lowlands described here, but the valleys and glens of the chain of the Andes, some 3,000 to 6,500 feet above the sea-level. The real calysaia, that which of all cinchonas contains most of the precious alkaloid, abounds especially near the sources of the Beni, while the species of the flats (*Cinch. Bergeniana*, *Cinch. Lambertiana*, *Cinch. macroenemia*, *Cinch. firmula*), though they certainly contain quinquina and cinchonin, are as yet of no importance to commerce.

A romantic tale has it that a Countess Chinchon, the lady of a viceroy of Perú, was the first European cured by the bitter bark, of a violent fit of ague, towards the end of the seventeenth century; and that it was a descendant of the Incas, who, prompted by love of the beautiful countess who was the wife of his hereditary foe, had given her the specific, until then guarded with jealous secrecy by the natives. However, it was not so much the physician as the confessor of the noble lady, or rather the mighty Order of which he was a member, who took advantage of the discovery by completely monopolising the cascarilha trade. For more than a century the pounded bark came only through the Jesuits to the European market, under the name of Jesuit-powder. In the total absence of regular means of communication with the interior, it was easy enough for the Padres to stifle any attempt at competition in their numerous Missions on the eastern slope of the Andes, where, without any restriction, they disposed of many thousands of Indians, and to ask any price they pleased for the more and more appreciated drug.

Like the seringueiro of the Madeira Valley, the cascarilheiro, or bark-collector, generally a poor half-civilised Indian or mestizo, is most shamefully cheated out of his small, hard-earned gains; the traders always contriving to get the bark at half-price, while for the load and powder, and the half-spoiled victuals, given in exchange, they charge double and treble value. Yet the cascarilheiro is fond of his wild, roaming life, the hardships and fatigues of which he will endure for months, cutting his way through the dense forest to get at the trees he seeks, and carrying his heavy bundle of bark over hill and dale only to be perpetually robbed in the next village. There the cascarilha, or bark, is sewn into large bags of untanned hide, and carried by beasts of burden to La Paz; whence it is sent by the Peruvian seaport, Arica, to Europe and North America.

When one considers the immense distances the bark has to travel from beside murmuring mountain rivulets,—from the valleys of Apolobamba, for instance, at the foot of the eastern slope of the Cordillera, over snow-covered passes of 14,000 feet above the sea-level to La Paz and to the Pacific, and round Cape Horn to Europe,—it is wonderful that the idea of following the course of these mountain streams to the Beni and the Madeira, and by the Amazon to Pará, has not before been taken into earnest consideration. It is true that, in this direction also, the difficulties are not inconsiderable. The middle and the upper course of these rivers are almost totally unknown; one of them, the Madre de Dios, till within a few years ago, was believed to be a tributary of the Purús, whereas it is one of the Beni and the Madeira. The Indians on their shores are a race of treacherous savages; and the falls and rapids of the Madeira are not, all of them, easy of passage. To take a valuable freight, in the charge of a score or two of untrustworthy Indians, down such a venturesome course, requires not a little courage; yet, after all, it seems as if the merchants of La Paz and Arica, whose interest, of course, lies the other way, had a great deal to do with this neglect.

During our stay at Exaltacion, however, a mercantile house of La Paz (Farfan & Co.) made an attempt (and, as we afterwards learned, a successful one) to take a large and most valuable cargo of cascarilha, collected in the Sierra of Apolobamba, on light rafts down the Beni to the Mission of Reyes; and thence on ox-carts, over the campos on the watershed between the Beni and the Mamoré, to the Jacúma, a tributary of the latter. At the former Mission of Santa Ana, boats were freighted with it: and they got safely through the Mamoré, the Madeira, and the Amazon to the port of Pará. The expenses of this route, though by no means an easy one, were about half of those incurred by way of Arica;* and assuredly, as soon as the Madeira

---

* It is strange that even Bolivia, though named after the "Libertador," and called by him (in the high-flown, soaring style of these nations) "the dearest of his daughters," should have been treated so illiberally in the matter of seaports when the boundaries were fixed after the Declaration of Independence. It seems as if the poor country is to be cut off from the rest of the world, or put under the everlasting tutelage of Perú. While the latter extends over one hundred geographical miles down the navigable Solimões, or Amazon, and has several excellent seaports on the Pacific,

railroad is ready, all the bark will go by the Amazon Valley to Europe. Then will an increased export of bark take place; and the forests on the slopes of the Andes will be gradually invaded and explored, to the closer arrival of that period when the danger of the complete rooting-out of the useful tree may be anticipated. In this regard, surely, attention should be devoted to the planting of this blessing to suffering humanity in countries wherein it is indigenous, seeing that the attempts made by the Dutch and English Governments in Java, Ceylon, and on the Himalayas do not seem to have been quite satisfactory as to the quality of the bark in respect of quinquina. In Brazil several plantations of cinchona have been made on the Serra dos Orgãos : but they are still too young to allow of our judging of the result. As the Bolivian Government has forbidden, under the severest penalties, the export of the young plants and seeds, it is very difficult and expensive to get saplings. Seeds, indeed, are easier to obtain; but they offer less chances of success.

Without a very strong impulse from without, neither the Bolivian nor the Peruvian Governments, alternately in the hands of spur-clattering usurpers and ambitious lawyers, will make the slightest effort; and, as there is small hope of long diplomatic debates being held in the behalf of fever-shaken humanity, things will remain *in statu quo* for many years to come.

Bolivia lost Arica, which should, by all means, be hers, and now is perfectly isolated in that direction, as Cobija, being situated in a waterless desert, never will be of any great service to commerce. And hardly better are its natural communications with the Atlantic. There Brazil, owning both shores of the Madeira far into the region of the rapids, and the Argentine Republic claiming the right shore of the navigable Paraguay up to the confines of Mato Grosso, exclude it from the navigation of the two chief highways of trade—the Amazon and the River Plate—and hinder the growing of staples near their territory. Almost all the Bolivian trade goes by way of Arica, the Peruvian Government levying heavy taxes; so that the opening of the Madeira road will, indeed, be the source of life to all Bolivia: and the cession of some hundreds of square miles of (as yet useless) primeval forest to Brazil, thus removing its frontiers on the Madeira from Santo Antonio to the mouth of the Beni, that is, from 8° 49' to 10° 20' S. lat., appears a trifle in view of the advantages derived. It looks almost like madness on the part of the Brazilian Government to continue to add to the ocean of forest it owns already on the Amazon, especially as there is no strategic point of any importance on the claimed territory, as in the contested land on the Paraguay between the Apa and the Mondego. The only pretext for it can be that Perú, the ever-threatening enemy of Brazil, regards itself as the heir of Bolivia (so to say), and will be so much the poorer for it some day. Of course there was no want of Peruvian protests and expressions of the deepest indignation, which sounded strange enough from that quarter; and Brazil, in some future contest with the Argentine Republic, may surely count on seeing Peruvian men-of-war coming down from Iquitos to test the solidity of the walls of Tabatinga, on the Solimões.

K

Let us return, however, from the snowy heights of the Andes to the hot lowlands of the Amazon, where, in the shade of endless forest, there is many a herb of mysterious virtue, as yet known only to wild Indian tribes, while the fame of others has already spread over the ocean. Who has not heard of the urary, or curare, the quick arrow-poison which, in the hands of clever physiologists and physicians, promises not only to become a valuable drug, but to give us interesting disclosures on the activity of the nerves?

The wondrous tales of former travellers regarding the preparation of this urary have been rectified long ago. The venom of snakes is not used for it, but the juice of the bruised stems and leaves of several kinds of strychnos and apocyneas is simply boiled over a coal fire, mixed with tobacco juice and capsicum (Spanish pepper), and thickened with the sticky milk of some Euphorbiacea to a hard mass. This manipulation, moreover, is not undertaken by the old squaws of the tribe, devoting themselves to a painful death thereby, as the old stories ran; but, as there is no danger whatever, by the young wives of the warriors, who look upon it as part of their household duties, or by the men themselves. There are about eight or ten different poisons of similar, but not identical, composition and preparation, of which the urary of the Macusi Indians, and the curare, from Venezuela and New Granada, are considered the most powerful.

This dark brown, pitchy substance, usually kept in little earthen pots, is lightly spread over the points of the weapons, their long arrows, their light spears, and the thin wooden shafts, of about a foot long, which they shoot through immense blow-tubes (sarabacanas). Immediately upon the diffusion in the blood of the slightest portion of the 'poison the limbs, one by one, refuse to work, as if overcome with torpor, while the mind apparently retains its activity until death ensues,—which it does in a few minutes' time, from palsy of the lungs. It is strange that only those nerves are affected which regulate the movements depending on our own will, whereas those movements we cannot control, the beating of the heart for example, continue unaltered to the very last. Experiments made by French physicians upon animals have shown that, if the lungs are artificially kept in activity for several hours, the poison will be rejected by natural means, and no bad consequences will ensue. Of late the principal objection to the employment of the urary in medicine—its unequal strength—has been completely overcome by the effective alkaloid—the curarin—being extracted. This is about twenty times as powerful as the urary, and has been used successfully in the treatment of tetanus. The Indians shoot birds and monkeys, which they wish to tame, with very weak curare, rousing them from the lethargy which overpowers them with large doses of salt or sugar-juice; and this treatment is said to be very effective also in the reduction of their wildness.

It is a remarkable fact that the Indians on the right shore of the Amazon neither prepare nor use the poison, though the plants that supply the chief ingredients are certainly found there as well as on the left shore, on which tribes differing widely in customs and language use the subtle weapon. It would be difficult to say by what chance their ancestors first came to prepare it, as the poisonous qualities of the plants, before their sap is concentrated by boiling, are by no means very striking.

It certainly was a great invention in aid of their hunting, on which chiefly they depended for food; and we can well imagine that they took some trouble to improve it: but how came they to prepare the guaraná, resembling tea and coffee in its effects, from an insignificant-looking dry fruit of the forest? Some weary and famished hunter must have tried the unpalatable beans, and found that they wonderfully strengthened and refreshed him, and thence must have ensued the collection and bruising of the fruits and the planting of the seeds near their cabins.

The guaraná, prepared from the fruit of the *Paullinia sorbilis*, is a hard, chocolate-brown mass, of a slightly bitter taste, and of no smell whatever. It is usually sold in cylindric pieces of from 10 inches to a foot in length, in which the half-bruised almond-like seeds are still distinguishable; the more homogeneous and the harder the mass, the better is its quality. To render it eatable, or rather drinkable, it is rasped as fine as possible on the rough, bony roof of the mouth of the sudis gigas (pirá-rucú), and mixed with a little sugar and water. A tea-spoonful in a cup of warm water is said to be an excellent remedy in slight attacks of ague.

The taste of this beverage, reminding one slightly of almonds, is very palatable; still it scarcely accounts for the passionate liking entertained for it by the inhabitants of the greater part of South America. It must be the stimulating effects of the paullinin it contains (an alkaloid like cafeïne and theïne) that render it so indispensable to those who have been accustomed to it. All the boats that come lightly freighted with ipecacuanha and deer or tiger-hides, from Mato Grosso down the Arinos and the Tapajoz, in face of the considerable cataracts and rapids of the latter, take their full loads of guaraná at Santarem; and the heavy boats of the Madeira also convey large quantities of it to Bolivia; for at Cuyabá, as well as at Santa Cruz de la Sierra and Cochabamba, there are many who cannot do without their guaraná, for which they often have to pay 30 francs the pound, and who prefer all the rigours of fasting to abstinence from their favourite beverage. On the other hand, the mestizo population on the Amazon, where it is prepared on a large scale by the half-civilised tribes of the Mauhés and Mundurucús and sold at about 3 francs the pound, are not so passionately attached to it; they rather take coffee, and a sort of coarse chocolate, which they manufacture for themselves.

The stimulant most in use with the Indian population of Bolivia is the coca.* The thin leaves (about 1¼ inches in length) of the coca bush, which already is largely cultivated in Bolivia and Perú, are dried in the sun, and, with the addition of some fine ashes and a bit of red pepper, are chewed by the natives. It is said to render them less sensible to the cold on the icy heights of the Andes, and to reduce the severity of the soroche, that painful oppression of the chest with nausea caused by the rareness of the air on the mountain-passes. The Quichua Indians, indeed, will not venture there without a plentiful provision of coca leaves; and all travellers concur in admiring their strength and endurance in carrying heavy burdens over the steepest and roughest paths, with no restorative save their highly prized coca. How indispensable it is to them is evidenced by the fact that one of the last presidents of Bolivia, who, in a fit of reforming zeal, conceived the idea of serving out coffee and brandy in lieu of their coca ration to his Indian and mestizo army, was forced by the outbreak of a mutiny to withdraw his ukase and to let them have their beloved herb as they desired. The Indians on the Upper Amazon and the Solimões also know it under the name of ipadú. Taken as tea, it has a slight aroma of camomile.

These facts considered, the question naturally arises, how it has come

* *Erythroxylon Coca.*

about that nations living so widely apart and so mutually antagonistic have, out of the rich tropical vegetation, selected plants that have analogous, if not identical, effects on the nervous system, such as the maté, cacáo, guaraná, coca, coffee, and tea; and this, moreover, at a time when even the rudiments of natural science were not in existence. The process of satisfying this craving for stimulants, which seems to be so deeply rooted in mankind, has without doubt been the means of promoting the advance of civilisation. Our knowledge of the facts connected with pre-historic American cultivation being so indefinite, it is the more to be regretted that the precise period at which some American Noah first made his lucky discovery of maté or coca will probably continue to be as doubtful as the exact date at which some serious Arab first brewed the reviving black drink of the Levant.

Whether these first movements of civilisation, visible in the use of such treasures, reach as far back in America as they do in Asia, cannot, therefore, be decided à *priori;* the same impenetrable darkness covers both. But, notwithstanding their subsequent disparity, it is certainly possible that the natives of both the Old and the New World reached, at about the same time, a sufficient degree of civilisation to enable them to appropriate to the use of themselves more of the surrounding gifts of Nature than a few wild fruits and easily-caught animals; they only began the battle of life under unequal conditions. Besides higher mental gifts originally, perhaps, allotted to the Caucasian race, the advantages of more favourable climate, and the topographical superiority of part of Asia and Southern Europe, have enabled nations on the shores of the Mediterranean, more than two thousand years ago, to attain to so high a degree of civilisation that its achievements are our models to this very day, while the natives of the New World still remain wild and half-wild fishers and hunters.

Only in Mexico, Central America, and Perú, have favouring circumstances helped the red-skins to pass, by an easy transition, from the condition of hunters and nomads to that of cattle breeders and agriculturists, and thus to reach a higher degree of civilisation; while, on the contrary, in the rest of America, immense tracts of forest rendered cattle breeding impossible, reduced agriculture to a minimum, and necessitated the dispersion of the various tribes, in small hordes, to secure their maintenance by the produce of the chase. Of course, every such separation was rendered permanent by the difficulty of communication;

and this must be regarded as one of the principal causes of the infinite number of languages and dialects in the New World; which, in their turn, were additional serious drawbacks to general progress. Languages which have not been reduced to writing must change rapidly. Even the bodily peculiarities of different families, the shape of their lips, &c., will suffice to form an idiom, differing materially from the original one;* and such changes must have contributed to keep the separated hordes asunder, especially as the principle adopted by all people living in a state of nature seems to be: whoever does not speak my language is my foe.

Their division into so many hundreds of tribes and hordes, and the great number of their languages and idioms, made Martius, the learned explorer of Brazil, think that the state of the autochthons of America, though a primitive, is not their original one; that they are not a wild but a degenerate race, the degraded relics of a more perfect past, whose dissolution had begun thousands of years before the Conquest.

There is no doubt that this process has, since then, been accelerated by bloody wars and persecutions, reduction of their hunting-grounds, contagious diseases, and want of physical and moral comforts; but I do not believe there is any reason to date this decay from pre-historic times. When the hordes of Spanish adventurers destroyed the realm of the Incas, they found a prosperous and improving country; and their proud temples, as Martius urges in further proof, were by no means in ruins then. In additional support of his hypothesis, he points to the remains of hierarchical and monarchical institutions among all, even the most savage tribes, and the state of many of their plants, which nowadays are not found anywhere growing wild. But might not these vestiges of institutions be the beginnings as well as the remains of a civilisation? And might not nations standing on a very low level

---

* A very clever and learned monk of the Order of St. Benedict, Frei Camillo de Monserrate, custodian of the National Library at Rio de Janeiro up to the time of his death recently, and who, in his long voyages on the West coast of America, had had ample opportunities for comparative study of Indian languages, expressed himself in a conversation with me, to the effect that everything in this respect was to be accounted for by natural and material reasons; and that he was sure that "el," for instance, a final syllable recurring very frequently in the Mexican language, had arisen from the custom of the old Mexicans of pricking their tongues, in a sort of religious frenzy, with the long thorns of a large cactus, so that this organ was continually affected with many of them, and caused them to lisp and stammer, ultimately producing the strange syllable.

have brought these plants to the state of culture we see them in now, unintentionally and almost involuntarily? To the present day, even the wildest hordes have plantations of Indian corn, tobacco, cotton, plantains and mandioca, near their cabins; not on a large scale, of course, as that would be impossible with their roaming mode of life and inferior implements. No one can doubt that the improved form exhibited by these plants is the result of a very ancient cultivation; but there is no proof in it of an extinct higher civilisation on the part of the planters, though it must be confessed that the analogy with our own nutritious plants, brought from the seats of the earliest civilisation, is rather tempting; and the contrast between the very primitive mode of life of half-naked savages and the existence of such treasures is, at first sight, very striking. Another proof of the very ancient influence of man on these plants is the fact that some of them (as the banana* and the pupunha-palm) no longer produce seeds fit for germination, but are entirely dependent on the human hand for their propagation; and so is the existence of a great variety of others, the Indian corn for instance. Of this, several tribes have favourite varieties, which they cultivate exclusively. Thus the Guaranis of the Southern provinces prefer the small stripes with red and bluish speckles, whose grains are easily pounded to a palatable flour, while the Coroados only plant corn with large stripes, red on the lower and yellow at the upper end.

To reach their present state of perfection, all these plants required human tending the more that, with the single exception of the pupunha, they were of the class of tender herbaceous plants, of short-lived duration, incapable of thriving in the close mato virgem or primeval forest, and whose light-green leaves and slender white stems offer a striking contrast to the latter's hard column-like trunks and dark-leaved underwood. Their first requirements are air and sunshine, whereas the shade and protection of their own leafy canopy are so vitally necessary to the plants of the mato virgem that, if seeds are planted in the ground on a space cleared beyond design, they do not germinate, but make room for a secondary vegetation, longing for air and light.†

* The Musaceæ (*Musa paradisiaca*), and the other East Indian varieties imported by the Portuguese (*Musa sapientum* and the like), have numerous shoots if the chief stem is cut down; and nothing grows easier than the banana in these climes: yet its range would be a very limited one if it were left to multiply only in this way.

† In our European forests something similar is going on, though not in so striking

Only after the lapse of some fifty or sixty years, when daylight shall have stolen somewhat through the dense leafage of the capoeira (as the Brazilians call the second growth), which never rises, however, to any considerable height, here and there perhaps some seed of a palisander or a bertholletia may shoot up; and two hundred years afterwards the proud, dark, primeval forest spreads again over the ground that once was its own.

a way. If an old oak-forest is felled, useless and worthless shrubbery first springs up, and is replaced by better timber only afterwards.

CHAPTER VI.

THE WILD INDIAN TRIBES OF THE MADEIRA VALLEY.

The Múras.—The Aráras.—The Mundrucús.—The Perentintins.—The Caripunas.—Our First Meeting with the Latter.—Their Malocca.—Their Way of Burying the Dead.—Former Attacks on the Madeira, Javary, and Purús.—The Unknown Waylayers at the Mouth of the Mamoré.—Future of these Indians.—Their Languages and Religious Views.—Their Pajés.—An Old Settlement.

THERE is a proverbial saying diffused over the whole Amazon region: "lazy like a Múra who sleeps on three cords;" that is, who does not even take the trouble of making a proper hammock; and indeed the saying is right. The Múras are the laziest of all the lazy Indians of these parts. They are despicable alike to white and coloured men; and notwithstanding their well-known skill in hunting, fishing, diving and "similar free arts," any other Indian or mestizo would think it the gravest insult to be taken for one of these pariahs. Once they were a powerful tribe; but bloody feuds with the Mundrucús, at the end of the last century, reduced them to the poor condition we now see them in, leading an unsettled, gipsy life on the Amazon and the lower course of its tributaries; on any of which their light pirogues, sometimes in flotillas of twenty and thirty, may be seen gliding swiftly along. Owing to the accession of runaway slaves, they exhibit somewhat of the mulatto type; and their degeneracy has been so complete as almost to have extinguished their original character; which, said to have been a warlike and courageous one, now fitfully breaks out in daring robberies and treacherous murders. In less than a hundred and fifty years even their last remnants will probably have vanished entirely, not much to the detriment of the country, which can well spare a stubborn element, incapable of adapting itself to the new order of things fast approaching.

At Sapucaia-Oroca, on the right shore of the Madeira, at about 125 miles from its mouth, there is a Múra settlement, which consists of about a dozen miserable sheds, scarcely large enough to tie the celebrated three cords underneath, in which they repose after their fishing or thieving excursions. Below Sapucaia-Oroca, towards Borba and the mouth of the Madeira, the population is the same mixed one as on the Amazon. The light cabins, peeping picturesquely out of cacáo groves and banana plantations, are inhabited by mestizoes of all shades and degrees, and occasionally by a mulatto or sambo, all of them able to speak Portuguese just to the extent required for intercourse with the outer world. Assuredly the time is not far distant when easier communications, and the all-levelling influence of trade, will have erased the last traces of real Indian life from these regions.

The above-mentioned Mundrucús, formerly the mightiest and most warlike tribe of these parts, have only a few decaying settlements, of three or four cottages, on the Lower Madeira, their chief seats being on the Mauhés and the Tapajoz. After a long and most violent resistance, this tribe made peace with the Portuguese, at the end of the last century; and they have faithfully adhered to them ever since, even during the terrible "guerra dos cabános," so fateful to all the pale-faces. If proper attention had been devoted to some branches of their national industry, such as the preparation of the Guaraná and Pará tobacco, the manufacture of magnificent hammocks and feather ornaments, this tribe certainly would have had a prosperous career. At Manáos we saw some of their chieftains, with their faces tattooed all over in black. This unfortunately was the only item of their national costume. They wore—*horribile dictu!*—coloured cotton shirts, black coats and inexpressibles, and tall hats! Anything more ludicrous could not well be imagined. Generally speaking, there is nothing so conspicuous and ridiculous as coloured people (negro, mulatto, sambo, or mestizo) in what they consider Sunday apparel of unrivalled elegance. A pretty negro or mulatto girl (of the Mina tribe, for instance) looks quite a queen, in her way, in her costume of lace-trimmed chemise of dazzling whiteness, set off by the velvet-like dark skin, her gaudy short petticoat ending in points below; a white, yellow, or green kerchief, slung with inimitable grace turbanwise round her short ringlets; and a shawl they call panno da costa, with large blue, white, and black stripes, hanging carelessly over her shoulders or round her waist. Some coral bracelets, or ornaments of massive gold, which never saw the inside of a Pforzheim melting-pot, complete the outfit, whose brilliant colours and easy grace contrast strikingly with our fashionable black, brown, or grey strait-waistcoats. But when you see the same creature, after (it may be) her entering the service of some noble family as nurse or lady's-maid, in a tight black silk dress; her woolly curls twisted, with pomatum, scissors, and comb, into a shape slightly resembling the chignon of her mistress; in high-heeled boots, instead of her richly embroidered slippers; with some big, tasteless brooch, instead of her corals and heavy gold filigree;—the graceful creature is transformed into a hideously ridiculous monster: but squeamish Decency is not offended, and does not now, with averted head, hiss out—"Shocking!" The same happens with our own country people: how much more with the Indians!

The Mundrucús have long abandoned their supremacy on the Madeira. They left this river even before the Conquest, I believe, to another powerful tribe, the Aráras, who also nowadays are not held in the same fear as they were formerly. Towards the end of the last century, more than once they seriously menaced the former Mission of Araretama, now Borba; and the whole lower course of the Madeira was haunted and rendered unsafe by them: but now they have totally retired to the forests on the right shore, whence they break out only now and again, appearing and disappearing with the rapidity of lightning. None of the settlers, however, will venture into one of the smaller lateral valleys, where they are still kept in awe by the strong bows and long arrows of the former masters of the territory. The immediate shores of the main stream are tolerably safe now for many a weary day's voyage, as one may readily conjecture from the cottages of the peaceable seringueiros thinly scattered along, until one has reached the domain of the ill-famed Parentintins, anthropophagous hordes, always ready for robbery and murder, and evidently the closest guardians of the rich seringaes (caoutchouc woods) on their territory, for the chances of being murdered and roasted are heavy odds against the acquisition of a few pounds of india-rubber.

Usually the traveller sees so little of these dangerous neighbours, the Aráras and Parentintins, that he might be tempted to take the fearful tales of the caoutchouc gatherers for mere inventions of their awe-stricken fancy; but a few light pirogues of the former, which drifted down a lateral affluent, and the total absence of any settlement on the domain of the latter, disposed us to think otherwise. Moreover, the black corner-posts of a burnt cottage near Crato (marked as a town on the geographical maps, but in reality but one house and a few sheds), told their own tale of a whole family having been murdered and roasted there a few years ago by the Parentintins.* As in such cases nothing at all is done by the Brazilian Government, whose principle (very different from the fire-and-sword policy of the Portuguese) it is to spare the natives as much as possible, the few unprotected settlers must make room if they would not incur the danger of sharing the fate of their neighbours. The only mode of evading the difficulty thus created, of uniting humanity towards the natives with a sound protection of the settlers, so necessary for the future prosperity of the country, is to found Indian colonies—Aldeamentos or Missions —among the Indians themselves. But this gigantic work, as is well known, has been undertaken successfully only by the Jesuits, and even by them under particularly favourable conditions.

* As I write, I learn from the President of the Madeira and Mamoré Railway Company that a small number of Englishmen in the service of the Company have been attacked by the Parentintins at St. Antonio; and a few days afterwards an outpost a little higher up, consisting of a few Mojos Indians, headed by an engineer, were driven back by another troop of savages. As in both cases these escaped without any loss, not one shot having been fired at them, while the Company had two Mojos Indians killed, they are sure soon to return, and will not, by their visits, add to the comfort of the little colony. However, the hiring of a larger number of workmen, principally Europeans—say to the extent of two thousand—and of as many Mojos Indians from Bolivia (which might easily be effected), besides being absolutely necessary for the prosecution of the works, will finally have the effect of putting down these attacks.

Under the energetic rule of this Order (whose evil influence in civilised countries I have not forgotten, by the way), numerous Indian settlements, or Missions, had been created on different points of South America, in the sixteenth, seventeenth, and eighteenth centuries, whose crumbling fragments still excite our admiration and wonder. In the midst of pathless wildernesses, on the shores of rivers showing more than their full share of rapids, cataracts, and other obstructions to navigation, and scarcely ever heard of before, there sprung up flourishing settlements, with extensive plantations of Indian corn, mandioc, cotton, sugar-cane, and Ilex Paraguayensis, and numerous herds grazing around; in short, containing all the germs of future prosperity, and the sound development of agriculture and trade. The difficulties the Padres had to overcome, too, were greater by far than they are now. There were then no proud steamers ploughing these gigantic waters in the tenth part of the time taken by *their* slow sailing-boats; and a traveller or a missionary can now reach at least the *boundaries* of these out-of-the-way places in vigorous health, and unworn by the fatigues of the way. Diligent inquirers have familiarised us somewhat with the languages and customs of a good many Indian tribes; and we know, at any rate, what we have to expect from them; and, even if the certainty be not always a very comforting one, it spares us the pang of disappointment, and enables us to prepare for all eventualities.

In spite of the improved condition of things, the present Catechese dos Indios (as the Brazilians call it), mostly in the hands of Italian monks who have formerly been clerks and schoolmasters, yields but poor results, such as not to encourage the Government to further efforts.

The following literally true narrative of an occurrence will throw a pretty clear light on the present position of affairs. Some six or seven years ago, the inhabitants of a small cottage on the Rio Negro, above Manáos, were found murdered. As the tibiæ of the victims, which are used for flutes by a neighbouring tribe, had been taken out, there could not be any doubt left as to the identity of the murderers. The Government, reluctantly yielding to the petitions of the surrounding families, resolved to send a missionary; and one of the Italian Capuchin monks at the Hospice of Rio de Janeiro was ordered to go. At Manáos he provided himself, at the expense of the Government, with a large number of presents for the sons of the forest, such as scissors, knives, beads, and small looking-glasses, and demanded a well-armed escort of twenty men, with a sergeant or cabo. Though this seemed to look rather suspicious, the new apostle to the heathen was humoured, and he betook himself to his post of danger, relying for his security on his lofty mission and his bayonets. Nothing apparently had taken place there from the date of the last attack; the blackened posts, which once had supported the light palm-roof of a happy family, pointing sadly to the sky, and around the devastated mandioca plantation the silent density of the forest uninvaded by the trace of either friend or foe. It would require one to have felt all the heart-sickening loneliness, all the dreary melancholy of such a desolate place, to understand thoroughly the thoughts which must have then assailed the poor Brother, and how, not quite prepared to become a martyr, and with a secret yearning for the dull cell he had left behind him in the convent, he must have stealthily examined his shin-bones at night to see that they were there all right.

But an Italian friar has ingenious brains; and had not he considered and studied, theoretically at least, all the difficulties a modern missionary has to encounter in the Old and New World, even before he had left his convent at Genoa? Besides, he had twenty stout negro and mulatto boys behind him; and he thought it best to make the most of *them*, and to reserve for himself the supreme finishing-stroke, such as the christening of the subdued chieftain, with all his family or even all his tribe. So the cabo, with six men, was ordered to ascend a small affluent of the Rio Negro, whose shores gave signs of being peopled by the expected Indians, and, as an introductory measure of conciliation, to leave there some of the presents. The sergeant, who probably saw his way somewhat more clearly than his holy master, was lucky enough to discover near the mouth of the little river the opening of a narrow Indian path; and there he hung up his beads, scissors, &c., on the surrounding bushes, as if they were German Christmas-trees. On the next day he returned to fetch his answer; and he got it; but in the unexpected shape of a thick hail of arrows showering from out the very bushes whereon his presents were still suspended. Luckily the ungrateful waylayers had taken aim too hastily; the sergeant and his men leaped out of the boat, and screening themselves behind it as with a shield, drifted slowly down the river to where the Frater waited impatiently for them. The holy man had not even the satisfaction of curing a wound got in the strife, and had to content himself with showing the arrows sticking in the boat as *corpus delicti*. His wisdom, however, was at an end; and he could not hit upon any better plan than asking the President of the province for one hundred soldiers more, with a view to taking more energetic measures. Of course he was given to understand that the Government by no means intended opening a campaign against the Indians; and, even if such had been the case, Sua Reverendissima should certainly not be troubled with the conduct of the military operations. The champion of the Church, who, perhaps, on that field might have given better proofs of capacity, returned, rather offended, to his convent; and the mestizoes of the Rio Negro, prizing their tibiæ somewhat, help themselves as they did before; that is, they kill every wild Indian they can set hands on, and everything remains in the old bad state.

Very different from these Indians, and the above-mentioned Parentintins and Aráras, are the Caripunas, who live a little higher up, in the region of the Madeira rapids. They also do not enjoy a very high reputation for peaceableness: but, at least in our case, they condescended to have friendly intercourse. Perhaps their good behaviour was influenced by our numbers, six white men armed with guns, and eighty Indian paddlers with knives and bows, though they certainly must have known that the latter are not much to be feared in case of a fight. As we passed one morning the smooth below the rapid of Caldeirão do Inferno, we saw three bark canoes, full of Indians, half-hidden under the overhanging boughs of the opposite shore. Before we had time to think of the course we should pursue, one of them was turned round, and in a few moments had reached us. There were two Indians and a very corpulent female in it, all quite naked, save a small apron on the latter. They were strong, well-shaped figures, of middle size, with long black hair hanging down to their shoulders; one of the men had it twined into a big plait. They had the long curved fore-teeth of the capivara* stuck through their ears, and both males and female wore small bunches of red feathers, looking like scarlet mustachios, in their noses, which gave them quite a queer and strange appearance even to us, who had

* *Hydrochœrus Capivara*, a rodent of the size of our tame pig, and much resembling the Guinea-pig, is found in numerous troops on the shores of almost all the South American rivers.

already seen others of the brown sons of the woods.* They had no arms whatever with them; and this fact, and the company of one of their spouses, were to us sure signs of their friendly intentions. Yet

BARK-CANOE OF WILD INDIANS (ARARAS AND CARIPUNAS).

our Mojos Indians, who appeared quite respectable and decent in their long bast shirts, when compared with our new acquaintance, looked

---

* Caripunas-Indiani penem ad præputium linis ligatum et sursum tractum destinatumque ad lineam ventri circumdatam ita gestant, ut perpendiculari ratione erigatur. Miri istius moris quæ sit vera causa, non satis compertum habemus. Mojos Indianos tamen, qui pertinent ad Missiones juxta Mamoré fluvium, novimus præputium eodem modo præligare; scilicet quum fistulæ uriualis os velant prorsus satisfecisse se pudicitiæ legibus credentes.

OUR FIRST INTERVIEW WITH CAMPUNA INDIANS (Madeira).

shyly and suspiciously at them from under their large-brimmed hats. "No Christianos!" whispered in my ear Remigio, our bigot capitano and steersman, in whose mind the doctrines he had been taught in the former Mission of Trinidad had fallen on but too fertile ground. Probably he meant it as a last, though unsuccessful, protest against any intercourse with his unbaptized naked cousins. He, whose ancestors less than two centuries ago must have presented about the same appearance, could not discover any worse fault in them than that they were "no Christians," while his own Christianity, of which he thought so highly, barely went beyond hearing mass, mumbling his rosary, and singing endless litanies.

However, our heathens did not seem to heed the sulky looks of their brown relations since they were received kindly by the white-faces; and, without waiting for a further invitation, the steersman of the nutshell, as soon as he had put her alongside of our heavy barque, leapt over with an engaging grin, and sat down among us just as if he were an old friend. He was a lively fellow of twenty-five or thirty years. With a quick eye he took in everything around him: our arms, guns, cutlases, and wood-knives, suspended beneath the palm-leaf awning of our boats, seemed especially to interest him; and I am sure he did not forget to mention them in his report to the chieftain. Unfortunately, our conversation, carried on for the most part by signs, was perforce a very limited one, and though "The Driving Cloud," or "The Tiger's Claw," or whatever else he might be called,* did not disdain to accept a knife, a little mirror, and a row of white beads (of which he already wore such a quantity round his neck that they formed a sort of cuirass on his chest), we could only make out of his gibberish that "at home" they had much sweet macacheira, that is mandioca; which we regarded as a sort of rustic invitation.

The Mojos—our most Christian Remigio even included—obeyed the order we gave them to follow the bark-canoe, shooting rapidly ahead, with better grace than might have been expected. Mayhap the behaviour of the "no Christianos" had not struck them as being so very ferocious and cannibal-like, or the mention of the greatly longed-for root sounded sweet in their ears. As we approached the opposite

* With the Coroados of the South, such names as "Falcon's Eye," and the like, reminding of the North American red-skins, are very common, while the softer Guaranis call themselves after fruits, trees, stars, &c.

L

shore, we saw the whole tribe, about sixty warriors and as many women and children, waiting for us under the shady roof of orchid-covered figueiras, interspersed with slender palms and magnificent fanlike strelitzias. In the first row stood the chieftain, a strongly-built, short man of about fifty, shouldering his long bow and two or three arrows. His broad face, framed within thick masses of lank black hair, was painted black near the large mouth; and his appearance altogether

PORTRAIT OF A YOUNG CARIPUNA INDIAN.

could be called anything but lovely. Besides the thick cuirass of beads and the graceful trinkets in ears and nose, he wore a magnificent diadem of yellow and red toucan feathers; and it must be confessed that he wore it with the dignity of a king.

He seemed to be inclined graciously towards us, probably in consequence of the report of his ambassador, who in his feather-light craft had arrived a little before us; and with a majestic wave of the head he invited us to approach and to follow; which we did, surrounded by a dense crowd of laughing and chattering squaws and children, serious and respectable-looking old men, and young warriors. The chieftain marched slowly ahead, and led us along a narrow but carefully cleaned path, bordered with a vegetation by whose profusion we had never before been so impressed. Trunks of gigantic size, graceful palms of every variety, blooming creepers and bromelias, orchids of the strangest shapes, and light ferns, with the warm sunbeams breaking through the dense leafage at intervals, and suddenly setting off some brilliant flower, some scarlet feather ornament, or the white glittering beads on the brown skins of our new friends—all combined to make it a picture none of us shall ever be able to forget. Our own myrmidons followed, looking not over-confident in their own strength, and completed the long cortége, the end of which was lost in the darkness of the forest.

At the distance of about half a mile from the shore we reached a clearing in the wood, with three large cabins closed in on the sides, and a smaller open shed, which evidently was the meeting-hall of the men. We were desired to take seats there in hammocks, not very remarkable for their cleanliness, and we forthwith began the distribution of our knives, scissors, fishing-hooks, red cotton handkerchiefs, &c.; in barter for which we got a good quantity of macacheira and Indian corn, half-a-dozen long bows and a bundle of arrows.* On the whole, they did not seem to be as greedy for the produce of our industry as we had seen other more civilised tribes, for example, the Tapuyos on the Amazon, and the Mojos of Bolivia. They had not yet had enough iron in hand to understand its value thoroughly. Their arrow-points of bamboo or hard wood, and the sharpened edges of a river-shell,† evidently appeared to be quite as effective to them as our

* The bartering for a pretty cotton apron tastefully adorned with feathers was a little more difficult; yet one of our companions at last succeeded in getting one for us. The brown beauty, who had dexterously replaced it with a heliconia leaf, looked rather abashed on the ground, in spite of all the paradisaic innocence of the clothing.

† The Caripuna squaws give birth to their children before the whole tribe, but without the assistance of any one, and themselves cut the navel-string with the sharpened edge of a river-shell. The Cayowa women of the South go unattended to the wood when their hour of labour arrives, and return with the baby, when all is over, to discharge their household duties, and to wait upon the husband, who for a week lies motionless in his hammock, and behaves himself as if he were the patient. On remonstrances or railleries of the white faces, he only answers with a pitying smile.

knives;* and if they graciously accepted our glittering steelware, it seemed to be more out of curiosity than anything else. Very different was it with the glass beads, which they prized highly, and which seemed to be a sort of money with them, and the place of which, before their intercourse with the white race, is said to have been supplied by the small hard seeds of certain plants.

Besides the hammocks there was no "furniture" whatever in the Parliament-house, save some long thin drums,—for their festivals, probably,—a few pretty baskets of palm-leaves with feather ornaments in them, and some bows and arrows suspended to the beams; the former of the dark wood of the paxiuba-palm, the latter of the light stems of the ubá reed. Some slight cavities in the ground, with flat stones in the middle of each, showed us clearly that the Caripunas followed the custom of many other tribes, of burying their warriors in large earthen urns (or igaçabas) in the cottages. We counted five of them; and it was easy to see that soon the burial-ground would have to be enlarged, or the whole tribe would require to shift, if they were all to have the same honours. The latter course will probably be adopted, as by stress of the scarcity of the game they scare away the Indians are compelled to change their abodes from time to time. The Coroados, in fact, do so every few years, and burn down their light sheds on account of the vermin.

As the igaçabas were barely covered with earth, we suppose that they contained only the clean bones of the dead. We could not, of course, think of excavating one of them or even of looking closer at the tombs; the more so as a characteristic incident revealed to us the degree of respect and awe with which they regarded whatever has to do with their dead. I asked one of the younger Indians to give me, in exchange for a pair of scissors, a very queer-looking instrument, consisting of a thin board of half a yard length, which, when whirled about by a slender cord drawn through the middle, must give a whizzing sound. The boy, immediately turning round to one of the elder Indians, explained to him my request, in a tone whose excitement

---

On closer acquaintance, however, they used to say that it is necessary for the welfare of the child, who would infallibly fall ill if the father did not observe a strict regimen.

* The Coroados fasten old knife-blades at the end of the arrows they use for tiger, tapir, and wild-hog shooting. Formerly they had flint points, quite identical with those found in the Pfahlbauten. Hundreds of them are sometimes discovered together on the sites of former settlements.

contrasted strangely with his former self-possession and impassibility. With a very serious face, but with a sort of quiet politeness which I could not but admire, the old man tried to make me understand that these instruments, whose howling tone he imitated while marching slowly and majestically round the burial-places, were used for their lamentations over the dead, and could not be parted with like any profane object. Such an exhibition of sentiment by a real naked savage, in a real dense primeval forest, struck me indeed even more than the solemn manner in which the announcement was delivered.* I afterwards prevailed, with some difficulty, upon the same young Caripuna to keep quiet for a few moments in one of the hammocks, until I had drawn his profile. His hesitation did not seem to arise from any superstitious fear—the "civilised" Tapuyos at Manáos were far worse in this respect—but I fancy he simply thought it dull work.

But the hour for parting came, when the whole tribe accompanied us to the river-shore; the women carrying great quantities of mandioca-roots, and heavy bundles of yellow and red maize in baskets suspended on their backs by broad glossy stripes of bast, which passed over their forehead. They carry their babies in similar contrivances slung across their shoulders.

We parted evidently the very best of friends; and we were fully confident that such attacks as our old mulatto hunter had spoken of were not now likely to happen again. But we were the more disagreeably surprised when we learned, on our return to Manáos, that the same tribe had, only a few months afterwards, attacked the boat of a Bolivian merchant, and had killed the proprietor and five of his paddlers, while his wife, though badly wounded, had succeeded in

* Some years before I had witnessed a similar scene in the province of Paraná, on the shores of the Paranapanema, when the old Cayowa chieftain, Pahy (in the Aldeamento de Santo Ignacio), on our taking leave of him, presented us with a fine bow, adorned with toucan-feathers. I thanked him heartily, and, in acknowledgment of his gift, assured him, with as serious a face as I could muster, that I always should use it in war and in hunting, and remember him by it; but looking quite frightened, he took the bow hastily from my hands, and, handling it like a sceptre, moved round us with pompous measured strides, at the same time, with uplifted head, singing long-drawn notes of ear and heartrending harmony. He could not be quieted until I had promised, when I at last understood what he meant by some broken words in Portuguese like "Caça não! Guerra não! Amigo! Santo!" that we would ever keep sacred the gift of our brown friends, and never soil it in war or hunting—a promise which I can with good conscience declare we have always faithfully observed.

making her escape with the rest into one of the canoes, in which they drifted down the river, instead of continuing their voyage upwards. Without doubt, this had happened while the Bolivians were busy dragging their boats over the rocks, when the dispersion of the crew did not allow of any serious resistance. We could not ascertain whether in this case any provocation on the Bolivian side had preceded the outrage.* Behind the "padrão's" back the paddlers might rouse the wrath of the Indians, especially by brutal behaviour towards the squaws, who are regarded with jealous eyes by very many tribes (not by all, it is true); and their vengeance does not always fall exactly upon the offenders, for the fury of the Indians then turns on all the whites, and the innocent suffer in common with the guilty, even as the settlers, to revenge an onslaught, will shoot down any red-skin they can encounter.

Very often, what are trifles in our estimation are to them the springs of fatal feuds. Thus, for example, a few years ago a Brazilio-Peruvian expedition started for the purpose of determining the boundaries, under the conduct of Captain José da Costa Azevedo, and was attacked by a numerous troop of Indians on the Javary (an affluent of the Solimões,

* An incident that occurred in 1860, in the province of Paraná, is too characteristic to be omitted here, the more so as the facts were related to me by two of the principal actors in the drama.

On the ruins of the former Jesuit Mission of Nossa Senhora de Loreto do Pirapó, on the shores of the Paranapanema, the Brazilian Government had founded a colony (or Aldeamento) of half-civilised Guarani Indians, and had confided it to the direction of an old Portuguese major, one of whose legs had been stiffened for life by some Miguelistic ball about forty years ago. The Guaranis had their cottages a little apart from the Director's house, which sheltered, besides himself, a white overseer, six negroes, and four negresses. One day, quite unexpectedly, appeared a troop of Coroados before it, about eighty men, women, and children. They seemed to be quite peaceably inclined, received and gave little presents, and partook freely of a meal served to them at the fire in the courtyard, until nightfall, when some of the squaws, who had become more intimately acquainted with the negroes, laid their greedy hands on their comfortable woollen jackets, and would not give them up. A general tumult ensued, in which the Coroados advanced upon their enemies with the glowing firebrands they had rashly seized. The impossibility of explaining themselves, the Director's want of pluck, and, above all, the deep aversion existing between blacks and Indians, in spite of temporary friendships, could not but lead to a bloody crisis. One of the elder blacks, the tall Ambrosio, had silently prepared his gun, and, at the moment of the highest confusion, firing from behind a corner, shot the Indian chief right through the head. Some of his friends had apparently only waited for such a signal. Three more loaded guns with coarse shot were immediately fired into the densest crowd. The effect was magical. The smoke had not yet quite disappeared, when the Indians, silent as ghosts, had vanished, taking their wounded with them; the dead chieftain alone was left lying close to the house; and the expiring fires shone

running along the frontier against Perú from the parallel of 10° 20′ of south latitude), because they had destroyed some of their primitive bridges, that is, felled trees which lay across the river, to the obstruction of the passage of the boats. While they were dragging their canoes over a shoal, an overpowering number of savages broke in upon them with fearful yells. The situation was a desperate one, their ammunition having been damped by the upsetting of a canoe on the previous day. When at last they succeeded in getting their boats afloat, the second in command, Lieutenant Soares Pinto, lay dying in one of them, while, in another, the Peruvian commissary, Roldan, writhed with pain from an arrow-shot in the leg, besides several of the paddlers who were more or less wounded. After a dreadful voyage of many days, they reached the steamer stationed at the mouth of the Javary, which conveyed them to Manáos; but the poor Peruvian was in such a state that the physicians thought amputation necessary, the setting-in of gangrene being apprehended in this hot climate, and after the sorry nursing he had received.

Another case, involving the guilt of both parties,—the disregard of human dignity on the one side, and treachery and barbarous violence

only on his grim features and the dismayed faces of the Director and his blacks. They retired speedily to the house, apprehending an attack at dawn of day; but morning came without the Coroados: so, after having well searched the place, and, to their surprise, discovered that the Indians had taken away, during the night, the body of their dead chief from under the very windows, they all crossed the river—there about 600 yards wide; for the Coroados are indifferent boatmen, and could not easily pursue them. The Guaranis of the settlement, who until now had scrupulously kept aloof from the whole affair, followed their leaders, and a few days afterwards had to sustain a bold attack of their hereditary enemies the Coroados; the Major and his men having already left the place for Curitiba, the capital of the province, where, after a strict investigation, he was dismissed; and Ambrosio, the white overseer, and one of the blacks, were sent to prison for many months. In the skirmish on the shores of the Paranapanema, the gentle Guaranis, with the aid of a few fire-arms and swords, got the better of their bold assailants. We afterwards brought over one of their trophies, the skull of a Coroado woman, which showed a deep sabre-cut. It is now in the collection of skulls belonging to the Medical Faculty at Freiburg, in the Breisgau.

In almost every case of bloodshed between the white and the red men, it has been found that the latter would not be molested on their hunting-grounds by the white intruders, or that they were refused the indemnification they asked for them. Twenty and more years ago, before the law was in force which gave to the Government all tracts of land the titles to the possession of which could not be proved, every estanciero, or cattle breeder, in the thinly-peopled Southern provinces longed for new campos for his increasing herds. One of them, living near the Passo Fundo, on the Uruguay, discovered a magnificent prairie, capable of pasturing thousands of cows, which was divided from the older possessions by a tract of forest some miles wide only. It was a perfect godsend; and the estanciero forthwith set about opening a

on the other,—is this:—When the brave English traveller Chandless, whom we had the pleasure of meeting at Manáos, explored the Purús in 1865, his servant, an Italian, informed him on the way that he had decided on not accompanying him farther up, and that he was going to return alone to the Amazon Valley. Chandless, who knew his man well, and who guessed rightly that it was not so much the increasing hardship of the voyage as the desire to make a good bargain for the Indian children a little lower down the river which caused this sudden resolve, tried to dissuade him from his purpose, but in vain! He went, and—never reached the Amazon. His master, on his return, found pieces of his canoe near an Indian malocca on the shore, and there heard the particulars of the horrible tale. The Italian had, immediately upon his arrival, begun bargaining for an Indian boy, and had at last purchased him for a hatchet; but, as he was conveying him to his canoe, the child began to scream piteously; upon which his mother, running up, rescued him, and would not give him up. Hereupon the Italian demanded his hatchet back, but was haughtily refused. A short skirmish ensued and the white man was killed, and, I suppose, roasted and devoured.

way to the new campo for the transport thither of a few head of cattle, without heeding in the least the protest of a horde of Coroados who had been in the habit of visiting him from time to time, and with whom he had always been on a friendly footing.

When the Indians saw that their old hunting-ground, the abode of numerous herds of stags and deer, was lost to them, they demanded an indemnity first of five, and at last of two, Spanish ounces (about £15); but they got for answer nothing but a sneer and hard words. They tried several times to block up the new path by felled trees; but, as they saw that the negroes of the estancia removed the obstruction with less trouble than they took to make it, they seemed to give up the task, and did not appear for some time.

However, when the young animals of the new herd were to be counted, and to be branded with the mark of the estancia—a festive occasion, on which the proprietor and all his family went to a light house erected on the new possession—the Coroados made their appearance again, and were kindly received by the master, in spite of warnings from his subordinates. He offered the chieftain a piece of roast-meat, and, upon his request for a knife, handed to him his own dagger-like one, which was stuck in his girdle, after the fashion of the place; whereupon the Indian, with a movement quick as lightning, drove it into his chest up to the very handle; and, as if this were a concerted signal, a crowd of armed Coroados poured in from all sides, and, after a short resistance, killed eight white people, women and children included. Only one boy of fourteen years old escaped by a window; and he, throwing himself on one of the horses without, spread the horrible news. In an expedition undertaken by the neighbours to avenge the murder, a few Indians were killed; but the greater part of them escaped, and retired farther into the interior of the forests.

Another bloody encounter—let us hope the last—occurred in 1862, in the so-called

THE WILD INDIAN TRIBES OF THE MADEIRA VALLEY. 153

But to return to the Indians of the Madeira. The most dangerous footpads on its whole course are a tribe whose real name even is not known, scarcely any individual of whom has been distinctly seen, yet who do not allow the traveller to breathe freely until their domain is passed. Scarcely a year goes by without one of their bold well-calculated surprises, or the treacherous murder of some traveller, or Mojos Indian from the Missions, descending the river to gather cacáo. They seem to live chiefly near the confluence of the Mamoré and the Guaporé, along the shores of the latter to the old fort of Principe da Beira, and on the campos east of the Mamoré towards the Itonama. Not even the best gun is of any use against them, as the sharpest eye cannot penetrate to their well-chosen ambushes behind the dense boughs, whence their never-erring arrows are always the first to proclaim their presence. Hence the only possible protection against them are light cuirasses of hard leather, or other stout stuff, such as were worn by the Portuguese troops not many years ago in their combats with the Botocudos on the Rio Doce. But who will ever think of putting on such things in that climate without the risk of absolute and immediate danger?*

The Indians of the old Missions, most exposed to them by reason of their frequent voyages on the rivers, live in constant dread of them; and around the fires of our Mojos every evening might be heard

Sertão de Guarapuava—that is, the immense wooded region extending west of this little town to the shores of the Paraná, and even farther on. An enterprising Paulista had settled there in the face of all warnings, and, by constant vigilance and cautious behaviour, had, for six years, held the Coroados, his neighbours, at a respectful distance. One day there appeared a large troop of them before the palisades with which he had encircled his house, clamorously demanding Indian corn, and trying to force their way in after they had been refused; and in the contest that ensued, one of them was killed by the son of the proprietor of the house. In a renewed attack some time afterwards, a great number were shot by the Brazilians, who were well protected by their palings against the arrows of the Indians. They were again obliged to retire, and were not heard of for years, though one or other of the Brazilians, who never failed to keep a sharp look-out, even while working in the fields, swore he had seen some lurking in the bushes.

Some years after this, a son-in-law of the old Paulista, having bought the produce of a corn-plantation a few miles off, belonging to the military colony of Chagú, just then given up by the Government, went there with wife and children and some of his brothers-in-law, eleven persons in all. It was the moment of revenge so long awaited by the Coroados! None of them ever returned; their corpses were found lying near the burnt cottages.

* Dr. Eiras, from Rio de Janeiro, has already been mentioned as one of their victims in 1869.

whispered tales of their horrid deeds. Several times the savages attacked and killed the soldiers while fishing in the Guaporé, near the fort of Principe da Beira, nay, under its very guns, though these are by no means so formidable as might be supposed;* and the commanding officer had to prohibit such excursions, save in sufficient numbers and under due precautionary arrangements. The Bolivian traders would annihilate the whole tribe without any scruple, if they could. More than once, they have tried to get up a general insurrection, and have invited the commander of Principe da Beira to take part in it; but, even if he had consented (which he could not without acting against the clear wishes of his Government), its success would have been very doubtful. As it is now, the son of the forest has decidedly the upper hand, and scarcely ever gets what he deserves for his murders; but, twenty or thirty years hence, perhaps the tables will be turned, and then will ensue what happens everywhere when the white race and the red get to close quarters. Every stroke of the settler's axe will be as a nail driven into the coffin of the native; for, at every such stroke, he will be thrust farther away from the main sources of his life—the principal rivers and the hunting-grounds near

* It is almost incomprehensible that the Brazilians should abandon to decay a fort which the Portuguese built with so much trouble and expense (in 1780), and which, in case of war with Bolivia, would be of great importance. Well-informed Brazilians have told me that the soldiers of the garrison not only pulled out the strong cramp-irons of the parapets, but also stripped the chapel of all its rich wood-carvings, in order to get at the nails, &c., which they gave to Bolivian traders for brandy. The doors of the fort still are scrupulously shut every night, especially since the soldiers, with the aid of a hill of rubbish situate against the wall, are not impeded by them in their nightly visits to the brown beauties living outside in their frail palm cottages; but certainly not one of the heavy guns, whose transport up the Madeira and Guaporé must have been no light work, is ready for use. It is no idle boast of the Bolivians, who, sneering at the harmless monsters marked with the escutcheon of the Bragánzas, vow they will have the old fort by means of a single barrel of cachaça (sugar-brandy); upon which provocation the black defenders, proudly exhibiting their blunderbusses, swear they will with them open such a fire on the Castelhanos that there shall be no need of the artillery. However, such is the dependence of the fort on Bolivia for its supply of provisions that it would be the easiest thing in the world to starve it out in the event of war.

All the little forts on the southern and south-eastern borders of the realm were in similar condition at the time of the war with Paraguay; indeed, in all South America there is not a single fortress which at all answers to modern requirements, not excluding the renowned Humaitá itself, whose chief strength lay in the deep swamps surrounding it. With the exceedingly high wages of workmen, and the great difficulty of getting a sufficient number of them to such distant places, iron forts made in Europe would be advisable—one near Santo Antonio, on the Madeira, and another near the mouth of the Beni or the Mamoré.

them; and, as soon as the shrill whistle of the locomotive shall sound through the clearing, and proud steamers rock on the rivers, he will be totally undone. He never will submit readily to the entire abandonment of his old ways, and never will take to agriculture, an employment which he despises as belonging to the lot of his humble enslaved wives, unless he be compelled to adopt it, or unless he be brought up to it by patient degrees, with a combination of paternal kindness and unswerving firmness. The unalterable course of his thoughts ever will be that he had a better claim to the soil on the ground of priority of residence, and that it was asking too much of him to change his mode of life in favour of the intruders; and the white man (I mean the settler, the uneducated man) will always look haughtily down on the brown "animal," and will be only too happy to execute his mandate: "Get hence to make room for me and my family!" A violent contest, carried on from both sides with treacherous* weapons, must ensue; but its end cannot be doubted, and another nation will soon have ceased to exist.

An intelligent Guarani Indian of the Aldeamento of San Ignacio, on the Paranapanema, once asked me: "Why do not the white people leave us undisturbed in our forests? Why are we to live like them? Is there not room enough for us all?" And what could I reply? He would easily have refuted any sentimental talk about the blessings of civilisation by simply pointing to the importation of the measles, just then decimating his village; and it would have been cruel to insist upon the naked truth that by the highest right in the world, the right of might, we should in time drive them to still greater extremities. The schoolmaster-like advice, to keep on good terms with the white man for his own benefit, was all I could give the honest fellow. To sum up our observations on the future of the South American Indians, we may briefly note that, whenever they have come into contact with the white race, their doom has been sealed. Like their more energetic northern brethren, they are visited with physical and moral destruction;

* If a tale we heard on the Rio da Pomba (an affluent of the Parahyba) be true, the palm of treachery must be conceded to the *white* race. Planters who had been occasionally troubled by little thefts committed by the Indians, but who, otherwise, lived in peace with the numerous hordes of the vicinity, had the woollen jackets and blankets of their negroes, who had been swept off in an outbreak of small-pox, carried into the woods. In accordance with the design, the effect on the Indians, who of course availed themselves of the clothing, was terrific. Nearly the whole tribe was destroyed.

the rate of which can be retarded only by founding aldeamentos after the plan of the former Missions, but with the condition that less care be paid to the religious, and more to the agricultural and industrial, element.

CARIPUNA INDIAN HUNTING.

It is impossible to overestimate the civilising influence which might especially be exercised over the women by a kindly active lady, versed in the several branches of household industry, and which would thus get diffused through them over the whole community. In every village, in fact, there should be a female teacher for the long-neglected squaws. A new generation would then arise, which, if not endowed with the energy and activity of the European population, would at least become tolerable neighbours to it; and by amalgamation with which, in process of time, it might contribute to the formation of a stable race adapted to the climate.

To many it may appear that such mixed races bear in themselves the germs of destruction, nature generally having a tendency to return to the pure types; but closer observation of the present (so-called) white population of the northern provinces of Pernambuco, Ceará, Parahyba do Norte, Maranhão, and Pará, will clearly show that so much of the Indian element has survived there that more than one-third, or a fourth part, of the whole population must be ascribed to it. Even if it be more and more diminished by increasing immigration, and should it at last be discernible only by an experienced eye, yet there it is, and it has been the means of profit to the thinly-peopled country; and surely no one will assert that the black-haired, dark-eyed mestizoes of these countries are less fit to live and work under the glowing rays of the tropical sun than the fair sons of the North.

However, I am still far from joining in the unwarrantable lamentations of novel-writers over the impending extinction of a mythical red race, far superior to the white in heroic virtues and noble qualities of heart. Such a red race exists only in their imaginations. The indolent, sensual, and sometimes treacherous race of real life will and must give way to the growing exigencies of over-peopled Europe. The titles of possession enjoyed by the autochthon, important as they may be in his own narrow and childish judgment, are abolished in the Court of Appeal which takes cognisance of the wider needs of the world. And to ultra-sentimentalists of the novelist type I should like to put this query: "Is not the prosperity of the family of some hard-working settler, trying with the sweat of his brow to create a new home for his children and his grand-children, of more importance than the comforts of a set of savages, with which that prosperity might possibly interfere?" Moreover, by way of justifying this complete extrusion of an unwilling race, a really higher civilisation, in the form of agriculture and regular industry, should replace the hitherto prevalent system of wild robbery; the hidden treasures of the country should be explored for the benefit of mankind at large, and the last traces of that narrow Spanish-Portuguese system of destruction, which took only its own ego and the immediate span of time into consideration, must for ever disappear. In the United States, we may well wait patiently for the completion of this process, which draws to a close with the inflexible rigidity of a law of nature. There the waves of immigration already touch the foot of the Rocky Mountains. There the wigwam is destroyed to make room for the railway station or the streets of nascent cities, and Indian savagery and modern culture, unable to exist side by side, *must* daily come to bloody conflicts. But in the South American States, in Brazil especially, which owns provinces, with a population of only 40,000, larger than Germany, all hands, be their number never so small, should be turned to account, particularly as the bulk of European emigration is not likely to turn in that direction for the present. The association of the Brazilian Indians with useful communities in aldeamentos, on a larger scale, is also favoured by the consideration that their character, on the whole more gentle and peaceable than that of the North American Indians, does not offer insuperable obstacles to earnest and persevering attempts. What the speculating spirit of the Jesuits conceived and brought about, should we despair of achieving through the agency of a Government animated by higher views?

One of the chief difficulties of such an undertaking is, as already mentioned, the great number of South American idioms: and it must be reckoned a capital idea of the Jesuits that their missionaries, instead of teaching Spanish to their Indians—which would have turned *that* way the torrent of European adventure—did all they could to make the Guarani language, the richest and most flexible of those idioms, the prevailing tongue. Though they may not have been quite successful, yet the Guarani has spread, through their labours, over an exceedingly wide range; and, to the present day, there are many Guarani words in the language of the ordinary population of Brazil (quite independently of their colour and descent), and at places where Guarani was not the language of the autochthons.

As to the language of the Caripunas, MARTIUS gives a short vocabulary of it from which I take the following:—

Water, *oni passna*.
Tree, *jui*.
Bow, *cannáti*.

Head, *mapo*.
Waterfall, *saschu tschama*.
Knife, *mané pacca*.

Teeth, *está*.	Arrow, *púa*.
God, *oará*.	Moon, *ursche*.
Day, *sabaka*.	Tapir, *au ana*.
Sun, *baari*.	Dog, *tschaspa*.
Son, *wakö*..	Stag, *tschassú*.
Daughter, *jussawakö*.	Tiger, *kaman*.
Madeira river, *Munnu*.	Alligator, *kapuena*.
River, *énne*.	1, *aares*.
White man, *cariba tschikö*.	2, *eranbué*.
Fire, *tschú*.	3, *kimischá*.
To die, *makö*.	4, *eranbué nardbue*.
He has died, *naia makö*.	5, *musken túna*.

We should have much liked to ascertain whether our friends the Caripunas have the same mode of conveying their thoughts as the Coroados in Paraná, especially as the "written rocks" of the Madeira seem to be beyond their comprehension now. In the immense primeval forests extending between the Ivahy and the Paranapanema, the Paraná and the Tibagy, the rich hunting-grounds of numerous Coroado hordes, one frequently encounters, chiefly near forsaken palm-sheds, a strange collection of objects hung up between the trees on thin cords or cipós, such as little pieces of wood, feathers, bones, and the claws and jaws of different animals.

In the opinion of those well versed in Indian lore, these hieroglyphs are designed as epistles to other members of the tribe, regarding the produce of the chase, the number and stay of the huntsmen, domestic intelligence, and the like; but this strange kind of composition, reminding one of the quippos (knotted cords) of the old Peruvians, has not yet been quite unravelled, though it is desirable that it should be, for the naïve son of the woods also uses it sometimes in his intercourse with the white man.

Settlers in these countries, on going in the morning to look after their very primitive mills near their cottages, have frequently discovered them going bravely, but bruising pebbles instead of the maize grains, while on the floor of the open shed the names and purposes of the unwelcome nocturnal visitors have been legibly written in the sand. Among the well-drawn zigzag lines were inserted the magnificent long tail-feathers of the red and blue macaw, which are generally used by the Coroados for their arrows; and, as these are the symbols of war and night-attacks, the whole was probably meant for a warning and admonition *ad hominem*: "Take up your bundle and go, or beware of our arrows!"

On the Iguassú, one of the mighty affluents of the Paraná, there still are a few wild, little-known tribes living side by side with the sparse population of civilised cattle breeders. The German colonists of Blumenau, their eastern neighbours, include them under the Portuguese name of Bugres, while the Brazilians falsely call them Botocudos.

Driven into straits upon all sides, and particularly averse to friendly intercourse with the white race, they retire farther and farther; and, as the progress of cultivation deprives them of one tract of wood or rich campo after another, they protest in their own fashion, either by a sudden night-attack or by one of these puzzling proclamations. Thus, a few years ago, when the Iguassú was getting a little livelier with trade, they set up a long bamboo in a conspicuous spot on its shore, with a big bundle of feathers, bones, &c., waving at the top like a huge scarecrow. Unfortunately the floods had carried all off some time before we passed there, and so we were deprived of the pleasure of trying our wits at the strange riddle.

In the same drastic way, in ages long gone by, the nations of Asia must have written their first letters, until the palpable symbols were supplanted by images and signs, which in their turn were replaced by syllables and letters with the higher gifted races and tribes.

If by the words of Goethe—

> "So wird erst nach und nach die Sprache fest gerammelt.
> Und was ein Volk zusammen sich gestammelt,
> Muss ewiges Gesetz für Herz und Seele sein,"

the *sounds* are meant in the first place, yet the process of slow "fest rammeln" is the same for the *written* language; and those first "stammerings" of any nation are not devoid of interest.

Are not the sounds and the visible signs for them so closely linked that it seems as if a language cannot rise beyond a certain degree of development if the letters do not come to its aid? The American languages, above all, cause such thoughts to arise. They all are polysynthetical, that is, formed by agglutination, or a loose adding of formal elements to the word-root.

MARTIUS says, in the Portuguese preface to his "Vocabulary of Brazilian Languages:"—"The monosyllable or bisyllable radical words of these languages are loosely put together to express a more or less complicated notion. Yet, in all of them, are missing the flexions which are intended to convey the thought easily and clearly in all its sharpness and logical power to the spirit of the hearer. These flexions are substituted by certain particles,* that express the most necessary grammatical and syntactical notions. Of course they are less apt for the purpose; and these idioms cannot possess the beauty and precision of more civilised languages. While in the latter these flexions and composed words appear (so to say) as the results of an organic process, as a spontaneous emanation of the spirit, showing the laws regulating the course of ideas already in the construction of the sentences; the polysynthetical languages, on the contrary, having nothing of the kind, appear only as a loosely-joined conglomeration of words. This inflexibility and poverty characterize all the Indian languages of Brazil, even the Guarani, and the Lingoa geral do Brazil, or Tupi, which has arisen from it under the influence of the Jesuits; so that the eulogies lavished on it by the old missionaries seem to be applicable rather to its phonetic character than to its construction."

Thus far the excellent German linguist and botanist. At the end of his treatise he proposes the erection of schools for instruction in the Tupi language, thinking that thereupon the greater part of the native population, or rather the half-civilised descendants of the autochthons, would not regard the white men as strangers and intruders any longer, and would join them in larger numbers. Well-meaning wishes! If I conjecture aright, Brazilian statesmen must have thought: "If we but had schools for our own descendants! In a short time the last remains of the natives will, notwithstanding all our efforts, have vanished, and the low degree of civilisation to which they were capable of advancing by their own unaided efforts certainly did not warrant bright hopes of them!" So it is always the same vicious circle. They are not helped because they do not progress; and they do not progress because they are not helped.

* The following passage is taken from the Introduction to the "Tesoro de la lengua Guarani, que se usa en el Perú, Paraguay y Rio de la Plata. Por el P. Antonio Ruiz (de Montoya) de la Compañia de Jesus. Madrid: J. Sanchez. 1639."

"Among the chief difficulties of this language are the particles, many of which have no meaning by themselves, but only when joined to some other word, be it entire or maimed by the composition. For this reason there are no particular forms for the verb, which is conjugated by the particles: *A, ere, o, ya, ña, pee*, and the pronouns—*che, nde*, &c. The verb, *ñemboé, e.g.*, is composed by the particles, *ñé, mó*, and *e*. *Ñé* is reciprocal; *mó* is an active particle; and *e* means cleverness, aptitude; the whole together meaning to exercise, to learn. 'I learn' is expressed by *A ñemboé*."

However, when we judge of the civilisation, or rather of the aptitude for it, of the South American Indian tribes, particularly of those in the valleys of the Amazon, the Paraná, and the Paraguay, we must not forget the impossibility of their achieving *per saltum* the great advance from a life of wild fishers and hunters to a life of cattle-breeders, in the midst of those endless forests, and in the total absence of domestic animals comparable with our cattle. When we remember that the semi-cultured condition of a great part of Asia, and of some parts of Africa, is based entirely on the existence of

---

For the benefit of readers particularly interested in Guarani, I here add a dialogue on Christian Doctrine, as it was taught two hundred years ago in the Spanish Jesuit Missions:—

Priest. How ought a man to behave in this world to free himself from hell and to get into heaven?
Mará oicobope acé icó ara pube anhañ garata çüi onhe pyçyrô pota ybaky pe oiere raço ucar?

Pupil. He must believe in God, be christened, and follow his commandments.
Tupã rerobiar inhe mom garay pa; Tupã nhe ënga rupi oicobo.

Priest. Is there a God?
Oicobepe Tupã?

Pupil. There is.
Oicobe.

Priest. Do you believe in this God?
Pererobiarpe aë Tupã?

Pupil. I do.
Arobiar.

Priest. Who is God?
Mbaë Tupã?

Pupil. He who has created all things.
Opacatù mbaë tetiruã monhang ara.

Priest. How has he created all things?
Mbaë pupe Tupã opacatú tetiruã oimonhang?

Pupil. Only by his word.
Inheenga pupe nhote.

Priest. Has God a body like us?
Cetepe Tupã açei ãbé?

Pupil. He has not.
Naçetei.

Priest. Has God ever had a beginning?
Ni y py pe eri mbaë Tupã?

Pupil. He has not.
Ni y py i.

Priest. Was he from eternity?
Ceco abanhe pe cecoi?

Pupil. He was.
Ceco abanhe.

Priest. Will he be for ever?
Aujera manhepe çecoi?

Pupil. For ever.
Aujeramnnhe — ne.

Priest. Where is God?
Umamepe Tupã rece?

Pupil. In heaven. On earth there is no place where he is not.
Ybaky pe, yby pe noico mbaë amo çecoabëyma.

Priest. Can one see God?
Ei catupe açe ykebe Tupã repiaca?

Pupil. One cannot.
Ndey catui.

Priest. Why?
Maranamope?

Pupil. Because he has no body.
Cete — ëy m — nhe.

Priest. Where can one see him?
Mamepe açëo çepiak — ne?

Pupil. In heaven. When we get there we shall see him.
Ybaky pe iande çoreme — oçepiaky ne.

Priest. And those in hell will not see him?
Anhangara tape o ço mbaë rama ndo — çepiak — xoerene?

Pupil. By no means.
Ndoçepiak.

Priest. Why not?
Maranamope?

Pupil. On account of their sins. &c.
Inhëenya abyagoëra repyranmo. &c.

different domestic animals, and how the Zulu Caffre, despite his negro brutality, seems a Crœsus with his fat herds, when compared with the Indian who depends on his luck in the chase, the primitive immobility of the latter is not so very incomprehensible, even if we altogether disregard the difference of race.

The only animal fit to become domestic, of all the rich fauna of Southern America, is the tapir; but its habit of isolation may be a difficulty in its cultivation.

The all-stifling luxuriance of tropical vegetation, against which man is quite helpless without iron implements, was, at least in the densely-wooded valleys of the Amazon and the Paraná, and of the innumerable smaller affluents of the Atlantic, one of the chief obstacles in the way of development; and, if at the time of the Conquest the Indians of the Pampas also were on the same low level as their cousins of the wooded regions, the reason must be sought in the afore-mentioned want of domestic animals, which did not suffer them to live otherwise than by fishing or hunting, and the scanty produce of their very primitive and limited agriculture. The intermediate connecting link of cattle-breeding, that, since the introduction of European cattle, has acquired so high an importance in these countries, was then totally missing; and without it there was no possibility of getting on for a not very highly gifted race.

The religious notions of all these nations cannot be very exalted; and, moreover, it is an extremely difficult task to make them out. Besides the difficulties of the language and the difference of individual convictions, the Indians sometimes take a sort of malicious pleasure in wilfully misleading troublesome questioners; and the missionaries, both the old and the modern ones, who might have been expected to pay special attention to this matter, have always treated their poor, childish religious fables with scorn and disdain. On the whole, it seems as if the Indians belonging to the great Tupi family had somewhat better notions in this respect; and part of the early success of the missionaries was owing, perhaps, to their innate awe of a mysterious spiritual world, and of the priests mediating between it and them.

The Coroados, whom I have so frequently mentioned, though in many respects above other tribes, seem to be almost void of religious feelings, certainly according to the judgment of our good old friend Frei Timotheo do Castello Novo, Director of the Aldeamento São Pedro d'Alcantara.

With a pitying shrug of the shoulders, and meaning it, perhaps, as an apology for his own rather passive conduct, he narrated to us the shocking story of a Coroado with loud voice once asking him, during mass, for a plate of farinha! "Since that time," added the grey-bearded father, with a melancholy smile, "I have been rather disenchanted, and have refrained from asking my savages to hear mass." But even this matter-of-fact nation of Coroados I cannot believe to have no religion at all; and the question whether there are any such nations at all seems to be an open one still, and likely to remain so for some time.

Even the Tupi tribes have no kind of religious service; and, whatever their ideas on the surrounding Nature and the reasons of its phenomena may be, they certainly do not rise above the childish notions of demoniac powers, hostile rather than friendly, which may be conjured and rendered harmless by their Pajés, or charm-doctors. These sly impostors, who sometimes may delude themselves into believing at least in their sacred mission, if not in the infallibility of their medicines, play quite a conspicuous part with all the independent Indian tribes; and it even seems as if the awe within which they know how to shroud themselves was shared by the Portuguese-speaking mestizoes and zamboes.

As with the Shamans of the North-Asiatic nations, the influence a Pajé may secure over his tribe depends entirely on the success of his cures and his more or less imposing personal qualities. Woe to him if by some unlucky ministration or fatal advice he forfeits his prestige. The hate of the whole tribe turns against him, as if to indemnify them for the fear and awe felt by them until then; and often he pays for his envied position with his life.

And an influential and powerful position it is. His advice is first heard in war and peace. He has to mark the boundaries of the hunting-grounds; and, when quarrels arise, he has to decide in concert with the chieftain, sometimes even against the latter's wishes. By a majestically distant demeanour, and by the affectation of severe fasting and of nightly meetings with the spirits of another world, these augurs have succeeded in giving such an appearance of holiness to the whole caste, that their influence is a mighty one to the present day; even with the Indians of the Aldeamentos, where contact with the white race is sure by-and-by to produce a certain degree of scepticism.

When I was at the Aldeamento of San Ignacio, on the Paranapanema,

Cuyabá, chieftain and Pajé of an independent horde of Cayowá Indians, made his appearance; and I had the honour of being introduced to this magnificent sample of a conjurer. He was a man of about fifty, with large, well-cut features, framed within a dense, streaming mane of long black hair. The long xerimbitá on his under lip (a long, thin cylinder of a resin resembling amber), a great number of black and white beads, covering his chest in regular rows like a cuirass, and a broad girdle holding his cheripá (sort of apron), which was fringed all round with rich woven ornaments, gave him quite a stately, majestic appearance.

Though he had never seen white men before,—the few officials of the Aldeamento being all more or less "amulatados," that is, showing the mulatto type,—and though our expedition could not but interest him in more ways than one, he did not deign to show the least surprise, or anything like it, and on our invitation took a seat at our table with such a quietly supercilious self-possession that we ourselves nearly forgot the *nil admirari* and our duties as hosts.

In an interview he had with the Director of the Aldeamento, who wished him to leave his forests and to join the whites, who had plenty of knives, hatchets, salt, and even powder and lead, and among whom only polygamy was prohibited, he owned,—gravely nodding his head and repeating over and over again, "Mesmo, mesmo" ("Likewise, likewise," used affirmatively), which had already gained for him the nickname of "Capitão Likewise,"—that what the white capitão had said as to the power and riches of the white men was all right and true; and that even polygamy had its disadvantages; but that, nevertheless, on account of his people he preferred remaining in the woods, and coming only occasionally to the Aldeamento to trade with his white friends. "Yes; and to pilfer this and that," was savagely whispered into my ear by the Director, who had now, for the third or fourth time, been baffled in his attempts at "civilising" the sly fellow. "Whenever he comes here," he assured me, "I have to send a few spies after him, if I don't wish him, or his worse set of women, to take away an axe, or a knife, or even a gun to his canoe, in addition to the little bag of salt I always present him with."

"What do you think the rogue did some time ago, in the Aldeamento of São Pedro d'Alcantara, on the Tibagy? He knew that one of the Cayowá Indians there, one of his own tribe, was possessed of an excellent axe, not one of those imported ones, which are useless with hard wood, but a good solid one made in our own country. To get this axe was the subject of Cuyabá's dreams both by day and by night. By a clever use of all his worldly and spiritual authority, and with an eloquence he knows how to display in the right place, in spite of his usual curtness, he contrived to make the poor fellow promise to hand over to him the coveted weapon, on the condition of the Great Spirit, moved by Cuyabá's intercession, granting him an interview for the purpose of initiating him into all the mysteries of Pajéism. After a course of preparatory ceremonies, severe fasts, and mortifications, to which the zealous neophyte submitted with patient readiness, Cuyabá informed him that the great day had arrived, on which he was to recite the prayers and magical words he had been taught, from sunrise unto sunset, on a particular spot in the forest, with strict observance of the rule of abstinence from both food and drink. He should then be certainly favoured with the presence of the mighty Spirit, who would reveal to him the most wonderful things: but he, Cuyabá, must have the hatchet before the arrival of that great moment, as urgent business (Government affairs probably) called him thence."

With the earnestness of profound faith, the honest youth took up his position on the appointed spot, from early dawn until the beams of the setting sun gilded the tree-crowns around him and the returning parrot-flocks filled the valley with their shrill cries. His prayers and supplications became louder and more ardent from hour to hour; but the Great Spirit did not reveal itself to his weary eyes. So at last he returned sadly and slowly to his cottage, there to learn that the old impostor had left the settlement with his wives and—the hatchet of course, and was now far beyond his reach; his complaints to the Director being of no avail, as the old humbug never returned to São Pedro d'Alcantara.

He had more legitimate claims, however, on the gratitude "of the best of his time and tribe" than this conjuring *à la* Cagliostro.

The Director had once witnessed his cure of a bad case of rheumatism. Singing aloud his exorcisms, and shaking the maracá* (whose

---

* The maracá is a sacred instrument, much resembling a child's rattle, used only by the Pajés and chieftains on solemn occasions. It simply consists of a gourd, with

sound is said to be especially disagreeable to the ears of the bad spirit Jurupari), Cuyabá danced round his patient, a young Indian, the while smoking a cigar of immense size and of peculiarly miraculous potency, whose smoke he blew into the sufferer's face and over his naked body. Presently he began to stroke and shampoo him from top to toe with such wild energy, that in a short time the perspiration poured in streams down his own and the patient's limbs. After he had, by a steady course of stroking from the middle to the extremities, pretended to concentrate the disease in his fingers and toes, like one of our jugglers, he pulled it out with a sudden wrench, put it into his own mouth, and swallowed it with fearful grimaces. He then declared the sick man to be cured; and, as the latter without any doubt felt some relief after all that kneading and perspiring, the Indian public at large was more than ever convinced of the efficacy of the huge cigar, the maracá, and the magical words, and of Cuyabá's power over diseases and evil spirits.

I mentioned the xerimbitá as an integral part of Cuyabá's costume. It is a cylinder of from 5 to 6 inches in length, made of the transparent yellow resin of the jatahy-tree, inserted into a thin bamboo tube. It is polished afterwards, pointed at one end, and provided with a small horizontal piece at the other, which secures it in the perforated under lip.

This barbarous ornament, though in that form and of that material we found it only with the Cayowá Indians of the province of Paraná, must not be omitted in a description of the Amazon basin some 1,200 miles further off; for on the shores of the Mamoré, on a hill called the Cerrito, near the site of the former Mission of Exaltacion, three white quartz xerimbitás of about two inches in length have been found, identical with some of the same material fished out of the Tibagy near São Pedro d'Alcantara.

On this Cerrito, an elevation well suited for a settlement, as in times of extraordinary high floods it rises like a lonely island out of the widespreading muddy waters (and which at present is inhabited by a clever and active Brazilian, Senhor Antonio de Barros Cardozo; to whom we and the leader of a former expedition, Lieutenant Gibbon, are alike

an ornamented handle, filled with pebbles, and always reminded me (I beg the pardon of all good Catholics) of the holy-water sprinkler of the Roman Church. Like that, it is indispensable for the expulsion of evil spirits.

indebted), the showers have washed out, besides the heavy stone xerimbitás,* a great many fragments of old earthen pots, ornamented in their interiors with simple undulating lines.

If we must regard the easily made resin xerimbitás as the unmistakable evidences of a particular tribe, how much more the stone ornaments, which must have taken a deal of time and trouble to finish? And the circumstance of their being found in regions so widely apart from each other confirms the hypothesis of a once wider range of the Tupi tribes, or testifies to the extent of their victorious expeditions. All the members of the tribe most probably did not wear these quartz xerimbitás, but only the chiefs and the Pajés, who to the present day pride themselves on the particular length of them. One of the Cayowá Indians of San Ignacio once told me, with evident signs of a deep-felt awe, that some holy men (santos) were living in the far interior of the forests, who were distinguished from other mortals by the unwonted size of their xerimbitás.

Might not such holy personages have used the hard quartz in past "heroic" periods; and might not these time-defying signs of their dignity still be found, in large numbers, near their places of worship, not unlike our own Druid temples?

As for the multitude of earthen fragments found on the Cerrito, evidently an old Indian settlement and burial-ground, they may have their origin in the custom of breaking the earthen pots at funerals, even as our own ancestors are said to have done in prehistoric times. Nowhere in any of the present Indian Aldeamentos, though the women there bake the pots just as they did ages ago (but where many of the rites may have fallen into disuse), did I see such a quantity of broken vessels accumulated as on that hill on the Mamoré. But the white man has long appropriated to himself the old burial-ground or sanctuary. Dense cacáo plantations cover its foot, while on the summit the juice of the sugar-cane is boiled under large open sheds, or meat is cut in thin long slices and dried in the sun. Already a small steamer ploughs the yellow river, and soon its impatient puffing and whistling will warn the

---

* One of these, kindly presented to me by Senhor Cardozo, is now in the highly interesting ethnographical collection of Mr. Blackmore, at Salisbury. May many follow the example of this Mæcenas of Art and Science, who not only collects and preserves the historic and prehistoric remains at and near Salisbury, but tries to embrace the whole history of human development!

lingerers at Cerrito that it is time to get ready, if they would catch the train in Guajará, and by that the steamer at San Antonio, and, by that again, the Transatlantic Mail at Pará!

And then, after the lapse of another age, the Red Man will have gone, and nothing will be left of his transit but—a few broken pots.

CHAPTER VII.

THE MOJOS INDIANS OF THE FORMER JESUIT MISSIONS IN BOLIVIA.

Foundation of the Missions.
—Life there.—Severe Discipline—Their actual State.
—Bloody Episode at Santa Ana.—Consequences of the political Storm.— High Festivals and Processions.
—Visit of the Excellentissimo.—The Chicha.— Vocabulary.— The Missions on the Paranapanema and Tibagy.—Final Considerations.

ON the campos or prairies of Eastern Bolivia, between the Beni, the Mamoré, the Itonama, and the Guaporé, about 30,000 real unmixed Indians, the Mojos, still exist in the former Jesuit Missions,* fifteen large regularly planned villages. Totally cut off from the outer world —on one side by the ice-covered Cordillera de los Andes; and, on the other, by pathless wastes of forest, together with scarcely explored

---

* Trinidad was founded in 1687 San José was founded in 1691
  San Ignacio   ,,   1689 San Borja   ,,   1693
  San Javier   ,,   1690 Exaltacion   ,,   1704
In the church of the latter Mission may still be seen a small crucifix, with a tiny

rivers full of rapids and cataracts—and deprived, moreover, of their leaders and teachers, they live in a state of disheartening depression and bondage little removed from absolute slavery.

When their ancestors first lent a willing ear to the sweet words of the wary priests, and, finding themselves settled in places little suited to their former modes of life, gradually gave up all their old customs, they bent before a far superior mental power, which soon discovered the patriarchal severity of sway to be the form of government best suited as well to the selfish purposes of the rulers as to the childish intellect of the Indians.

If they felt their subjection, and if their proud chiefs had to bow before the Fathers, they were recompensed by the protection extended to them by the latter; which, especially during the slave-robbing expeditions of the Paulistas, was of great service to them. The ruinous feuds between the different tribes ceased; and materially they were better off than before in many respects, the planting of maize and mandioca on a larger scale, and the breeding of the smaller domestic animals, ensuring a more regular and equal course of life than that supplied by hunting and fishing.

The early stages of the work of civilisation must have been attended with great difficulties; and it is much to be regretted, in the interest of both history and psychology, that the scanty reports we have on them are too partial to be implicitly relied upon, coming as they do from the Jesuits themselves, and from their adversaries, who triumphed after the suppression of the Order. Our chief authority, out of the ranks of the latter, is Don Feliz de Azára, a Spanish astronomer and surveyor; who, towards the end of the last and in the beginning of the present century, visited these countries, and communicated with several of the Indians, who well remembered the government of the Fathers and their expulsion in 1767.

particle of the Holy Cross carefully secured within a crystal case, with the following words referring to the foundation engraved on a silver plate at its base:—

"S. Lignum Crucis, del que se adora en el Colegio de S. Pablo de Lima, le dió el Padre Provincial, Antonio Vasquez, al Padre Juan del Campo, quien como Rector de S. Pablo lo dio á otro Padre grave y este al P. N. de O., que con bene plácito de los Superiores lo applicó a la Reduccion de los Mojos de la Exaltacion de la Cruz que funda el Padre Ant. Garriga anno 1704."

The nine other Missions, Loreto, S. Pedro, S. Ramon, S. Maria Magdalena, N. S. de la Concepcion, N. S. del Cármen, S. Joaquim, S. Ana, and Reyes, were likewise founded in the beginning of the eighteenth century.

He even goes so far as to deprive the Jesuits of all credit for the foundation of the Missions; which, as he labours to prove, had their origin in the so-called Encommiendas, plantations of Indian slaves established by private persons, civil and military officers of high rank, under the protection of the Government; and whose success and continuance were rendered possible only by the dread felt by the still independent tribes of the terrible razzias of the Paulistas. But Azára is too prejudiced altogether. Surely the cruel treatment of the Encommiendas cannot be taken as having added to the prosperity of the Missions, institutions founded by the same hated white race; and the fear of the invasions of the Paulistas could not have been very great with the Chiquitos, and the Mojos for instance, living in the far West (the present Bolivia), though elsewhere it might have counted for something.*

The secret of the complete success of the Jesuits doubtless lay in the strict organization and discipline of the Order, the zeal and unselfishness of its members, the tact with which they treated the Indians; and in the docile temper and quiet humility which down to the present day characterize the tribes they chiefly experimented on, the Guaranis and the Mojos. Some attempts at reducing to submission other tribes, like the warlike Coroados between the Paraná and upper Uruguay, were quite unsuccessful; and in one case ended with the death of the daring missionary.

According to the notes of Azára, and of the Jesuits Dobrizhoffer and Charlevoix, the way in which these Missions (or Reducciones, as they were then called) were administered was as follows. On each of them were two priests; one apparently to attend exclusively to spiritual affairs, but in reality directing the whole concern, and the other to look after worldly matters, the administration in all its details. All the Missions within a certain district were under the superintendence of a superior, who resided at one of the principal ones—for the Paraguay Missions, it was Candelaria; for those of the Beni, S. Pedro—and formed the medium of communication between those outposts and the General of the Order in Europe.

The preliminary measures for the foundation of a new Mission are thus described by Azára. First of all, some Indians belonging to an

* Once only, in 1691, the Paulistas came as far as Chiquitos; but they were driven back, and have ever since left the Missions there in peace.

established Reduccion were sent with presents to the tribe to be "reduced," and the decoy birds were instructed to tell their wild brothers that a noble white man in the neighbourhood, who loved them dearly, greatly desired to come and live with them; that he would bring them gifts even more valuable than those presented; that they then would always have plenty of cattle, iron utensils, and wearing apparel; and that he would build houses for them, cure their sick, and altogether be of the greatest service to the whole tribe. The messengers, of course, were chosen from the best-looking and most intelligent of the Indians of the nearest Mission; their contentedness was in itself a strong inducement; and the promises of the white man usually sounded so prettily in the ears of the hearers, that they willingly consented to the visit of the Great Unknown who, naturally losing no time, made his triumphal entry in the malocca, accompanied by a considerable number of his former pupils, carrying presents, and driving a small herd of cattle before them.

In a highly elevated state of mind, generated amid festive dances and revels, the materials for which the Padre supplied with unsparing hand, the new village is planned, streets are measured out, a chapel and solid houses of pisé are built (of course, by the Indians of the older Mission, whom I can fancy laughing quietly in their sleeves), in place of the light open sheds; and, above everything, the surrounding country is planted with mandioca, corn, and cotton. The magnificent climate ripens the crops; new herds are brought over from the old Mission; and, when the season of harvest arrives, the delighted savage finds himself in the possession of an unwonted abundance, and in a short time gets so used to the new order of things that he does not think of returning to his old habits. Without much trouble, he now has plenty of everything; whereas formerly, especially in the rainy season, when the swollen rivers spread their thick floods far and wide over the plains, and the fishes, finding worms and insects to their heart's content, despised his baits—more than once hunger had stared him in the face, in spite of his exertions. The ague, which long had tormented him, has vanished before the powerful bitter medicine of the white man; the ugly wound, which had defied even the conjuring of his mighty Pajé, has closed with the balm supplied by the holy man. In short, the son of the forest has never before felt so rich and so happy.*

* Referring to the hearty appetite of the Indians and the course pursued by the

Then there is another element not to be overlooked. The female sex could not but profit by the diffusion of gentler customs, just as in the time of our own heathen forefathers, when St. Boniface and other pious sons of Erin's green isle first preached the Gospel on the Rhine and Fulda; and the squaws, having the satisfaction of learning from the Indians of the Missions that there the lords of the creation had to be content with one wife only, and moreover that, like themselves, they had to work in the fields, doubtless were the first to be won over to the new doctrine; and there, as in our own country, and then, as in our own time, became the most powerful auxiliaries of the white men in black gowns. Anyhow, we get nearer to the arrival of the period of decision, which will show us whether the love of freedom or the honeyed words of the Father will prevail; and some fine morning he calls together all his children, and, in well-known accents,* delivers the following speech, or one conducting to the same conclusion:—"Beloved ones, you see that it is quite a comfortable life you lead under my fatherly guidance. I hope you will now altogether give up your old life in the woods; only, as it is quite impossible, you know, that your brethren should go on working for you as they have hitherto done, you must yourselves lend a helping hand in the fields and with the herds; and, in short, you must do all I tell you."

Even if some of the elder Indians sulkily took up their bows, and turned their backs on the orator and his nearly complete Mission, the greater part of the tribe thought of the fleshpots of Egypt, and—remained.

Then a proud staff of overseers and assistants was named from among the Indians themselves, very likely, at first, from those of the

---

Jesuits, Dobrizhoffer says: "If, after the saying of St. Paul, faith enters by the ears with other heathens, it certainly enters by the mouth with the savages of the Paraguay."

* Already in the sixteenth century the Jesuits, Joseph de Anchieta and Manoel da Vega, had written vocabularies of the Tupi language, the Lingoa Geral Brazilica; and in 1639 followed several Guarani vocabularies by Montoya. They were intended to help the missionaries in their task, and also to render that comparatively rich idiom the general one, a sort of "lingua franca," in all South America. However, the Padres also took the trouble of learning less-spread idioms, when they thought it necessary for their success. One of our Mojos from Trinidad had a little book of well-written prayers in his own language, which is quite different from the Tupi. The original dates from the Jesuits, and the copies taken by the Indians themselves, as the proprietor proudly assured me, descend from generation to generation. In the Reducciones on the Beni, the missionaries had to learn, in this way, no less than seven languages.

next Mission; the Correjidor and the Alcaldes carrying silver-headed sticks as emblems of their exalted rank, and visiting the Director every day to receive his orders; the Major-domo de Collegio, who, as chief master of the household, had to look after the provisions of the community, and to distribute the weekly rations; then the masters of the different trades—the Capitano de los Carpinteros, the master of the carpenters; the Capitano de los Herreros, the master of the smiths; the Capitano de los Tejederos, the master of the weavers; the Capitano de los Rosarios (instead of Torneros), the master of the turners, so called because he had to make the rosaries worn by every one,* and was attached to the service of the church; the Capitano de la Capella, the Capitano de la Plata, and the Capitano de la Cera, the masters of the chapel, of the plate, and of the wax. Besides, there were the Fiscales, to look after the works in the fields; and the Cruzeros, a sort of sanitary police, recognisable by black crosses on their white camisetas, who had to take care of the sick, and to register the births and deaths.

The pomp of sacerdotal sway, which to the present day profoundly impresses the childish mind of all these nations, certainly contributed greatly to make them forget the loss of that golden liberty which the next generation never even knew; and the Fathers took special care to allot to the whole population as large and as active a share in its display as was possible, be it in the shape of the execution of sacred music or of processions, or of symbolic dances.

The churches, now half in ruins and bereft of the best part of their ornaments, in the time of their splendour must have surpassed everything till then seen in South America, in respect of magnificence at least, if not in artistic beauty; and as for the processions, Charlevoix relates wonderful things about them. Especially on Corpus Christi day, not only was there the display of a profusion of the richest carpets, banners, and standards, but even the luxuriant tropical vegetation was brought under contribution for the embellishment of the "Via Triumphalis;" and no activity of the teeming fancy of the artist is equal to utilising all the treasures *that* offers. How poor seems our Northern vegetation in that respect! Firs and birches are about the only things we use on such occasions; whereas with the palms, ferns, orchids, aroideæ

* Our paddlers, each of whom had two or three rosaries with them, cut very pretty beads of the Palo Maria with their long knives, and perforated them with three-edged needles; evidently reminiscences of their old industry.

and creepers of those forests, one might decorate doorways " fit to be the gates of Paradise."

Under high arches covered with palm-leaves and magnificent fruits and flowers, brilliantly coloured parrots and macaws, toucans, snow-white herons, and demure-looking falcons were chained up. Even the yellow puma, and the black and the spotted jaguar, were exposed in cages; and the scaly inhabitants of the neighbouring rivers were to be seen living in large basins. The procession itself—with its long train of musicians, and fantastically-clad sword-dancers wearing aureolas of long arara feathers, and carrying gold-embroidered canopies, banners, silver crosses, &c., and followed by the whole male population, armed partly with guns and partly with bows and arrows—must, indeed, have presented an imposing spectacle, even to minds less impressionable than those of the Mojos.

Other shows, which gratified their taste for the pomp of solemn sights, and at the same time served to keep up their required military exercises, were the sham fights, which were held once a week on the square before the church and the collegio; and in which the whole population, capable of bearing arms, had to take part. Horse and foot then engaged each other under the command of richly accoutred leaders, the whole being directed by the Correjidor as commander-in-chief; and the combatants are said sometimes to have warmed up to such a degree that it has been judged necessary to separate them by force.

These exercises—continued with even more zeal when the Spanish Government had, on Montoya's request after the invasion of the Paulistas, provided the Indians with fire-arms—enabled the Jesuits not only to send the latter back with bloody heads, but also frequently to assist the Spanish Government in the wars after the separation of Portugal from Spain; when, in Uruguay especially, there were hot fights about the so-called Colonia. This severity of discipline and of military regularity did not apply only to their exercises. Their whole life was punctually regulated in the Reducciones; and to each hour was allotted its particular function,* which was rigidly maintained. At dawn of day, a bell called the Indians to prayer; and, after the whole population had assembled on the large square, the musicians playing the

* Usque eo illic omnes res, vel maxime privatæ, ad certam quandam normam et constantem directæ erant, ut secundum morem in Boliviâ traditum conjuges Indiani mediâ nocte sono tintinnabuli ad exercendum coitum excitarentur.

while, those destined to field-work betook themselves to the scenes of their activity, under the guidance of their overseers, and carrying the image of a saint with them, while the artisans went to their shops with their capitanos or masters. To every one was appointed his daily task; and, with the perfect drilling and schooling they had undergone, we cannot suppose that it was often necessary to apply compulsion.

Yet compulsion was applied sometimes; and the whole scheme of education was so arranged as to emphasize the necessity of submitting to law, and to chastisement as the atonement inevitably due to the commission of an offence. On this head there still survives a tradition in the Missions, according to which one of the Padres themselves (probably one of the younger ones) had to submit to the discipline of a severe punishment, it may be for some imaginary crime. The course of reflection designed to be impressed upon the astonished Indians evidently was this: If this can happen with the green wood—the clever, reasonable white man, communing directly with the Divinity: how, in the like case, can the dry wood murmur and rebel—the poor sinful Indian?

Dark stories also are afloat of rebellious chieftains imprisoned for life, who, in their enforced leisure, pondered over their fruitless endeavours to cross the plans of the Society of Jesus.

And what were these plans?

Had they really the intention of founding an independent realm of Guaranis? Was it to be a refuge for them in the event of some storm sweeping them out of Europe? They have been charged with designedly excluding the Spanish language from the Missions (which is the more striking, as with that exception they devoted tolerable attention to the efficiency of their schooling), with the view of securing to themselves the monopoly of direction; and by this prudent measure, indeed, they rendered any instigation of the Indians by their enemies exceedingly difficult, if not altogether impossible. However, though they were well able to resist the royal decree of their expulsion, and to detach themselves and their domains from a State incapable of opposing them energetically (as did their mental cousin, the memorable Francia, in Paraguay.), they delivered up their Reducciones (which in Rio Grande do Sul, Corrientes, and Paraguay alone, are said to have numbered 100,000 souls) to the Commissary, who was attended only by a few horsemen and a couple of Franciscan monks, with a calmness and philosophy the grandeur of which we might admire, but for the suspicion which intrudes itself that the Fathers regarded the whole as only a passing storm, and were unwilling to incur the odium of rebels for nothing.

Or did they look upon their South American Missions as a milch-cow, which would give them the means of carrying out their ambitious plans in Europe?

At any rate, the speculation in the immense natural treasures of these countries was not a bad one. If, even at that early period of development, the opening trade in hides, cotton, Paraguay tea in the South, and cacáo in the North, proved to be the source of so much wealth that the churches of the Missions abounded in plate, richly-ornamented sacred vessels, and chasubles, the remains of which are still treasured up and jealously guarded by the Mojos on the Beni as heritages of the good old times, what might not have been the condition of these unparalleled colonies, after the lapse of half a century?

The trade in Paraguay tea, which is so indispensable to high and low on the River Plate, would alone have yielded an immense revenue, as it nowhere thrives so well as it does there, not to speak of the cattle and, in the Northern provinces, the sugar-cane, coffee, cacáo, &c.

The Missions would have become the grandest and the best-administered agricultural institutions the world had ever seen, for there can be no doubt that the Jesuits would have succeeded in bringing them down to our own time in almost unchanged condition; only a ceaseless stream of immigrants, a far-extending net of roads and railways, and a general activity of trade (such as has been observed to spring up within the last ten years), might have interfered with the continuance of the patriarchal system: but, in any case, it would have taken some time to abolish it entirely.

After all we have seen, the condition of the Indians during the prosperity of the Missions differed from real slavery only in the particular that they were not exposed for sale; and it almost sounds ridiculous when Jesuit authors like Charlevoix speak of Christian republics, in allusion to the institutions of early Christianity. The Indians certainly were held on about the same low level as slaves. There was no private property in the community, save their trifling household goods; the soil was cultivated jointly; and they were strictly prohibited from selling to strangers the produce of their industry during their hours of leisure. The community of goods, therefore, existed only in favour of their masters; into whose pockets all the profits of the common work went, and who gave to their subordinates only such share as they pleased or thought absolutely necessary.

Whether such treatment was at all Christianlike, or not, the famous disciples of Loyola must have been the best judges themselves: but Republican it surely was not; and our Socialist theorists, not to speak of the firebrand-wielding disciples of the same school, will hardly assent to this interpretation of their principles. On a review of all the circumstances, we cannot look upon the Missions in the same rosy, ideal light as Jesuit authors did; yet, when we observe the state of degeneracy and misery in which the descendants of those Indians (who in the narrowness of their views certainly felt themselves happy) exist, within a century of the great change in their affairs, it strikes us that the seeming advantage of the greater liberty they now enjoy has been too dearly purchased. If the Jesuits did take advantage of them, it was after a cleverly-conceived system, calculated to bear fruit for a long season. Their existence, at least, was ensured to them; whereas now they are cleaned out, ruined physically and morally, after no system at all, by hundreds of pitiless adventurers, who have no concern whatever for their future welfare.

While under the rule of the Fathers, they were, it must be owned, in a condition of tutelage not exactly favourable to their future development; but the time of emancipation would have arrived to them also, perhaps under better auspices than the present; for let us hope that the sun of real civilisation will some day shine upon unfortunate Bolivia, continually disturbed with internal storms, and that her latent treasures will yet emerge to the light.

In the present state of things, the Indians are entirely in the hands of a horde of lawless adventurers, intent upon their own gains; from the vain but crafty Bolivian, and the fugitive defaulter from Rio de Janeiro, to the ignorant Polish pedlar, and the dirty Neapolitan tinker. Under pretext of trading, these cheat and defraud the artless red-skins in the most shameful way. And withal it seems as if these people had all sworn to do as much injury as they could to the morals of these children of Nature. The vigarios (the priests of the Pueblos) especially do their utmost to undo the work of their predecessors. To them neither the silver vessels,* nor the wives nor the daughters of their parishioners are sacred;† and, with the innate frivolity and sensuality of the natives, such examples of depravity must exercise the saddest influence on their habits.

These introductory remarks will serve to continue my reference in Chapter II. to the present state of the late Missions, now called Pueblos, that is, villages. They are under the superintendence of Correjidors, officials appointed by the Government and sent over from La Paz, Cochabamba, or Santa Cruz. But, as the Departamento del Beni, in which these Pueblos are, is regarded as a sort of exile, and as there usually are few aspirants to the office, the Government, having small choice, frequently entrusts the post to totally unfit hands.

As in most of the South American republics, the endless political disorders, which are caused by personal interests, and not by the conflict of political feeling, must also have contributed to make the remote Departamento a sort of forlorn outpost, undeserving of any, even the least, sacrifice. Had even competent Government officials taken greater interest in it, and been inspired with the desire to do something towards its progress, the short interval between the pulling down of one President and the fall of his successor, the excitement produced by these always more or less bloody dramas, and the subsequent changes in the offices, have not admitted of the execution of any wide improvements. If, for example, the importance of a regular line of communication between the Mamoré and the Amazon had not been impressed from without, Bolivia never would have done anything for it; and for ages to come the few imported European goods would

---

* In a conversation I had at Trinidad with the Superintendent of Police, respecting the treasures still existing in the Pueblos, he dwelt upon the enormity of the vigarios, over whom he had no authority whatever, who secreted one after another of the vessels, had them melted down, and then sold the silver. Besides, added he, with a characteristic movement of the hand, as though he were crushing some basin, they sometimes so disfigure the delicately-ornamented and carved vessels that they impudently use them at their own tables.

† Sexuum inter se consuetudo cum apud nullam Indianorum gentium Austro-Americanarum magna cum severitate exerceatur, tum apud Mojos Boliviæ verecundia imprimis laxata est. Maritus si post sex vel octo mensium absentiam domum rediit, dummodo ei uxor novam "Camisetam" novumque lectum suspensum texuerit, miti animo audit mulierem cum hoc vel illo rem habuisse se narrantem, ac tum demum indignabitur, si forte corpus miscuerit cum aliquo ex Albis.

Quæ cum ita sint, syphiliticos morbos atrocem in modum ingravescere, facile intelligitur; atque ii vel præcipue in causa sunt intermorientium paulatim aut marcescentium eorum, qui Alborum consuetudine utuntur, Indianorum.

have continued to be carried over the desolate paths of the Cordillera, while the rich products of the country would have been left to decay and ruin, like its poor brown population.

Only twice, in a space of more than forty years, did the Government at La Paz deign to remember its subjects on the Mamoré; and on both occasions they designed only the robbery of the Missions. In 1830, or thereabouts, the Indians of the Pueblo de Santa Ana rebelled against their Correjidor, whose brawling son had killed their chieftain in a scuffle. The criminal escaped, and in his place the incensed Mojos murdered the father, whose house they burned down at the same time: but their vengeance soon cooled; they quietly laid down bows and arrows, and returned to their wonted occupations.

Nothing could have been easier than to find out the ringleaders, to bring them to trial, and to have them severely punished. The Government of the Republic, however, had other intentions than to make an example of them. They had long waited at La Paz for an opportunity of getting hold of the silver treasure of the Pueblos; and now it had come at last. Some hundreds of soldiers were despatched to the Departamento, charged to seize half of the plate of all the fifteen Pueblos, the remotest of which, perhaps, had not even heard of the committed crime, and to bring it as satisfaction to La Paz. As the want of sympathy between the seven different tribes of the Missions, which might have been insidiously encouraged by the Jesuits, put the idea of an organized resistance out of the question, the pilfering soldiery went from Pueblo to Pueblo, and had but to pack up the sacred vessels and to load their beasts of burden with them. How much was carried off in this way cannot now be exactly ascertained; but it may be presumed that it was not less than the prescribed half; and at the present day there are, in the fifteen Missions together, nearly 100 arrobas, that is 3,000 pounds, of silver.*

But when President Melgarejo†—a brutal man, a murderer, and a

---

* The church in the Mission of S. Pedro alone had 2,000 lb. of silver in the time of the Jesuits.

† Nothing bears witness more strikingly to the sad political condition of the country than the number of its Presidents since the Declaration of Independence, or, perhaps, the way in which most of them retired from the scene of politics and—life. They were:

    1. The Libertador, Simon Bolívar, born in Carácas 1784, died 1830.
    2. Marshal José Ant. de Sucre, born at Cumaná 1793, murdered 1830.

drunkard, who by pitiless oppression of the financially ruined country secured the means for his life guards—also conceived the idea of robbing the churches in the Pueblos on the Mamoré and the Itonama for a second time, and of making clean work of it once for all, the Indians of Trinidad rose as one man, and obliged the lieutenant and his little troop, who had been sent thither for a start under an evidently erroneous conception of things, to beat a hasty retreat without fulfilling their mission.

Save these sporadic and, as will be allowed, not very profitable interventions on the part of the Supreme Government, the Indians, who do not meddle with the regularly recurring political revolutions, are completely abandoned to their own indolence and to the mercy of the traders I have already named, upon payment of the annual tax of 4 pesos, about 20 francs, per head.

In illustration of the reckless indifference with which the amplest sources of wealth, that might powerfully contribute to the country's future prosperity, are left to ruin, let me give the following narrative: On the campos near the Missions there were innumerable herds of half-wild cattle, the descendants of those bred in the time of the Jesuits, and under their iron government so jealously guarded that the Indians never dared take more of them than the Padres graciously permitted.* It was a stock which, though sprung from small beginnings, had in the course of two hundred years increased to an immense total; judicious

    3. General D. Pedro Blanco, murdered 1838.
    4. General D. Andres Santa Cruz.
    5. General D. José Miguel de Velasco, died 1860.
    6. General José Ballivian, poisoned at Rio de Janeiro 1851.
    7. General Manoel Isidoro Belzu.
    8. General George Córdova, murdered 1861.
    9. Dr. D. José Maria Linares, died at Valparaiso 1861.
    10. General José Maria Achá.
    11. General Mariano Melgarejo, murdered 1872.
    12. Dr. A. Morales, assassinated 1873.
    13. Lieutenant-Colonel Adolfo Ballivian, elected 15th May, 1873.

Only two of these formally surrendered their supreme office to their successors. Some were murdered immediately after their fall; others on their flight, after it; some of them even on neutral territory.

* According to a tradition still current in the Pueblos, the Jesuits, in order to utterly spoil the Indians' appetite for beef, and to give their newly-imported herds time to increase, tried to make them believe that the meat of the horned monsters which had come from such a distance was injurious to the red man; and it is added that, by way of emphasising the statement, they were careful to let them have some poisoned pieces. Who is not reminded by this of the well-known Jesuitical principle?

management of which would have continued to yield increased results. But "el Supremo Gobierno" at La Paz—adopting *Après nous le déluge* for its motto—apparently prefers immediate profit to all the bright visions of the future, and has for twenty-five years past allowed a set of adventurers, coming mostly from Santa Cruz de la Sierra, to carry on a war of destruction against these cattle. The payment of a tax of one peso per head purchased the right of any one to kill as many as he liked or could catch; and, if he understood his business, and hit on the right way of addressing the controlling Correjidor, he paid, let us say, 300 dollars for 3,000 head of cattle.

But as this mode of destruction was perhaps found to be rather a slow one, twelve years ago a well-organized company purchased, for the round sum of 5,000 dollars, the monopoly of slaughter on a large scale, for a period of ten years, on the campos of the Beni and the Mamoré; and it must be confessed that the utmost was then done, even for South America, in the way of beastly brutality and thoughtless waste.

In these cases, generally, only the hides and tallow were made use of, the meat being left as worthless to the vultures. To be sure, neither the hands nor the appliances for cutting, salting, and drying—such as may be found in the great saladeiros of the Argentine Republic, Uruguay and Rio Grande do Sul *—could be easily found in Bolivia, and the preparation of Liebig's extract of meat, in the absence of machinery, has been, of course, quite out of the question.

This summary mode of doing business, though it may be sometimes justifiable, will always be opposed to European sentiment, especially when disclosure is made of the disgusting particulars. The abovementioned company, for instance, caused to be erected † strong fences, extending widely over the campos, and narrowing gradually towards the end. Into this waterless "corral" the flying herds were driven by mounted Indians, and the poor animals, distressed with fear and thirst, died in such numbers that, under the glowing tropical sun, the greater portion of the hides and fat was spoilt long before the hides could be

* In some saladeiros, or charqueadas (that is, factories of charque, or carne secca, *dried meat*), from 800 to 1,000 oxen are slaughtered daily, and their meat cut with a dexterity that surpasses belief.

† The palings of these fences are bound with strips of untanned hide, which is used in these countries for the most different purposes. Laços (slings) are made of it; beds and chairs are covered with it; and the cat-o'-nine-tails (the guasca) is a bundle of slightly-twisted strips of it.

taken off. But, where one of these abominable chases proved ruinous rather than profitable, others, effected with more circumspection, proved successful; and many thousands of the valuable and easily-transported hides, when sold, brought such a plenty to the country, that a perfect Fools' Paradise ensued.

The caballero, who galloped proudly along in his red-striped poncho, with the large sombrero on his black hair, and silver spurs to his tall deer-skin boots, but showing none of the grand qualities of his Spanish ancestry save unbounded vanity and dandyism, then lost and won immense sums, and hundreds of hides, at dice. These he always carried with him on his rides over the campos; and, at a moment's notice, the saddle-cloth was spread on the ground, and the blind goddess was tempted. In the Pueblos the lazy Indians burnt tallow instead of fuel, and yet there remained such vast herds of cattle that a fat cow did not cost above two dollars. So the Government, always embarrassed for money, and thinking this source of wealth to be inexhaustible, had the effrontery to pay their officials in the Pueblos on the Mamoré (the correjidores, vigarios, and schoolmasters) with bonds for so many head of wild cattle, leaving it to their own judgment whether they caught them themselves, or sold their bonds at a considerable abatement to the professional slaughterers.

Hundreds and hundreds of fat, easily-domesticated animals could be had in this way for little more than the trouble of capturing them; but unfortunately the example of our old friend, Antonio Cardozo, who acquired such herds and made them the stock of an estancia near Exaltacion, has not as yet found many followers among the Bolivians; and this is the more to be regretted as the consequences of such an inconsiderate policy soon began to show themselves. The herds were gradually reduced until their last remains have retired, under the guidance of proud bulls,* to remote corners of the campos, where, by reason of the wild Indians, they will be

* The Bolivians say that the strongest of the young bulls, after bloody fights with his competitors, forms a new herd, at the head of two or three dozens of cows, while the weaker bulls also unite in troops of some dozens. It is a strange fact that the hide of these wild bulls is far superior to that of the tame, in respect of toughness and durability, and therefore is always much valued, especially for the lasso-making. Every year a great number of Gauchos come over from the Argentine Republic, from Salta and Tucuman, to buy these hides for making the indestructible nooses so indispensable to them for the seizure of the half-wild horses, mules, &c., on their pampas. As the so-called tame cattle of Bolivia, as well as of the Argentine Republic, are as little stabled as the wild bulls on the Mamoré and the Beni, the difference in the toughness of the hides can arise only from the tame bulls being coupled with a far greater number of cows than the wild ones.

left in peace for some time to come; and thus has a country, particularly adapted for cattle breeding by its immense natural prairies, excellent climate and sparse population, been most brutally deprived of one source of future national wealth and prosperity.

With the wild cattle have also vanished the stags, the deer, and the troops of long-necked emus,* which once lived on the campos in the immediate vicinity of the Pueblos. All have been sacrificed to the wild greed of the white man, and the thoughtlessness of the Indians; durable profit being postponed to the advantage of the moment. One thing only, strange to say, survives amid all these sad changes—the practice of the Government in Sucre and La Paz of paying the officials in the Pueblos by bonds on wild cows; these gentlemen evidently shutting their eyes resolutely to the reductions they have already effected; and I should not at all wonder if, on occasion of some future loan, European capitalists were offered the wild herds on the campos as supplementary securities to the treasures to be dug out of the silver and copper mines in the mountains, and to the taxes and tolls to be levied on roads and railroads yet to be built.†

At present it is impossible even to calculate the extent of the damage that has been done; but it is quite certain that the Indians of the Missions, who till now were well fed, are already so far degraded as to seek greedily for earth-worms, which they dry on cords before their cottages for their own consumption, and that they have begun to decrease in an accelerated ratio; which is surely effected, among other causes, by physical want.

While, on the one side, the wild cattle are destroyed with a zeal worthy of a better cause, on the other, no pains whatever are taken to turn the rich vegetable treasures of the country to account. Not the least effort is made to extend and improve the culture of the cacáo, sugar-

---

* The American ostrich, Ema or Emú, also called N'handú, by the Mojos Pi-yu (*Rhea Americana*), is still frequently found on the remoter campos of the province of Minas. Its eggs are about two-thirds the size of African ostrich-eggs.

† Since writing the above, I have seen the Concession of the Bolivian Government, authorising Colonel G. E. Church to run steamers on all the rivers of the Republic belonging to the Madeira basin; and, sure enough, in it was an article (No. 3) which ran as follows:—The Bolivian Government concedes to the Steam Navigation Company the right of appropriating fuel and timber wherever it is not on private property, and of taking 8,000 head of cattle from the herds owned by the State in the Departamento del Beni (*sic*), on condition, however, that this be done in the way most advantageous to both the State and the Company.

cane, tobacco and cotton, or to make use of the magnificent dye-woods, timbers, and resins wherewith prodigal Nature has so lavishly endowed it. As little is done for industry, to wit, in the development of the extraordinary skill exhibited by the Indians in plaitings and weavings of all kinds, and which, if assisted somewhat by European culture, would justify the best hopes for the future. On the contrary, everything is done to dishearten them thoroughly in this respect. They are required to sell at the lowest prices the varied produce of their industry; solid palm-straw hats (the so-called Panamá hats), tastefully ornamented mats made of brilliantly-dyed rushes, and cotton weavings (macánas), which far excel European goods in quality of texture and harmony of colour, and which, moreover, are in great demand and fetch high prices in the towns, Cochabamba, Sucre, and La Paz;[*] and again, they are forced to buy, at six times their fair value, our gaudy cottons, printed with glaring aniline colours, which the fair sex vastly prefer to the spotless white, or to the subdued colours of their own manufactures.

No wonder, then, that a kind of lethargy creeps over the Indians, thus abused, and that with their good humour their skill at the work also gradually wears away. Indeed, experienced Bolivians have assured me that, of late, it was easy to observe not only a reduction in the quantity, but even a deterioration in the quality of their macánas.

The chieftains, of whom there is one in every Pueblo, usually negotiate in the more important matters; they hire the paddlers for your voyage to the Amazon, for instance, and are entrusted with the money paid in advance; but even they, as well as their inferiors, are exposed to frauds perpetrated by white men; and they have so often fallen victims to their own credulity that little may now be expected from their intervention. Only recently two of the richest of them, the one at Exaltacion, and the good old chieftain of Trinidad, had been swindled by unscrupulous rascals out of their whole fortune,—house and home, cattle and plate. The former, who to his misfortune took to dressing after the European fashion, was persuaded by an

---

[*] In the Brazilian province of Minas Geraes similar fabrics are produced by the wives and daughters, and sometimes the female slaves of the poorer planters, or cattle breeders. As these were always on a small scale, and therefore in larger demand than the supply, some merchants of Rio de Janeiro had them imitated in England, and imported great quantities of cotton stuffs exactly resembling them in colour, but of very different quality. The consequence was that all these fabrics fell into discredit, from which the modest Brazilian industry was not exempt.

itinerant Neapolitan jeweller that a man in his position should never wear less than two gold watches, with heavy chains. The poor fellow, accordingly, bought two third-rate Geneva watches, and other useless baubles, at stupendous prices;* and he was thereupon so pestered and dunned by his creditor that, in despair of otherwise satisfying him, he sold off his house and his herds, and all he possessed; and he now lives, a ruined man, in as poor and wretched a condition as the meanest in the Pueblo.

Besides the correjidor and the vigario, whose offices are not always filled, as at Exaltacion while we were there, the Government pays—it is startling to record the fact—a schoolmaster in every Pueblo; and, poor as the teaching may be, yet one occasionally finds an Indian able not only to speak but also to read and write Spanish. Among our eighty paddlers there were two who could read Portuguese almost fluently, and who accepted with the greatest pleasure some "books for the young" I had with me. Now, as the whole library at the disposal of the Indians in the Pueblos consists of a few written prayers, which have descended from father to son, from the time of the Holy Fathers, we may conclude that, with proper help, they would become tolerably good scholars.

From the same period date also the scores for the Missas Cantadas, fine old Sacred Music, and the musical instruments, violins, violoncellos,

---

* These pedlars, or mascates (a word sprung probably from the intercourse between Goa, which is still under Portuguese rule, and Southern Arabia), with their worthless gewgaws, are absolute plagues and nuisances in Brazil. Their peculiar style of doing business is illustrated by the following authentic narrative of what happened some years ago in the province of Minas, at a fazenda on the Rio Preto, an affluent of the Parahybuna. Attended by his servant and his mules, a mascate arrived there one day, who might have founded his proposed attack on the experience he had acquired in previous visits. After selling a few trinkets, he remained, as usual, to dine with the family, to whom he was careful to signify his intention to start on the morrow. In the course of conversation with the gentleman respecting politics and the price of coffee, and with the ladies touching the latest Paris fashions, he suddenly stopped short, and took out his watch, which he kissed respectfully before opening it, and which, having kissed it again, he returned to his pocket. The Brazilian had noticed the manœuvre with amazement; but only after some time did he venture to ask about it. The mascate, who at first feigned some embarrassment and hesitation, finally told him that this watch, an invaluable family inheritance, and a matchless talisman, contained a likeness of "Nossa Senhora," which protected the wearer against disease, poverty, and misfortune of every kind, and that it had saved him already on a hundred occasions. Again reverently saluting the precious jewel with his lips, he showed to the fazendeiro, who had been listening with distended optics, a picture of the Virgin painted on the inside of the lid (which he gave it as his own judgment was probably executed by no less an artist than St. Luke), then re-kissed it, and carefully stowed flutes, harps, and their remarkable bajónes, a sort of trombones in the shape of huge Pan's pipes, made of palm-leaves skilfully pasted together. All these are preserved in the churches; and the Indians themselves take special care to keep up their practice on them, and their familiarity in reading the notes. A high mass at which I assisted in Trinidad was executed with a precision and correctness that did not show the least trace of decline, and reflected credit on the musical capacity of the red race. Altogether, that Sunday morning I spent in the old church of Trinidad is one of the memories I most like to dwell upon of all the voyage.

At early morn I left the house of my kind host, and walked leisurely through the lonely streets of the Pueblo to the square in which the church is situated. The rising sun was gilding the clay walls of the edifice, which, though devoid of all architectural beauty, yet contrasted effectively with the low mud-houses in its vicinity; sparkling dewdrops clothed the grass and flowers; and a refreshing cool wind swept in from the campos. Again I contemplated the naïvely-conceived frescoes on its front of St. Francisco and of St. Luiz de Gonzaga (albeit they were not executed by artists great in colours and lines), and the masterpiece of the tympanum, the mystic device representing the Holy Trinity. In a Mission singularly consecrated to this mystery, such an explanation, if we may be permitted so to call it, was rendered all the

it away. Yielding to the ardent entreaties of the fascinated fool, he consented, reluctantly, to entrust the watch to his keeping for a few hours; all his anxious proposals to purchase it being repelled with indignant resentment, which only served to inflame the planter's eagerness to possess the sacred treasure to such a degree that he continued to offer higher, and still higher, terms for it. This was exactly what the rogue wanted. After his repeated protestations that he never could be so degraded as to part, for dirty money, with his most sacred property, he at length consented to sell, or rather to exchange (*trocar*, to exchange, is the respectful Brazilian word for sale or purchase of sacred objects) his talisman for the trifling sum of £250, vowing again and again that nothing but the claims of an old friend reconciled him to the sacrifice. As soon as the bargain was concluded, our mascate, pleading urgent business, mounted his best horse, and, like a prudent man, took to his heels, followed by his servant and mules. And well he might hasten away! Hardly had he departed when there came friends and neighbours of the poor victim of superstition, who soon opened his eyes to the cheat that had been practised upon him; and their sneers and laughter roused his fury to such a pitch that, putting himself at the head of his negroes, he galloped off in pursuit of the impostor; but in vain. He had to do with an old fox, who did not intend to wait until he felt the point of a long Minas knife between his ribs. What has become of the effigy of "Nossa Senhora," by the hand of St. Luke, I cannot tell. At any rate, it was a *dear* family piece, and may perhaps avail as a talisman against future follies.

MISA CANTADA IN THE ANCIENT MISSION OF TRINIDAD (MAMORÉ).

more necessary by the fact that the red neophytes more than once perplexed the Fathers with unanswerable questions.

While I stood under the portico of the old building, philosophising and speculating upon the term of active vitality yet reserved for the operations of the spirit of the age in which the rude imagery was executed, by hands that have long rotted away below either the green grass of the campos or the dark vaults of the church, I was joined by two Indians, who emerged from one of the straight, long streets. They

THE MYSTERY OF THE TRINITY EXPLAINED BY A JESUIT ARTIST.

were the sextons; and almost immediately the bells of the campanile summoned the villagers to prayers. As in Brazil, they are not rung in our way; but several well-tuned ones are hammered on at the same time after a peculiar, usually very quick, rhythm. It does not sound very solemn; but the lively melody of the peals harmonises well with the blue sky, the bright sun, and the gaudily dressed congregation, which goes to church rather for diversion and for society than for devotion.

It is far otherwise, however, in the old Missions on the Mamoré, where both men and women approached silently and seriously; the former, without exception, clad in the classical camiseta of home manufacture; the latter already luxuriating in chemises of the gaudy, large-flowered cottons of Europe, with their long black hair flowing loose over the shoulders, sometimes down to the knees. Even the children, most of them lovely little creatures, walked as demurely as their elders, with rosaries in their chubby brown hands. For this auditory at least, church and divine service had retained all the glory and holiness wherewith the Jesuits of old had surrounded them.

From the music-gallery, facing the altar, I could easily watch the filling of the wide hall below, wrapped at first in a mystic twilight. In the first row, close to the choir, squatted the women on mats; after saying a short prayer on their knees; and behind them were the men. The few white faces, the secretary of the Prefect and two or three merchants, were completely lost in the crowd of Indians; and I almost fancied I was hearing mass in the time of Montoya or of one of his successors. In this gallery, which showed two small organs in richly-carved cases with painted panels, presently assembled the musicians, with their fiddles, harps, and bajónes, under the leadership of the master of the chapel, a venerable-looking old Indian, with large spectacles adjusted by a cord, with little round pieces of lead, passing over the crown of his head; and the singers with a small red flag had taken their post close to the solid wooden balustrade, to help the choir below in case of need. The priest now appeared before the altar, and the solemn tones of a fine old mass swept through the spacious aisle. It was the festival of some saint; and the altar exhibited its richest silver adornments, while slender palms, waving their graceful boughs from the pillars of the aisle and from the music tribune, added the charm of tropical vegetation to the fairylike picture.

An incident, partly comical and partly pathetic, served to intensify my elated frame of mind. While I leaned over the balustrade in the effort to seize as much as possible of the lovely spectacle, an elderly Indian with a brave little boy had knelt down beside me. The old man had looked neither to the right nor to the left, and the beads of his rosary glided swiftly through his fingers; but the child soon began to feel dull perhaps, and his wandering eye at last caught my watch-chain with the locket attached to it; yet he did not presume to extend his hand for it: but his smiling face and brightened eyes, when I took it off and gave it into his hand, clearly evidenced the delight he felt. The old man as yet had only looked askance over his rosary at our doings; but when, on my opening the medallion, he saw a picture in it, which possibly he took for that of some saint, he whispered a few hurried words in the ear of the little fellow, who, seizing the locket with both his tiny hands, carried it devoutly to his lips.

Quieter and more decorous behaviour than that of these Indians one could not witness. Here were visible none of those improprieties familiar in Brazil, where the free-and-easy ladies beckon to their negro boys to fetch them glasses of water during mass. As silently as they had come they returned to their cottages after the ceremony. Such indeed was

the stillness that I should have taken the village to be deserted during the rest of the day, but for some groups of children out at play.

Gorgeous festivals and processions were counted, as I have already explained, among the principal factors of a successful catechese; and at the present day, not only in Bolivia but all over South America, they are the shows which electrify the whole population.

In the North of Europe at least, one cannot easily form an adequate notion of the strange mixture of bigotry, childish delight in shows, and inclination to debauchery, which impels both high and low to take part in them.*

In the Pueblos, however, these spectacles derive a distinctive character from the prevailing Indian element, which strongly contrasts, in solemn dignity and a certain savageness, with the more childish, monkey-like conception of the negro-mulatto and mestizo population of the cities.

In the Pueblo of Exaltacion de la Santa Cruz, where several high wooden crosses are erected in different places, probably in honour of its name, a dozen of the sword-dancers (macheteiros), on the day of the consecration of a church, went singing and dancing and brandishing their broad knives and wooden swords, from cross to cross, headed by their chieftain, who carried a heavy silver cross, and followed by the whole tribe. They wore dazzling white camisetas, rattling stag's claws on their knuckles, and a fanciful head-gear composed of the long tail-feathers of the aráras and of yellow and red toucan's breasts.

At every cross, and before the altars of the church, they performed

* In some towns in the interior of Brazil, in addition to the scapegraces dressed as Turks, hangmen and Roman soldiers, an actress takes the part of Mary Magdalene in the Good Friday procession. Kneeling on a sort of richly-ornamented pedestal (called andor), carried by six men, with dishevelled hair and inflamed eyes, she fills the air with her lamentations and screams. The public, among whom unrepenting Magdalenes usually are very numerous, are seized with holy horror; even tears have been seen to flow here and there; but, on the whole, it is a wretched exhibition, which gives rise to scandals of every kind. At Barbacena, a little town in Minas Geraes that enjoys the worst of reputations as to the morals of its inhabitants, such of the women, both married and unmarried, as have to reproach themselves for any offence, on a certain day walk to a chapel boasting a particularly merciful image of the Virgin, bare down to their girdles, with hair loose, and carrying heavy stones on their heads. Even persons of the highest rank are obliged to comply with local habits in these matters; and at Rio, on Corpus-Christi day, the Emperor Dom Pedro II., bareheaded for two hours, accompanies the procession, which is preceded by St. George, a hideous doll of life-size, tied on a horse,—much to the disgust of his sons-in-law, who also have to submit to the torture, if they happen to be there at the time.

a sort of allegorical dance, with a great show of brandishing their inoffensive weapons, which they at last, breathless and perspiring, laid down, together with their savage diadems, at the foot of the crucifix; the whole evidently representing the submission of the Indians and their conversion to Christianity.

Old Bolivians have told me that these dances used to be executed by dozens of macheteiros, and that they would probably have ceased altogether if the chieftains did not exert the full weight of their authority in behalf of keeping them up, even forcing the young men, in case of need, to take part in them.

Self-inflicted tortures are occasionally witnessed in these processions, under the stimulus of religious fanaticism, apt to remind one of the great car of Juggernaut. It may be an Indian who, tied by his outstretched arms and by one leg to a heavy wooden cross, accompanies the *cortége* for hours in a painful crawl; or it may be devotees (women among them) who drag themselves along on their bare knees, until, fainting and bleeding, they sink down before the altar.

These festivals regularly end in sharp drinking bouts, in which they contrive to consume a very large quantity of cachaça (brandy), or of their national beverage, chicha; of which I shall treat below.

Among the chief "profane" occasions for shows and mirth-making are the rare visits of the Prefect of the Departamento, who resides at Trinidad, when he passes through the Pueblos on one of his circuits. Though it be no proud, richly-carved and gilt Venetian barge that carries him down the Mamoré, but quite an ordinary boat with palm-leaf awning, which at most boasts the green-yellow-red flag of the Republic, yet the grace and dignity with which the Excellentissimo accepts the homage of the crowd waiting for him in the "port" certainly recall the proudest days of the noble city on the Lagoons.

A volley of musketry is fired, and the high dignitary is solemnly conducted to the Pueblo, with a concert contributed by the fiddles, the pipes, and the inevitable bajónes, which on these occasions are supported by boys walking before the musicians, like the trombones of antiquity. Headed by their chief, the whole Indian population passes under the windows of Sua Excellencia, after which a solemn service is held; but the setting of the sun is awaited impatiently all the day. Then begin the entertainments, which reach their climax in a bull-fight of the most cruel kind, and terminate with the night.

MOJOS INDIAN, FROM THE ANCIENT MISSION OF TRINIDAD,
ORE THE ALTAR ON A HOLY DAY.

On the Plaza before the loggia of the former Jesuits' College, where the Prefect and the officials have taken their seats, an arena has been formed within a circle of stout palisades. At a given signal, a wild bull, captured on the campos for the occasion, is brought in, and the ring is carefully closed on all sides. The animal, at last disengaged of the several laços by which it was originally restrained, suspiciously looks around for a way out;—in vain! Nothing meets his view but endless palisades and the towering heads of a bloodthirsty crowd, intent, from his Excellency down to the lowest

MOJOS INDIAN OF TRINIDAD.

Indian, upon thoroughly enjoying the death-throes of the king of the prairies, and prepared to answer his loud roar with a stupendous shout of triumph, to which the swell of music shall be communicated by the violins and bajónes. Then chicha and brandy are liberally handed round in calabashes; and, after the worthy representative of the Supreme Government has thrown a few handfuls of copper coins among the excited crowd, the frenzy may be said to have reached the pitch required for opening the real business of the evening. Several athletic Indians, half mad with vanity and drink, vault with cat-like agility over the high palings; and with their long, pointed knives beset the poor animal upon all sides, which, infuriated by endless devices, ploughs up the soil with its horns. With lowered head it boldly charges the first adversary; whereupon another sallies forth from behind, who with a sharp cut of his knife opens a gaping wound on its back; and, as the bull, bellowing with pain, turns round upon him, the first assailant, amid the yells of the crowd, the applause of the Excellentissimo and of the attendant respectability, and the triumphant music, which now strikes in, literally cuts off a piece of flesh from his back.

MARIANO, MOJOS OF TRINIDAD.

Thus proceeds the brutal sport, which is sometimes fraught with the gravest risks to the fighters: but no casualty suffices to disturb the general hilarity for one moment. Should any of them be impaled on the horns, or tossed into the air, or crushed against the palings till their ribs are broken, they are dragged out, and their places are taken by fresh gladiators, bolder and more savage than the first set. Yes, even women, with flashing eyes and flushed cheeks, like frantic Mænads, leap into the gory ring, to cut off their slices from the carcase of the rapidly-expiring beast; which, when the final stroke is delivered that severs the sinews of the hind legs, sinks groaning and bellowing to the ground, where it rather resembles a bleeding mass of quivering flesh than the proud animal that had, an hour before, impatiently and defiantly stamped the sand.

Hereupon arise yells of triumph and brilliant flourishes on the bajónes. His Excellency expresses his warmest thanks for the elevating spectacle, and retires to his apartments; and the drunken Indians discuss their heroic deeds beside the fires, drinking chicha and devouring the meat of their tortured victim.

As night advances, the gentry assemble in the spacious rooms of the old collegio for a festive dance, though the rough floors, which are divided into regular compartments by rows of bones, are far from inviting, the Holy Fathers who had them laid down probably not having designed them for any such use.

A few musicians, seated in hammocks in one corner, relieve the monotony of their recitative—which is partly an amatory effusion and partly an improvisation suitable to the occasion—by thrumming on jingling guitars; and the caballeros and senhoritas pair off, either for the national fandango, or, as in these times of universal copying and aping is more likely, for the quadrille. A quadrille at the old Mission of the Beni! And the grocer, or the artist in waistcoats and great-coats who but yesterday mended our old poncho, in his shirt-sleeves, the *vis-à-vis* of his Excellency, with his little, gaudily-dressed, black-eyed senhora! And yet, why not? We must never forget that in South America the colour of the skin, all toleration notwithstanding, determines the social position, and that every white man, or whoever can pass himself off for such, with the assurance of the proudest Castilian, thinks himself to be of as good blood as the King himself.*

---

* This must happen in all countries where the Caucasian race mingles with the others, and the difference of race in such cases weighs heavier than all other considerations. I have known dark Brazilians in the highest positions at Rio de Janeiro, who would cheerfully have given half their fortunes and their influence for the white skins of the Portuguese water-carriers, who panted up the staircases of their palaces with their heavy loads to earn a few pence. Besides, there is no hereditary nobility in Brazil, whose Constitution is modelled after that of the United States; and *personal* nobility can only be bestowed by the Emperor, or bought; about £200 for a baronet's title, £600 for that of an earl's, and so on. Sharp tongues persist in affirming, that 25 years ago, when that clever philanthropist, José Clemente Pereira, the noble founder of the Lunatic Asylum at Rio de Janeiro, saw his work in danger of suspension from

The refreshments handed round, chicha and cáchaça toddy are so freely partaken of on all sides that most of the company will long for a good ride on the morrow over the fresh dewy campos; so, wishing them all a *boas noites*, we passed under the gloomy wooden colonnade which supports the verandah of the collegio, whence we got a view of the old church looming in the faint starlight, and sought repose in our own hammocks.

Except making a few feeble attempts at settling the ceaseless differences between the Correjidor and the chieftain of the Pueblo, and addressing emphatic injunctions to the former as to minding the yearly poll-tax of the Indians, and as to providing against their escape to Brazilian territory, I do not think the Excellentissimo Senhor Prefecto del Departamento had much business to transact with his subordinates on the following day; and we may well suffer him to continue in peace his circuit to the other Pueblos.

I have frequently mentioned the chicha—the national beverage of these countries, the naming of which instantly brightens the gloomiest face and relaxes the severest brow. It is but fair that I should give some information as to its preparation, though it be at the risk of shocking delicate minds.

In the first place, I have to say that this chicha must not be confounded with the sour beverage made from apples, which Gerstaecker encountered among the Araucanians, and which, on due consideration, is as much at home on the Rhine and the Main as in the South of Chile. Oh no! *La nuestra chicha* is made of the golden grains of Indian corn, which, bruised and moistened, are brought to a state of fermentation; but it is just this process of bruising and moistening which gives to it its peculiar national distinction, although the grinding-stones are to be found wherever human beings are. In short, they are no other than the masticatory organs of the ladies— in our case, of the Indian ladies. About the time of a festival, on passing by the always open doors of the cottages, you are sure to find three or four women (not always of the youngest or prettiest)

---

want of funds, he urged the Government to a more liberal dispensation of baronetcies, and, in the interest of the Asylum, to bestow them rather on open hands than on astute heads; and that, in consequence of it, the contributions came in so plentifully "que naõ tinha mãos a medir," that is, that he had not hands enough to relieve them all, as every coffee-planter, and slave or carne-seca dealer who had amassed wealth, was anxious to contribute his mite—to the Lunatic Asylum.

squatting and cowering round a large trough made out of one piece of wood. They are busily engaged in chewing the hard grains, which they take out of calabashes beside them, and in spitting them, after sound mastication, into the trough.

This thick mass, which is thinned with water, is poured into large earthen jars and left to ferment, which it usually begins to do within a very short time. How long this process should continue, in order

CAPITÃO PAY, CHIEFTAIN OF THE CAYOWÁ INDIANS.

to impart the particular flavour affected by Bolivian gourmands, or when and how it must be filtered, to separate stray grains from it, I am unable to say. Thinking it unlikely that the lovely drink would find many votaries in Europe, I did not inquire after the further details of its preparation.

However, it is an interesting fact that not only the half-wild inhabitants of the Pueblos on the Mamoré, but even the denizens of the more civilised trading towns, like Cochabamba, cannot do without the chicha, though there is no lack of either refreshing or intoxicating drinks, from the innumerable lemonades and refrescos to the most ardent spirits. Beer alone, when its brewing shall have reached the foot of the Andes, may contest the supremacy of the chicha; but it must be of a weak, agreeable quality, not the strong ale or porter of English export, which, overcoming all the difficulties of transport, has already found its way there.

CAPITÃO VEI-BANG, CHIEF OF THE COROADOS.

As to the taste of the chicha (for, a victim to my love of science, I tried the yellowish, turbid, slightly-pearling liquid—though only after having carefully ascertained that there were no fragments of grinders, but only bruised grains, at the bottom of my calabash), it reminded me of weak cider with the slightest addition of starch; and possibly, when one succeeds in forgetting all about its preparation, it may not be quite so objectionable as the warm water of the river, or the thick water of the corridges, or pools, which are full of organic matter of all kinds.

Of course nothing seems easier or simpler than the idea of doing the bruising of the grains in a mortar, or with a couple of cylinders; but an indescribable smile curls the lip of the true Bolivian when you are ingenuous enough to propose such a thing. With a pitying shrug of the shoulders, he will inform you that that was tried long ago, and that chicha prepared thus "artificialmente" was destitute of all savouriness,—in fact, was not chicha. And, indeed, who knows whether he be not right, and whether fermentation brought about by different means does not produce different effects? "Into the innermost secrets of Nature no created spirit as yet has penetrated;" and even the celebrated automatic duck of the late Hofrath Beireis may have awakened dubious thoughts in some of his fellow-professors, gifted with more delicate smelling-organs than the rest, as to the final result of its artificial apparatus of digestion.

The tenacity with which the Bolivians cleave to their old ways in such matters is evidenced by the following narrative of fact. Some years back a Frenchman erected at Santa Cruz de la Sierra a very simple chocolate mill. Notwithstanding the large consumption of the article, the cacáo beans used to be bruised by the poor Indian women, in wooden troughs, with the aid of common field-stones:—a mode which, besides being imperfect and laborious, involved the loss of time. Anywhere else the enterprise could not have failed to be a splendid success; but not so in Bolivia. The man was totally ruined. Nobody would buy his chocolate, for it was said to cause—*risum teneatis!*—violent colics, through the novelty of its "artificial" preparation; and the Indian women have therefore to go on with their Sisyphean work.

After these culinary diversions, let us return to the Missions, of which there are fifteen in the Departamento del Beni, inhabited by seven different tribes. Three of these, the Canichanas, Cayuabas, and Mobimas, live in one Pueblo each; while the four others, the Maropas, Baurés, Itonamas, and Mojos, have three or four villages each. Giving an average number of 2,000 souls to each Mission, we have a total of 30,000 Indian inhabitants of the Department.

In spite of the external similarity of the several tribes in respect of dress, customs, and habits—results probably due to Jesuit culture—there are marked distinctions which have resisted effacement. Thus the Cayuabas of Exaltacion, who evidently have suffered most from the corrupting influence of the white man, are still renowned as the boldest and hardiest boatmen; while the Canichanas of S. Pedro, who from the first struck us by their sullenly-stern behaviour and Mongolian type, are said to have given more trouble to the Reverend Fathers than all the rest, and to have occasionally indulged, up to a very recent date, in their anthropophagous appetites, to which they sacrificed more than one messenger from adjoining Missions, as he wended his weary way over the lonely campos.

The Mobimas, at S. Ana, near Exaltacion, arrest attention by their tall figures. Notably the squaws, as they stride powerfully along in their white camisetas, might easily originate fables like those respecting the giants of Patagonia; while among the Mojos* at Trinidad, Loreto, S. Ignacio, and S. Javier, there are to be found, not only figures of faultless symmetry and beauty, but the truest, the faithfullest, and the kindest of hearts.

An illustrative vocabulary of the various languages is given in the annexed table; and, regarding pronunciation, I have to remark that the spelling is the German one.

For the outward appearance and the physiognomical and other points of interest of these Indians, I refer to the illustrations. A sketch, be it never so hasty, cannot fail to impart a better idea of them than any verbal description. The two last sketches represent the chieftains of the Cayowás and the Coroados of the Province of Paraná; and they may be regarded with greater interest from the fact that the Guaranis and their kindred, the Cayowás of the district called Guayra (now included in Paraná), even so far back as the end of the sixteenth century, were the willing pupils of the Jesuits, as the Mojos became afterwards. The warlike Coroados, of an opposite character, at the same period were the trusty allies of the white settlers of the Province of S. Paul, helping them in their slave-robbing expeditions and in the destruction of the Missions of the

---

* In the Amazon Valley all Indians coming from the Bolivian Missions are designated by the name of Mojos; probably because the first crews that were seen there in their peculiar bast shirts belonged to this tribe.

Jesuits; who, in consequence of these repeated attacks, retired farther to the South, to the shores of the Uruguay and the Paraná, taking their disciples with them. After numerous conflicts with the advancing tide of culture, the Coroados were outlawed by the Portuguese Government; and only within the last twenty-five years have some of their hordes deigned to live with the hated white man on any other footing than that of war, and to take up their abode in the Aldeamentos, or Indian settlements administered by the Government. In some of these,—such as San Ignacio, and Nossa Senhora do Pirapó, built on the sites of the Missions destroyed by the Paulistas, in 1630; and São Pedro d'Alcántará on the Tibagy,—and in the heart of the endless region of primeval forest lying between the Tieté and the Iguassú, I was enabled to institute comparisons between the several tribes there living beside one another, in peace though not in amity; and there were these likenesses taken.

With the aid of the still visible elevations of the surface, attesting the remains of the ruined Pisé walls—which, like the ruins of Villa Rica on the Ivahy, were partly enveloped with close vegetation—we could easily construct the plan on which these several Missions were laid out; and it apparently was adopted, with few variations, in all of them: In the centre a large square, with the church and the collegio on one side, and the low Indian cottages disposed in long rectangular streets all around it; the strict regularity of the whole harmonizing well with the severe military discipline maintained therein. Only on the Paranapanema did we observe a peculiarity, of which the Bolivian Missions showed no trace—the remains of walls and trenches, slight fortifications evidently necessitated by the repeated attacks of the Paulistas.

When we come to review all that has been advanced on this subject, the achievements of the Jesuits cannot but strike us as having been grand and admirable, let their aims have been never so ambitious and selfish, and the means they employed never so immoral and disloyal. The degree of success effected by them appears the grander when contrasted with the existing condition of things under the modern Brazilian and Bolivian clergy. Indifferent as are the Governments to the union of the diffused remains of the aboriginal inhabitants, if they desire to incite them to productive activity and to save them

202   THE AMAZON AND MADEIRA RIVERS.

from complete extinction, recourse must again be had to the Italian Capuchin monks as missionaries; for there is not a single one, out of the many fat native bonzes who are to be found strolling idly through the streets of the towns, and scandalising all true Christians with the laxity of their lives, who would consent to exchange his rich prebend for the hard life of an Indian aldeamento.

VOCABULARY. 203

VOCABULARY OF INDIAN DIALECTS CURRENT IN THE BENI DEPARTMENT OF BOLIVIA.

	MOJOS. At Trinidad; N. S. de Loreto; S. Ignacio; and S. Javier.	BAURÉS (Chapacuras), At N. S. de Concepcion; N. S. del Carmen; and S. Joaquin.	ITONAMA. At S. Ramon; S. M. Magdalena; and S. José.	CANICHANA. At S. Pedro.	MOBIMA. At S. Anna.	CAYUABA. At Exaltacion.	MAROPA. At Reyes; and S. Borja.	GUARANI.
Man	Hiro	Kiritian	Umo	Enacu	Itilacna	Oratasi	Uni	Aba
Woman	Eseno	Yamake	Caneca	Ikogahui	Cutscha	Cratalorane	Yutscha	Cuña
Head	Nutchuti	Upatchi	Utschu	Eucucu	Bamacus	Nahuaracama	Mapo	Acang
Cheek	Numiro	Urutaratchi	Papapana	Eikokena	Kinto	Iribuju	Tamo	Tadipi
Eyes	Niuki	Tucutchi	Icatschi	Eutot	Sora	Niyoco	Huiro	Teso
Ear	Nutchoka	Taitatatschi	Moohtodo	Eucometo	Lototo	Iradike	Paoki	Apiçaqua
Hand	Nubupe	Umitchi	Malaca	Eutijle	Sojpan	Daru	Muipata	Mbo
Sun	Ssatche	Hnapuito	Apatsche	Nicojli	Tinno	Nharaman	Vari	Quaraci
Moon	Coche	Panaŝo	Tiacaca	Nimilaou	Yetao	Inave	Oche	Yaci
Water	Une	Acum	Huanuve	Nese	Touni	Ikita	Jene	Y
Fire	Yucu	Isso	Bari	Nitschucut	Véé	Idore	Tschii	Tata
Mountain	Mari	Pecun	Iti	Coméé	Tschampandi	Iruretui	Matchiva	Ibiti
Bow	Kaiporoku	Parami	Hualichkit	Niescutop	Tanilo	Iranpui	Canati	Guirapa
Arrow	Takirikire	Tschininie	Tschere	Itschnthuera	Tulpaendi	Irabibiki	Pia	Hui
Young	Amoparu	Ischuem	Viayachne	Eookelege	Oveniomca	Mamihuasi	Huekehue	Oumunbuqu
Old	Etschasi	Itaracun	Achni	Emmara	Bijau	Iratakasi	Tscheaita	Tuya
I	Nuti	Huaya	Oni	Ojale	Incla	Areai	Ea	Ndi-ni
He	Ema	Ariosu	Macuno	Enjale	Icolo	Are	Aa	Ae
Give me	Peeracano	Miapatschi	Ape	Sitchite	Caujleca	Piboloire	Eki ahue	Emboocho
To eat	Pinike	Cahuara	Conejna	Alema	Caiki	Pamii	Pihue	Acaru
To sleep	Migue	Huatschinaé	Ischavaneve	Aguja	Oroki	Pibilii	Ochahuan	Ake
I will	Pivoro	Mosi tschacum	Huatschi-tachvaco	Huarehue	Jirampana	Orichnhueuhua	Akekia	Potari
I will not	Voi-pivoro	Masi tschacum		Nolmach chus-éréhu	Cai-jiram-panasca	Yeitschuenhua	Oje amakia	Ndaypotari

APPENDIX.

THE SURVEYS—THE HYDROGRAPHICAL, HYPSOMETRICAL, AND STATISTICAL RESULTS—HOW OBTAINED.

Though in a few years puffing locomotives will be speeding through them, the districts we explored have till now been so detached from communication with the rest of the world, and have, notwithstanding their natural wealth, partaken so little of the influence exercised by commerce over the course of universal history, that it is likely more than one of our readers has had to refer to the map, to call to mind the exact position of the different points in the great Amazon Basin, or the Madeira, or the Mamoré Valley.

Nevertheless, with the opening of better means of intercourse, and with the exportation of their produce, these countries will acquire greater importance in the future. They should evoke at least as much interest as does Central Africa, for instance; which again and again attracts explorers and interests readers. Although, therefore, the results of our voyage may be incomplete in more respects than one, and though our investigations frequently were hurried, yet they may not be altogether devoid of interest, on the score of this having been the first expedition to these regions undertaken of late years. I now proceed to give a short summary of the astronomical, hydrographical, hypsometrical, and statistical results obtained.

The astronomical observations were made in the following way:—

Two ship's chronometers (by Poole, of London) having proved defective at Manáos, and former explorations having convinced us that these delicate instruments suffer materially, not only from their short transport on land, but also from the shocks and rockings of the rudder-boats, which soon disqualify them for determination of longitude, we resolved to base our calculations on observations of lunar distances. Though these (we always made two of them on important occasions) did not all prove to be of equal exactitude, we still had enough to ascertain beyond doubt the geographical situation of the chief line.

The latitudes were determined by the altitude of the sun and of the stars, taken almost wherever we halted, the nightly observations being greatly favoured by the cloudless serenity of the sky during the dry season. The instruments used were an excellent *cercle de reflexion* by Casella, and two sextants with artificial horizons; the one used in first line being a mercury horizon.

Between the principal points of the expanse of water thus astronomically determined, the detail of the river-course was obtained by means of a micrometer by Rochon and a prismatic compass.

An exact triangulation, extending over the whole width of the river, was necessarily out of the question, even if we could have found time for the measuring, properly so called, since the setting up of observatories and of trigonometrical signals in the dense forest, with the limited staff at our disposal, would have required the preparation of years.

The levelling was generally done barometrically, with two aneroid barometers and a hypsometer (by the temperature of boiling water), and on the chief breaks the difference was, besides, directly measured by the levelling instrument.

APPENDIX.

Exact transverse sections of the whole river, and measurings of its velocity for the purpose of calculating the quantity of the water, were taken on many points; and the deepest channel was fathomed throughout the explored course.

For the principal objects of our exploration, that is, for the comparative estimates of expenditure for a railroad along its shore, and for canalisation of the river, and for the completion and rectification of the geographical maps, this mode of survey was thoroughly adequate; and on the results so obtained the concession granted by the Brazilian Government to Colonel G. E. Church was based and worked.

The results of the measurings are as follows:—

1. LONGITUDE AND LATITUDE OF THE PRINCIPAL POINTS.

Names of the Points.	South Latitude.				West Longitude from Rio de Janeiro.		
On the Lower Madeira—Murassutúba	5°	37′	37″	0			
,, ,, Ilha das Baétas	6°	18′	28″	7			
,, ,, Espírito Santo	6°	43′	20″	5			
,, ,, Crato	7°	31′	3″	4			
,, ,, Domingo Leigue	8°	36′	4″	0			
On the Upper Madeira—Rapid of Santo Antonio	8°	49′	2″	6	21°	29′	8″
,, ,, Fall of Theotonio	8°	52′	41″	0	21°	30′	57″
,, ,, Rapid of Morrinhos	9°	1′	45″	0	21°	36′	30″
,, ,, Mouth of the Jaciparaná	9°	10′	9″	0	21°	42′	20″
,, ,, Caldeirão do Inferno	9°	15′	48″	0	21°	52′	14″
,, ,, Fall of Girão	9°	20′	45″	0	21°	54′	22″
,, ,, Rapid of Tres Irmãos							
,, ,, Rapid of Paredão	9°	36′	37″	7	22°	13′	4″
,, ,, Rapid of Pederneira	9°	32′	7″	0	22°	20′	20″
,, ,, Mouth of the Abuna							
,, ,, Rapid of Aráras	9°	55′	5″	8	22°	15′	20″
,, ,, Rapid of Periquitos	10°						
,, ,, Fall of Ribeirão	10°	12′	52″	1	22°	8′	30″
,, ,, Rapid of Madeira							
,, ,, Mouth of the Beni	10°	20′	0″	0	22°	12′	20″
,, ,, Rapid of Lages							
,, ,, Rapid of Pao-Grande							
,, ,, Fall of Bananeira							
,, ,, Rapid of Guajará Merim	10°	44′	32″	8	22°	3′	42″

2. DISTANCES BETWEEN THE PRINCIPAL POINTS.

Extreme Points.	Length in Statute Miles.
Developed length of the river-course from the mouth of the Madeira to Santo Antonio	560
,, ,, ,, Santo Antonio to Guajará Merim	225¼
,, ,, ,, Guajará Merim to the mouth of the Mamoré	102¼
,, ,, ,, the mouth of the Mamoré to Exaltacion	130
,, ,, ,, Exaltacion to Trinidad	188

The total of these distances, 2,412 miles, is the length of the journey, there and back, made by the expedition in canoes.

3. ALTITUDE OF THE PRINCIPAL POINTS ABOVE THE SEA-LEVEL.

(N.B.—Reduced on the Low Level of the River.)

Name of the Points.	Altitude above Sea-level in English Feet.
Town of Serpa, on the Amazon	59
Mouth of the Madeira	69
Manicoré on the Lower Madeira	92
Baêtas ,, ,,	131
Tres Casas ,, ,,	164
Ilha do Salomão ,,	174
Domingo Leigue ,,	177
Mouth of the Jammary ,,	184
Rapid of Santo Antonio (below the break)	200
Fall of Theotonio ,,	272
Rapid of Morrinhos ,,	288
Caldeirão do Inferno ,,	305
Fall of Girão ,,	335
Mouth of the Beni	402
Fall of Bananeiras (below the break)	450
Rapid of Guajará Merim ,,	475
Mouth of the Mamoré	493
Level of the Mamoré at Exaltacion	499

4. DIFFERENCE OF LEVEL AND EXTENT OF THE PRINCIPAL FALLS AND RAPIDS.

Name of the Rapid.	Difference of Level. English Feet.	Length of the Rapid. Yards.
Santo Antonio	3·93	300
Theotonio (principal break)	26·25	110—300
Caldeirão do Inferno	4	440
Girão	26·25	770
Paredão	3·5	600
Pederneira	3·31	280
Aráras	3·41	770
Ribeirão (principal break)	13·15	440
Madeira	6·72	980
Lages	6·72	820
Pao Grande	6·56	440
Bananeiras (principal break)	19·7	550
Guajará Guassú	3·5	500

The slope represented by eighteen larger and twenty-eight smaller rapids* is 227¼ feet in an extent of 12¼ miles. The total difference of level between Santo Antonio and Guajará being 272 feet, 272 ft.—227¼ ft.=44¾ feet; which yields the slope of the smooths between the rapids.

* The boatmen on the Madeira usually distinguish a Rapid by *cabeça, corpo, e rabo;* that is, head, body, and tail.

APPENDIX. 207

5. Width of the River, Depth, and General Proportion of the Slopes.

Slope.

1) Slope of the Mamoré between Exaltacion and the mouth . . . 1 : 32,104
2)   ,,   Madeira from the mouth of the Mamoré to Guajará . 1 : 30,000
3)   ,,   ,,   Guajará to Santo Antonio . . . 1 : 5,303
4)   ,,   ,,   Santo Antonio to the mouth . . 1 : 26,490

Depth of the deepest Channel at Low Level.   Feet

1) Mamoré at the mouth (maximum) 33
2)   ,, on the reef of Matucáre (minimum) . . . . . $2\frac{1}{2}$
3) Madeira between the mouth of the Mamoré and Guajará (maximum) . . 50
4)   ,,   ,,   ,,   ,, (minimum) . . $4\frac{3}{4}$
5) Beni at the mouth 50
6) Madeira, greatest depth above Theotonio 122
7)   ,,   ,,   at Sapucaia Oroca 121
8)   ,, on the reefs of Uroa (shallowest part of the channel) . . $4\frac{1}{4}$

Width of the Rivers.   Yards.

1) Mamoré, at the mouth, at low water . . . 323
    ,,   ,, at high water . . . 520
2) Guaporé, at the mouth, at low water . . . 550
    ,,   ,, at high water . . . 770
3) Madeira, average width above the rapids . . 480
4)   ,, minimum of width within the rapids . . 380
    ,, maximum ,,   ,, . 2,200
5)   ,, below the rapids at Sapucaia Oroca . 800
6) Beni 1,100

6. Elevation of the Banks—Difference of Level between High and Low Water—Quantities of Water.

Near Exaltacion the banks of the Mamoré rise on an average to 43 feet above low water level; and this is also about the height of the floods; but at its mouth the shores rise only to about 26 feet, and are inundated far and wide by the floods which there usually reach 30 feet in height.

On the Madeira the elevation of the banks varies considerably within the region of the rapids; and so do the high and low water levels. Immediately above each rapid they sink to about $6\frac{1}{2}$ to 10 feet; immediately below they rise to a maximum.

On the Lower Madeira the normal elevation of the banks is 23 feet above low water, that is, a trifle less than high water level. At some places, however, as at Sapucaia Oroca, the difference between flood and low water level is 40 feet; the elevation of the right shore 43 feet, and that of the left 33 feet above low water.

The quantities of water conveyed per second by the Madeira and its confluents at different levels are as follow :—

	Low Water Level. Cubic Feet.	Medium Water Level. Cubic Feet.	Flood Level. Cubic Feet.
Guaporé, at the mouth	23,415	66,270	180,818
Mamoré	29,500	89,350	248,060
Madeira, at the upper end of the rapids .	52,900	152,212	428,876
Beni, at the mouth . . .	48,842	153,412	463,000
Madeira, below the rapids at Sapucaia Oroca	146,278	517,090	1,351,065

APPENDIX.

By way of comparison, I give the quantities conveyed per second by the Rhine near Mannheim:—

	Cubic Feet.
At low-water level	19,600
At medium-water level	58,624
At high-water level	196,000

The surface of ground drained by the different rivers is, after the existing maps:—

	English Square Miles.
By the Guaporé	193,855
By the Mamoré	199,468
By the Beni	141,320
By the Lower Madeira	220,175
	754,818

Which shows clearly that the mighty Beni, until now, has been treated illiberally by map-makers, though its origin in the high well-watered Cordillera, which also supplies the Mamoré with a disproportionately great quantity of water as compared with the Guaporé, ought to have been taken into account.

Though out of several proposals made by us for the improvement of the ways of communication, only our plan for an economical railroad was finally adopted, the estimates of the other projects may be of some interest to scientific readers. They were:—

1) The construction of inclined planes, at all the larger rapids, to track the vessels; such as are in use in North America and Prussia.
2) The canalisation of the river with sluices.
3) The construction of a railroad along the bank.

The expenditure required for the first project (which, with a considerably increased trade, might soon have proved insufficient) was estimated at 900,000 milreis, or 2,340,000 francs. The second, the execution of which would have been attended with almost insurmountable difficulties, was estimated at 21,000,000 milreis, or 54,600,000 francs; and the third, which actually has been begun, at 8,500,000 milreis, or 22,100,000 francs.

As the length of the railroad to be constructed, with a minimum of gauge, is only about 174 miles (on easy surface, on the whole), the estimate may appear rather high, even for Brazil; but in thinly-peopled countries, hitherto entirely cut off from the rest of the world, and into which it will be necessary to import everything, with the exception of the timber, and workmen especially, the cost of various operations, particularly of constructive works like bridges, will swell to enormous sums.

In the total absence of reliable official returns, the number of souls living along the main river and near the extensive lake-like lateral branches (*e.g.* the Uaupés) can be estimated only roughly; and we place it between 5,000 and 6,000, the half-civilised Mundrucús and Múras included.

They subsist chiefly by the preparation of India-rubber, the collection of Pará nuts, and other fruit of the forests, and on the produce of small cacáo and tobacco plantations. Therefore supplies of provisions of all kinds (even of the mandioca root, which grows with scarcely any trouble) fail to be obtained in sufficient quantities in the most fertile valley in the world, and must be imported from afar.

For the singularity of the fact, I mention here that an *alqueire* of mandioca flour (about one and a third bushels) costs, at Rio de Janeiro and Pará, 2—3 milreis (4s. 6d. to 6s. 9d.); in Bolivia 1 (2s. 3d.); and on the Madeira 12—14 (27s. to 31s. 6d.) Proportionately high prices affect other products, the sugar-cane to wit, which would thrive excellently. If the caoutchouc industry may be called a gold mine, agriculture would prove equally remunerative as it did in California at the time of the gold fever.

APPENDIX.

Cattle breeding, with the exception of the very modest beginnings on the natural campos of Crato, has been quite unknown on the Madeira, and probably will continue so for some time to come. There are immense districts without an ox, or a cow, or a horse, or a mule, or a sheep, or a goat. Even a pig is a rare sight. Dogs and fowls only are to be seen near the cottages, usually associated with a crowd of the easily-tamed inhabitants of the woods—parrots, toucans, monkeys, several rodents, and even bristly peccaries. And yet the want of animal food is felt acutely by the dense population of the Amazon Valley, and will be daily aggravated by the increasing immigration of Europeans, who do not relish the eternal fish-and-farina dishes.*

On the campos of the Mamoré, Upper Beni, Itonama and Machupo, on the grassy plains occupied by the fifteen Missions, cattle thrive so plentifully that, with proper management, they would easily supply the whole country, as soon as the Madeira railroad shall have opened a market for them in the Amazon Valley; and the recently-started National Bolivian Navigation Company, as well as the railroad, may reckon on at least this considerable trade.

Besides hides, tallow, dried meat, live stock, sugar, brandy, and cacáo, the invaluable Peruvian bark also will then take its way down the Madeira to Pará, and the economical monstrosity of sending it to Europe over the Cordillera and round Cape Horn will cease. And the same observation applies to the produce of the rich mines of Bolivia; of which, by the way, only those of Potosí (the richest silver mines in the world) and the newly-discovered ones of Caracóles† are worked and doing fairly, while the excellent copper mines of Coro-coro are totally neglected. These crooked ways, of which the example of the Peruvian bark is sufficient evidence, injuriously affect not only the exports of the country, but also the import of European and North American goods; which are as indispensable to Bolivia as to the rest of South America.

Let us (by way of illustration) follow them from some European port to their place of destination, La Paz, Cochabamba, Sucre, or Santa Cruz de la Sierra. Having arrived, after a sea voyage of eighty or ninety days, at the Peruvian port of Arica, and landed as usual with average (as it cannot be otherwise with the defective arrangements there), they have first to pass the custom-house of the "Sister-Republic," which, in consideration of the sum of 500,000 dollars annually paid to Bolivia, has (by the treaty of 1865) acquired the right of levying heavy taxes on all classes of goods (about 30 per cent. *ad valorem*). From Arica they are carried by the railway to Tacna, where they are packed up in parcels that must not weigh more than 120 or 140 lbs.; and thence by beasts of burden over the steepest and roughest mountain-paths, in the most troublesome and tedious way, to La Paz. Arrived there, well shaken and, perhaps, saturated, the cost of the goods has amounted to 150 dollars, or about £30, per ton; and to reach Cochabamba, or Sucre, or Santa Cruz de la Sierra, costs about half as much more. All these towns, however, are situated near affluents of the Amazon, and will be accessible from its mouth in an easier manner, in a shorter time, and at half the expense, as soon as the short railway along the rapids of the Madeira is completed.

The following is a tabular statement of the trade to and from Bolivia:—

Imports.	£	Imports.	£
From England	528,000	From Argentine Republic	64,000
,, France	264,000	,, Perú	80,000
,, Germany	224,000	,, Brazil	56,000
,, United States	72,000		£1,288,000

---

* Fish-Lapland was the title bestowed on these countries by our factotum, Mr. O. v. Sch.

† It is a well-known fact that in the province of Alto-Perú (the present Bolivia) the Spaniards worked in 10,200 places for the silver ore.

APPENDIX.

Exports.	£	Exports.	£
Silver	720,000	Vicuña and alpaca wool	60,000
Peruvian bark	160,000	Tin	40,000
Copper	128,000	Coffee	6,000
Coca	128,000	Tallow and hides	2,000
Gold	80,000		
			£1,324,000

From this it will be seen that the imports have been considerably liquidated by the produce of the mines.* With improved ways of communication, a country, whose population is increasing so rapidly† without any immigration from without, and which owns provinces of surprising fertility, may well cover the imports independently of the mines.

Several attempts, or rather projects, have been made to force the barriers, and to open the country to commerce. Thus, the railroad which runs from Buenos Ayres towards the north (extended to Córdova now) will, by its contemplated prolongation to Jujui, connect the Southern part of Bolivia with that important harbour at the mouth of the River Plate; and another project has been mooted of opening a way by the Pilcomayo (navigable though it be only during the rainy season) to Asuncion in Paraguay, where the magnificent river of that name will offer the best of all media of communication.

A third project, the execution of which has been begun in right good earnest in the face of immense difficulties, is the railroad from the Peruvian port of Islay, by way of Arequipa, to Puno on the Titicaca Lake. It may ultimately become a rival to the Madeira Railroad; yet, as they will touch Bolivia at nearly diametrically opposite points, and as moreover the construction of a railroad over the wild, rugged mountain range,‡ with tunnels, viaducts, and galleries, will involve the labour of scores of years in these countries—during which time the Madeira line will be at work and gathering its harvest, though difficulties will not be spared to it either—the latter may well be recommended to the respective Governments and to the commercial world in general, especially since the agricultural produce of the fertile plains on the Madeira and its affluents will always go by the Amazon.

Thus before the powerful influence of steam will one barrier after another fall; and ere the lapse of another century iron rails will penetrate to the remotest corner of the new continent, now inhabited by wild tribes whose names even are unknown to us; from the forest-covered Amazon Basin down to the grassy plains of the Gran Chaco, to the retreat of the grim Pampas Indians, and to stony Patagonia; and the mixed population, which will have sprung up meanwhile, will be united to the rest of the world by the strong ties of interest and of commerce. But the red-skinned native of pure blood will have become a myth; the world will be the poorer for many an idyll; but, on the whole, mankind will have achieved a vast stride in the career of Progress.

* In the last eighteen months, the produce of the silver mines of Potosi and Caracóles has increased so largely that in 1872 it amounted to £1,350,000.

† The population of Bolivia amounted, in the first year after the Declaration of Independence, that is in

	1826	to	997,427
It has since progressed thus—	1831	,,	1,087,792
	1836	,,	1,181,169
	1841	,,	1,277,531
	1846	,,	1,373,896
	1851	,,	1,448,196
	1859	,,	1,950,000
	1870	,,	2,750,000

‡ The pass of Tacora, between Arequipa and Puno, is 15,000 feet above the level of the sea.

www.ingramcontent.com/pod-product-compliance
Lightning Source LLC
Chambersburg PA
CBHW021345230426
43666CB00006B/418